APPROACHING THE

CORPORATE
HEART

'Margot gives corporations, organisations, the workplace a new meaning. They become places for the hero's quest to heal ourselves and each other, to transform our being, our life and our world.'

ULRIKE KLEIN, FOUNDER, JURLIQUE INTERNATIONAL

'I salute Margot Cairnes in her mission to bring human values and spiritual integrity to leaders in the commercial world.'

CAROLINE JONES AO, JOURNALIST AND BROADCASTER

'This book speaks to me about optimism, a mature, positive outlook on life, not in naïve ignorance of the vicissitudes of life or turning a blind eye to many atrocities committed in this world. It is about an holistic approach to life and particularly to our working life, which for many of us constitutes the bulk of our conscientiously lived life. It is about linking our intellect and emotions. It reminds us that leaders, really good ones, care for the people they lead and remind us that working for the benefit of others is the really fulfilling aspect of leadership, enriching those led and the leader alike.'

DR ROLF STOMBERG, FORMER MANAGING DIRECTOR,
THE BRITISH PETROLEUM COMPANY PLC, LONDON

'Corporations reside in a key position between individuals, families and communities, and societies, nations and the planet. What could be more important than facilitating their returning to a "heart place" and responding to that heartbeat?
This book opens that door.'

ANNE WILSON SCHAEF, PhD
AUTHOR OF THE ADDICTIVE ORGANISATION,
MEDITATIONS FOR WOMEN WHO DO TOO MUCH,
WHEN SOCIETY BECOMES AN ADDICT,
BEYOND THERAPY BEYOND SCIENCE,
NATIVE WISDOM FOR WHITE MINDS

APPROACHING THE

CORPORATE
HEART

—— ♥ ——

Margot Cairnes

BALBOA.
PRESS
A DIVISION OF HAY HOUSE

Balboa Press books may be ordered through booksellers or by contacting:

Balboa Press
A Division of Hay House
1663 Liberty Drive
Bloomington, IN 47403
www.balboapress.com
1-(877) 407-4847

Because of the dynamic nature of the Internet, any web addresses or
links contained in this book may have changed since publication and
may no longer be valid. The views expressed in this work are solely those
of the author and do not necessarily reflect the views of the publisher,
and the publisher hereby disclaims any responsibility for them.

The author of this book does not dispense medical advice or prescribe the use
of any technique as a form of treatment for physical, emotional, or medical
problems without the advice of a physician, either directly or indirectly. The
intent of the author is only to offer information of a general nature to help you
in your quest for emotional and spiritual well-being. In the event you use any
of the information in this book for yourself, which is your constitutional right,
the author and the publisher assume no responsibility for your actions.

Printed in the United States of America

ISBN: 978-1-4525-3403-9 (sc)
ISBN: 978-1-4525-3405-3 (hc)
ISBN: 978-1-4525-3404-6 (e)

Library of Congress Control Number: 2011905964

Balboa Press rev. date: 22 September 2011

Dedication

*I dedicate this book to my clients; those who over
the years have trusted me to guide them on the hero's quest
and had the courage to stay with the process when the going got
tough. Thank you for the example you have set, for the
difference you have made and for the learning
we have done together.*

CONTENTS

Acknowledgments

I was initially commissioned by Simon & Schuster to write *Approaching the Corporate Heart*. The original paperback edition was well received by the business community and led to many exciting opportunities and many letters from appreciative readers. It is very exciting to be now releasing this revised edition as an eBook for the global market.

This revised edition has definitely been a team effort. I have been ably assisted by my research assistant, Lija Simpson, and my staff at Zaffyre International, especially, Martin Paech, Debbie Fowler and Barbara Fletcher.

The original edition of the book was developed with the support of commissioning editor Lynne Segal, who oversaw the book from inception to final manuscript. In preparing the manuscript, I was assisted by researcher Clare Jankelson, who in turn was ably supported by Robyn Hanson and Vicki Kaplan. At Simon & Schuster, Siobhan O'Connor assumed the editing role. In the meantime, I received valuable input from my early readers, Professor David Russell, Father Gerald Coleman and many of my dear clients.

Without any of these people, this book would be less than it is. So I offer my wholehearted thanks to each and every one of them.

Author's Note

What an opportunity it is to bring out an eBook edition of *Approaching The Corporate Heart*. The response to the paperback editions was overwhelming. We received emails, letters and faxes by the hundreds. Many were heartfelt, offering gratitude that someone had said what they themselves were thinking, affirming what they themselves had experienced. Other messages were from people wanting to move into the area of corporate coaching, or from leaders wanting to explore new ways forward. One of my favourites, a fax written in the Australian vernacular, simply stated: 'Bloody ripper of a book–thank you.' My reply: 'Bloody ripper of a fax, thank YOU.' Apart from warming my heart and encouraging me to keep going, what all this mail taught me was that authors don't always know best about their own work. In the first edition of *Approaching the Corporate Heart* I gave people instructions on how to approach the book. The feedback from enthusiastic readers was that they mostly ignored my advice and got a huge amount out of the book by reading it their own way. So, in this edition there is no pompous advice, just my very best wishes that you enjoy what you are about to read and my hope that this book enriches your life in the same way that it appears to have enriched the lives of others.

The Cast of Characters

Every book must have a cast of characters. The cast in this book are the leaders of major organisations around the world—men and women who have generously agreed to share personal and professional details of their lives and business. I have, of course, changed names, places and identifying details, while staying true to the flavour of each character and the nature of the lessons they have to teach us.

The Benefits

I find it hard to express clearly how profound an impact the material in this book can have if you let it. The level of breakthrough success that is possible for individuals and organisations that take the heroic path is so startling it is often beyond imagination as we set out. Business leaders around the world declare they want quantum leaps in performance and results, yet they go on doing what they have always done. If you do what you have always done, as the proverb goes, you will get what you have always got. This book reveals a new, transformational way forward. With my clients I get to see the benefits to them as their heroic journeys unfold. As an author, I don't have the opportunity to walk beside you on your quest and to see your life blossom... this I regret. But I believe that if you are reading this book, then your own heroic quest is about to begin, if it hasn't done so already. I encourage you to honour the wisdom in these pages and I rest happily in the knowledge that your heroic quest will be fulfilling and rich beyond measure.

Chapter 1

A Heartfelt Quest

*Fear not that thy life shall come to an end, but rather
fear that it shall never have a beginning.*

J. H. NEWMAN

In the past few decades, organisations around the world have been re-engineered, reinvented and downsized. If you are one of the shrinking pool of people who still have a government or corporate job, you are probably now expected to do more with less. If you are self-employed or working in a small family business, you are probably finding that being a little guy in the land of the giants means long hours, hard work and a lot of resourcefulness; in small business, you have to do so many things yourself. Whether you work from home or in an office, alone or surrounded by people, it is likely that you feel a sense of loneliness and from time to time find yourself wondering if the money is worth the angst, the stress and the problems.

But who is to blame for what appears to be an increasingly depersonalised workplace? Is it heartless bosses, blinded by ambition and greed, or is it demanding shareholders who will transfer their investment dollars to more lucrative organisations if yours doesn't continue to perform at ever increasing levels of profit and growth? Perhaps it is the rate of technological change, rising customer expectations, increasing global competition or the always changing maze of government regulation?

All these things are part of current reality, but who said life was meant to be easy? Although we tell ourselves fanciful stories of times when life was simpler, easier and more stable, we know history is cluttered with wars, plagues and economic upheavals. Life has never been smooth for very long. Yes, we are currently experiencing an exponential rate of pervasive change, but even that has historical precedent. The Industrial Revolution was a time of social, political and economic transformation, similar in proportion to that experienced today. The French Revolution, the American Civil War, World Wars I and II and the advent of communism in Russia and China were all seismic upheavals. The truth is, people, when they come together, create communities, organisations and nations that are as complex, diverse and susceptible to change as they are themselves. While the features of our society and its places of work may change, the depth, diversity and intricacy of human nature does not. People go on being themselves, manufacturing all sorts of challenges for themselves and each other.

Of course, there have been times when, despite ourselves, things seemed easier. These times, however, are the exceptions—although this is not always the way we see it. We want to hold on to the 'good times', make them the standard, and see everything else as an aberration that we somehow have to 'fix'.

'I want things to go back to normal,' Peter was telling me.

'What did normal look like?' I questioned. 'I haven't felt normal for years.'

'Well, there was a time when it was like we were riding a wave. Work was easy to get. The company just kept growing. We could afford extra support and I had time to build up a whole range of interests outside of work. Then the wave crashed.' He paused.

'Actually, looking back, it was all an illusion—an historical accident, really. Now, we're still moving forward, but it's harder work, we have less cushioning. I feel more stressed, more narrow in my focus.'

'Normal', it turns out, is often an illusion. Even the scantest review of history tells us that change is constant. Sometimes it brings comfort, sometimes hardship. What is fascinating is that we accept the good times as the standard by which our lives should be led and others as 'problems' that need to be solved. So we race around looking for cures for life itself. We see the changing tide of experience as a series of hiccups interspersed with more comfortable periods to which we all strive to cling and constantly seek to return.

In other words, we spend a huge amount of time chasing an illusion, treating reality as a distraction that is somehow keeping us away from having what we want. We then spend a disproportionate amount of time attending to the symptoms of a disease that turns out to be the social fabric of life. Unfortunately, this keeps us from enjoying the richness, fullness and diverse wonders of the world in which we live. Always looking for ways to 'solve the problems' of conflict, change and fluctuating fortune that are the very material of life itself, we fail to experience fully and immerse ourselves in the wonders of the process of living.

Leadership guru Warren Bennis writes in *Behavior Online Conversations*:
Technologically we are very advanced but psychologically we are babes in the wood. We don't know ourselves or anyone else very well.

This is because we generally fail to look—we are too busy dealing with the inconvenience of living.

Could I possibly be suggesting that we should simply accept social problems such as the rate of crime, family and social violence, homelessness, unemployment and poverty? Am I picturing a society where people sit around like 'flower children', absorbed in their inner experience and ignoring important social Issues? Hardly. I'm merely saying that an instant replay of what we call the 'history of civilisation' tells us that people have been abusing themselves and each other since time immemorial. It appears that this is how people behave. So, if we want to move forward both individually and collectively, we had better get to understand people better and find transformational ways of working with our humanity.

'Oh,' I've been told, 'that's easy for you to say, Margot, but do you realise that people are just too busy, too tired, to do any more than cope?' It would seem that fatigue, depression and a deep sense of loneliness are endemic in our places of work and throughout society in general. Stress-related illnesses, relationship breakdowns and a sense of powerlessness seem to be the order of the day, as they were of a good many yesterdays.

Reality, it turns out, isn't always the way we would like it to be. Living is full of ups, downs and sideways—bumps, glitches and trials. Nowhere would this seem more so than in the workplace, where most people feel controlled by external factors and continually under pressure from customers, shareholders, bosses, unions, colleagues, markets, suppliers, employees and, increasingly, technological innovation and information overload. At work, people are frustrated by organisational politics, daunted by ever increasing workloads and always feel under threat of retrenchment and redundancy due to slipping performance or some external change or strategic restructure.

I have found that this is exactly why work is such a wonderful learning place for personal, emotional and spiritual transformation. In the workplace, simply functioning at some kind of human level is so challenging that it becomes almost impossible to ignore the many facets of human interaction and personal expression. Moreover, because it is imperative that we produce something tangible when we are in the workplace, there is incredible incentive to face reality full on and then transform it into measurable outcomes. Work has provided me and many of my clients with the stimulus, challenge, incentive and support to move to higher levels of personal aliveness and relationship and material success. This may seem paradoxical given the dehumanising terminology that abounds in the workplace: people are referred to as 'human resources' who can be 'upskilled', 'multiskilled' or 'reskilled' (a bit like reprogramming a robot), and 'outplaced' when they are no longer needed. However, we don't *have* to let our circumstances define who we are.

While Victor Frankl was interned in a Nazi concentration camp, during which time he was starved, beaten and otherwise mistreated, he decided that he did have choices. His captors may have had control over how he was treated, but he had control over how he reacted to the reality of the situation in which he was placed. No matter how bad or how good we judge any situation, we always have control over how we deal with it—this is the secret to personal freedom, joy and peace of mind.

Comprehending this possibility requires a special kind of intelligence. Accepting reality in all its shades and nuances, and then working with what is, in a humanising and personally transforming way, is not a path for the lazy or dull. Nor is it for the timid or apathetic. Transforming experience on the emotional, spiritual and material planes requires commitment, energy, time and application. It also requires considerable skill and a willingness to look at things differently. If you choose to revolutionise your world (and quite likely the world of many others if you take this path), you will find that life will go on doing its own thing regardless. You, however, will experience this as an exciting, enlivening, joyous and rewarding journey. Not that this means it will be easy. Adventures worth having are rarely without danger, challenges or difficulties: that's what makes them so memorable.

The Hero's Quest

There is a lot of literature about the heroic journey. Master myth scholar Joseph Campbell has popularised myths such as that of Ulysses and has derived from these myths the archetype of the hero's quest.

The hero's quest is the search for the best that is within us all. It involves viewing and participating in life in new and enriching ways as we delve into the depths of our own being and come to terms with our own psyche—befriending our private demons, learning to accept and work with our own limitations and developing our deepest human potential. Heroes achieve this by gaining self-knowledge as they pit themselves against a series of real tests, challenges and hurdles that take them beyond what is currently known.

The heroic journey is always highly personal and unique. Robert J. Holder and Richard N. McKinney, remind us in their article "Corporate change and the hero's quest" it is not possible to replicate the journey of anyone else; trying to do so diminishes your chances of success on your own quest. The heroic cycle involves a separation from the mundane as the hero passes through a series of trials and initiations (usually mysterious and involving deeply based personal transformation) before reintegration into the world that he or she has left. The world to which the hero returns has rarely changed radically; the heroic quester, however, having seen new lands and having transformed him or herself so fundamentally, experiences life, even the mundane, in a very different way.

We so often think that happiness involves things being different. We believe we will be content when a relationship changes, we get a new job, change our place of living or acquire another material possession. The hero knows that we can each be happy here and now. The difference isn't in the world in which we live, but in how we see that world. The great gift of the hero's quest, as heroes discover through the trials of their adventures, is the hero's own mental, emotional and spiritual essence.

Once we have found our own true selves, everything is different. Happiness, joy and contentment are no longer elusive, they are our everyday companions. It's not that the lives of returned heroes are easier, smoother or less challenging—on the contrary, living the everyday life well can often be the greatest challenge of all. However, heroes, blessed with knowledge of their own essences, now see what was once 'mundane' as an enriching part of their personal journeys.

The hero's quest is always into the unknown. It is an uncertain, highly experiential odyssey; one that requires exploration rather than planning. The key to success is to trust oneself on a radically deep inner level; this connects us to others and to reality in a new and transforming way. On this level, we hear the call of our own true destiny, which pulls us out of the mundane and entices us to go in search of all that we can be. Organisational scholars Holder and McKinney tell us:

> *The quest is both a spiritual and a physical process. The spiritual dimension involves an inward renewal. This inward change directs the creation of the physical change.*

This is why work provides such a wonderful arena for an heroic journey. Many people, through contact with the New Age or mystic teachers, have engaged in involved inward journeys. Therapy also can lead us into greater awareness of our inner being. However, the most powerful transformations occur not while you are sitting quietly in solitary splendour, nor even when you share your deepest secrets with trusted others, but when you take the learning from these personal experiences and put them into action, working with them in some physical form. As our work demands action and tangible output, it is the perfect venue for anchoring our personal shifts into reality. This makes work a spiritual as well as a physical experience. It makes work the stuff of heroes.

In their confronting and challenging book *We've Had a Hundred Years of Psychotherapy - And the World's Getting Worse*, James Hillman and Michael Ventura discuss how therapy has largely resulted in the separation of the realms of personal experience and social action. People sit around in their millions at support groups, sharing their personal experiences, giving and receiving advice, but doing very little to change the reality of the society in which they live. I constantly hear reference to the 'me' generation, which I take to mean those people who have become fascinated by their emotional and spiritual process while remaining disconnected from the world around them. This not only robs society of the valuable input from caring and aware people but it also robs people of an opportunity to anchor their personal journeys in social and physical reality. It's a bit like the theorist who is unable to make practical use of his or her knowledge.

Some years ago, faced with more work opportunities than time, I recruited a number of people to help me. I realised that the work I was wanting these people to do would require them to use the full range of their emotions, spirit and mind, so I chose people who had a history of spiritual growth (one had been a swami), emotional development (they were all trained and experienced in some therapeutic field) and intelligent endeavour (they all had higher degrees). What absolutely stunned me was the incredible difficulty these gifted people had in putting their years of study, spiritual practice and psychological training to use. It was as if they had separated their personal development from the work they did and were unable to Re-establish the link between how they operated in the world and the commitment they had made to their personal being.

Actually, as a society we have made an art form of separating who we are from the work we do. This unfortunately has robbed our work and, in many ways, our lives of meaning. Reversing this process is not straightforward or easy. It is, however, possible—but not through the means we normally associate with either work or social interaction.

I am the grateful recipient of some ten years of higher education. I have studied science, business, education, economics, politics, psychology and philosophy. In all these disciplines, I managed to excel in the opinion of those who graded my work. However, all those years of training have faded for me into a colourless blur. While I do remember the excitement of discovering and discussing new ideas, I also remember the flatness of living for years in an intellectual realm. I may have been developing an insightful, analytical mind, but I was also losing my spirit.

Psychiatrist Alexander Lowen in *The Spirituality of the Body* tells us that the link between the mind and the body (which he claims houses the spirit) is feeling. Feelings were absolutely off-limits in my academic training. I can remember being ridiculed at business school for being 'too subjective' when I dared to interpret leadership situations through the filters of my emotional experience and reality. It was made very clear that emotion and business were never to meet.

This lesson has been taught to me again and again by my clients. While working with groups of senior executives around the world, I have been praised by my students for talking about feelings and for having actors demonstrate emotions. However, if I dared to ask them, the executives in training, to feel any emotions, I was verbally attacked. The strength of the prohibition on experiencing, as against theorising about, emotion was made stunningly clear to me when working with employees of a large bank. Over a three-year period, some 300 of the bank's senior managers were being put through a year-long executive development program. This program included a one-week live-in course where twenty managers at a time were subjected to intensive training in leadership, strategic thinking and personal survival skills such as fitness, relaxation and public speaking. In the first year, I was asked to address a number of groups for one day during their residential week. During that day we talked about emotion, did intellectual exercises on emotion and worked with actors who showed us what emotions looked like and how they could be used to optimum benefit in work and personal relationships. The course participants were asked to rate each session and my one-day sessions received full marks from nearly every participant. On the strength of this, the following year I was asked to work with groups from the same pool of 300, still in groups of twenty, on the one-week live-in course. This time, however, I was allocated a two-day segment.

I decided to use the extra day at my disposal to take things one step further: instead of just asking the group to postulate about feelings, I would have them feel some. So, using exactly that same material that had been so warmly received the previous year, I structured the two days to have the executives experience the emotional reality of their personal and professional lives. I was shocked at how hostile people became when faced with their own emotional experience. Rather than realising that their hostility arose from feelings of anger and alienation resulting from the pressures of their daily lives, the executives became very angry with me. They complained bitterly about everything that I said and did and gave my sessions the lowest rating. The message was clear: intellectual debate about feelings was fine, experiencing the reality of their everyday life on an emotional level was not.

This is yet another message that has been brought home to me repeatedly. Working with leaders of a multibillion-dollar business on a two-day workshop, I asked the participants twice on the first day to tell me how they felt about particular issues that were of special relevance to them. When I dared to ask about the state of people's emotions on the second day, one manager barked, 'You have made us feel twice already, you are not going to get us to feel again.' As both spirit and emotion are largely 'off-limits' in a business setting, I was unable to convince these managers that they were actually denying their ability to operate as integrated, whole human beings—as people who enjoyed connection between their mind, their body and their spirit. No, these people fiercely defended their right to remain physically, emotionally and spiritually disjointed.

Ironically, all of these people also had great need for and difficulty in finding a new way forward through the maze of dramatic changes that were occurring in their specific industries. They were fighting hard to retain a linear way of thinking and operating that was actually blinding them to the possibilities inherent in the world being transformed around them. They were aggressively protecting their prerogative not to take the hero's journey. They wanted new ways forward, but they were too frightened to explore the parts of themselves with which they had long lost contact—they wanted to stay in the realm of the intellect where they felt safe and in control. Unfortunately, by staying in this domain, they were denying themselves access to both the fullness and the richness of emotional and spiritual aliveness. Simultaneously, they blocked their own discovery of the answers to their vexing business dilemmas.

Psychiatrist Dr Carl Hammerschlag in *The Theft of the Spirit* informs us that the spheres of analysis and spiritually empowered human action are often mutually exclusive. If we insist on understanding everything analytically, we are likely to remain in the world of theory and be unable to bridge the gap between discussion and action. How many times have I heard people in a business setting complain that their supervisor, leader or co-worker did not 'walk their talk'. One of the biggest complaints in any organisation is the dichotomy between the rhetoric and the reality. Most organisational participants exhibit a sharp disconnection between the domains of thinking (closely associated with talking) and action. Moreover, while people continue to reject basic human emotion, the dichotomy between thinking and behaviour will remain, as will the label of hypocrisy that accompanies the discontinuity between words and actions.

To regain contact with our spirit, to recover our inner wholeness and integrity, and transmit this through congruent action, we have to learn again how to feel. That's why the most effective heroes' journeys are really journeys of the heart.

The Heart's Journey

I particularly like working with leaders because they are committed to someone other than themselves. In my experience, leaders genuinely care for the people they oversee. For me, this provides a wonderful opening into the world of the heart. In isolation, people will give up, lose courage and wimp out; in contrast, when someone believes in us, depends on us and trusts in our ability to lead the way, it is amazing the creativity, energy, courage and persistence that unexpectedly surfaces and takes us forward.

This fact is widely known and utilised. I was told by self-defence experts who train police officers for some of the toughest areas in New York that one of the surest ways for police to ensure their own safety is to keep a picture of their loved ones prominently displayed in their patrol cars. When they are going into a potentially dangerous situation, the officers are trained to look at a photograph of their families or sweethearts and say, 'For you, I go into this situation and for you I come out safely.'

These same self-defence trainers told me of a man whom they had met at a survivors' group. This man had been asleep in his house when he was attacked with a hatchet by an intruder. His assailant had, in fact, mistaken him for the man next door, against whom he held some vendetta. Mistaken identity or not, the poor man was struck some seventeen times with the hatchet before his attacker drew a knife and started slashing him. What made the victim survive? Apparently all the time he was being hacked, this man was giving thanks that it was him under attack and not his wife and children, who were also in the house. It was his love for his family that gave him the will to live and thus saved his life. This accords so strongly with my own experience.

Some years ago I found myself living as a single mother raising two young children. I was not fortunate enough to have any support from my extended family, and one of my children had a life-threatening disease that meant she had to be hospitalised frequently and for long periods. At about this same time, my father developed cancer, which slowly and methodically took his life. His illness made it necessary for him to live with me and my young children in our very small home. Nursing my daughter and father made it very difficult for me to work. With medical and living expenses, we soon accumulated a large debt.

At the time that all this was happening, I can remember thinking, *If I can come through all this having learnt something, I can achieve anything.* So I concentrated on using every piece of the experience as a learning process about life, relationships and myself. All the same, I felt terrible. My daughter's paediatrician suggested that I was suffering from depression. I suggested that I was actually exhibiting a huge dose of sanity, since I *was* in a rather depressing situation and my mood simply demonstrated that I was in touch with the reality of my plight.

Within ten years of that experience, every dream I ever had came true for me. With the wisdom of hindsight, I can see that what I achieved I owe to my children and my father. You see, if I had been on my own, I would have had no incentive to stretch myself to the limits. Without needing to nurse my child back to health, I would never have understood the joy of sacrifice, which one learns staying up night after night beside a sick child in hospital. Without my father's illness, I would never have learnt the wonder of farewelling someone I truly loved and the gratitude of knowing that I had helped him die peacefully. Without the incredible debt I accumulated, I would never have had the incentive to strive so hard to bridge the gap between my knowledge and experience, and the needs of the business world. Without my desire to provide my children with a better future, I would never have looked again and again for new ways forward—I would never have persisted when I was criticised, or searched so hard for new technologies, ideas and support systems. If I had only myself to think about, I would have taken the easy option of putting myself and my own comfort first. Without my children, I would never have taken the hero's journey. Mind you, I never felt like a hero, just a mother doing her best for her kids. My best, however, was greatly extended because I wasn't just working for myself.

When we hear stories of cultures and times when people felt a pride in their work, in historical moments when work still retained a connection with the life and soul of the worker and the wider community, we recognise the feeling of somehow being more because others depend on us. This is the heart's journey, the path of feeling. Ironically, given current attitudes to emotion in public life, it is also the route to true leadership.

Heartfelt Leadership

In his book *Why Leaders Can't Lead: The Unconscious Conspiracy Continues*, Professor Warren Bennis implores:

> *Roosevelt, who challenged a nation to overcome its fear; Winston Churchill who demanded and got blood, sweat and tears from his people; Albert Schweitzer who from the jungles of Lambarene inspired a reverence for life; Albert Einstein who gave us a sense of unity in infinity; Gandhi, David Ben-Gurion, Golda Meir and Anwar El Sadat who rallied their people to great and human causes; Jack and Bobby Kennedy and Martin Luther King Jr, who said we could do better—all are gone now. Where are their successors? Why have we not had any true leaders in the White House for a generation? Why are there no potential presidents who inspire or even excite us? Where, for God's sake, have all the leaders gone?* (page 59).

He then tells us that for today's leaders: 'There's no such thing as the common good or public interest. There's only self-interest.'

What Bennis and so many others have failed to realise is that self-interest and the common good are part of the same equation.

If what we want is health, which increasingly is found to involve physical, emotional and spiritual connection, then we are well served by working in the interest of others. If we crave personal, spiritual and emotional fulfilment, if we seek joy, happiness and peace of mind, then having others depend on us is a great blessing. If by self-interest we mean increased material wealth at the expense of others, then we are deluded. How can it be self-enhancing to operate in a way that supports our remaining restricted and fragmented as human beings?

Leadership is a great privilege because it opens the gate to the heart's journey—it provides us with incentive to embark and remain committed to the hero's quest. In other words, it provides us with the impetus, challenge and support we need to unlock the key to our own wellbeing, fulfilment and highest potential. Sure, it's hard work; of course, it can be painful, difficult and uncomfortable. From what I see, however, that's a pretty good description of the reality of people's lives now. So, we can stay where we are and fiercely defend our right to remain disjointed, alienated people, or we can step forward as leaders, listen to our heart's desire, give thanks that we have a role to fulfil and embark upon the hero's quest.

This is the way not just to our own wellbeing, but also the way to transform society. Transformation happens when people operate effectively in their own areas of influence, while remaining in relationship to the whole. As we now live in a global society, that means committing ourselves to understanding the interconnections of global systems while seeking to operate at maximum effectiveness at a local level.

This means having the self-interest to learn how to feel deeply as we dare to embark on experiencing the journey of life. As we reconnect with ourselves, we will begin to unite the realms of body and mind, thus spreading our growing integrity to those around us through the congruence of our actions and speech. Integrity breeds trust, trust breeds commitment and commitment breeds courage. Surely these are the things that are so sorely missing, not only in governments and business, but also in families and communities around the world. Hence the way to the corporate heart is through the heart of those on the hero's quest, those with enough self-interest to want life to be more than a drab repetition of disjointed experiences. Those lucky enough to have people depending on them (and who doesn't, if they so desire) will find within themselves the courage, spirit, energy and persistence to be more, thus simultaneously creating a richer, fuller world, both inside and outside themselves.

These are the people to whom I dedicate this book; to you, as a helping hand in the journey to creating a life filled with meaning, joy and inner calm for yourself and the people you lead.

Chapter 2

Approaching the Corporate Heart

*'He who provides for this life, but takes no care for
eternity, is wise for a moment, but a fool forever.'*

JOHN TILLOTSON

Who is a Hero?

QUESTION: HOW MANY PSYCHOLOGISTS DOES IT
TAKE TO CHANGE A LIGHT BULB?

ANSWER: ONLY ONE, BUT THE LIGHT BULB
REALLY HAS TO WANT TO CHANGE.

Outstanding performers are characterised, according to Harvard professor of psychiatry Albert Rothenberg in *Creativity and Madness,* not by intelligence, temperament, personality type, introversion, inheritance, early environment, inspiration, obsession or mental disorder. The only attribute that is common 'absolutely, across the board' in those who excel in life is motivation. To be a hero you have to want to be a hero.

The whole notion of the hero's journey is premised on free will. Ulysses suffered shipwreck, capture, torture, loneliness and personal loss. Yet he was compelled by his own 'better judgment' to go on the hero's quest. He heard the call of destiny, the invitation to be all that he could be, and he could not contain it. Like so many heroes, Ulysses started his hero's journey in response to an accident, an error of judgment. However, once on the journey Ulysses chose to lay aside his warrior perspective to explore parts of his personality, parts of his psyche, that he had previously ignored. He was, along the way, assisted by heroic guides. However, it was Ulysses himself who went questing. He heard and responded to his inner voice—a voice that encouraged him to make the most of life, even if that meant leaving the conventional wisdom, thinking outside of the boundaries and spending years in fantastic, often terrible, places. What made Ulysses a hero was that he chose to heed the call to go exploring. What's more, he took personal responsibility for how he responded to everything that happened to him along the way.

Heroes, therefore, are those who elect to take responsibility for their decisions and actions. More than that, heroes choose to see life as an adventure and a voyage of discovery. They resolve to immerse themselves in the process of living, to be where they are and feel the true force of what it is like to be fully alive. Heroes elect to feel what it is like being themselves, living their life. This means heroes choose to be fully present—emotionally, spiritually and intellectually—in the 'here and now', drinking in and savouring all that life has to offer; the good, the bad and the ugly. This is such a wonderful way of living that heroes invariably become leaders. Regardless of class, education, intelligence, sex or training, heroes capture our attention and inspire us to action.

Becoming a Hero

For the past two decades I have served as an heroic guide to business leaders. I have done this with individuals, with corporate top teams and with whole organisations. Typically, I am approached by a would-be heroic leader, someone with an ambitious vision and the courage to do the inner personal and outer worldly work necessary to bring that vision into reality. Some of these leaders realise that if they are to lead their people to new levels of achievement and wellbeing, they, the leader, must be prepared to pave the way—so they come seeking leadership development and the skills to develop a leadership strategy for themselves and the achievement of their vision. Others approach me to gain help in changing 'their people'. If I can convince such people that the first place to start is with themselves, the leader, we proceed and wonderful things happen.

David Judd

I discovered this to be true early in my career, when I was lucky enough to work with a man who, faced with the terror of personal destruction, used the experience to find within himself a depth of humanity, creativity and strength that stretched his previous limits and allowed him to lead an industrial site and a whole township to new possibilities, at the same time setting the global benchmark for business excellence.

I recall addressing a conference on managing organisational change. There were about 50 participants and I was the first speaker after lunch. I sat in on the conference in the morning, listening to speaker after speaker talk at the audience, all saying much the same thing. Somehow I just couldn't get up after lunch and lay another monologue on the increasingly bored assembly. So, during the lunch break, I had all the tables removed from the meeting room and the chairs placed in a semicircle.

When the delegates reassembled, I asked them to sit in small groups and picture each other as animals. I then asked them to tell each other what animal they had projected on to whom, and why. The results were startling: these people, mainly men, who had barely met each other, were floored by how much insight apparent strangers had into who they were. I used their learning to facilitate a discussion on how strongly we unconsciously communicate who we are, and yet how in organisational change programs we generally try to change our behaviour while ignoring our being, thus creating a growing discontinuity between what we say and the messages we are sending. This inspires distrust and bedevils communication at the very time when honest, open communication is of vital importance. My intentions, apart from keeping people awake after lunch, were to suggest that perhaps we were looking for the answers to our 'change questions' in the wrong places, and to encourage people to widen their perspectives and look in less conventional places for their insights in order to achieve quantum shifts in their thinking.

During afternoon tea I was approached by two men, one of whom said, 'Our boss, David Judd, needs you. He's our greatest asset and our biggest liability. We think you can fix him up.' Today, as a financially successful advisor with a book full of clients and more than enough work on my hands, I might have smiled at these guys, thanked them for their belief and changed the topic. Back then, however, I was saddled with debt and was in the process of rebuilding my business after my daughter's illness. I needed their boss just as much as he needed me.

So, within a few weeks, I was flying to Portland, a small town in the Australian state of Victoria. At that time, Portland was home to some 10,000 people and one of the world's largest aluminium smelters. David Judd was the operations manager of that smelter. I spent a day talking individually to the various managers, while awaiting my introduction to David. During that time, I found out a number of things.

First, David had life-threatening cancer. He was, in fact, supposed to be at home recovering from a recent operation to remove a brain tumour. He was, however, true to form, at work. I was warned that he was more problematic after lunch, because while in convalescence his energy levels ran down during the day, amplifying his resentment of his illness. A problematic David, I was told, was a challenge. He had, by all accounts, a ferocious temper and didn't like consultants. In spite of this, his managers seemed to care for him deeply—they saw that he had a brilliant strategic brain and a good heart, if only he wasn't so unreasonable in his demands (on himself and everybody else) and if only he could do something about that temper.

If there is one thing I would rather avoid, it is angry people. Nevertheless, I needed this assignment and mustered all my courage as I went in to meet this obviously incredible man. David was physically very imposing: he stood at about 193 centimetres (6 foot, 4 inches) tall, and, although his limbs were thin, he had a huge gut. (I later found out this housed a monstrous tumour.) During our entire meeting, he looked even more massive because he sort of hovered above his desk, not quite sitting and not quite standing. (I later discovered that this was what he did when he didn't like people and he wanted them to go away.) He told me that he had a dream. He wanted to make his aluminium smelter the best smelter in the world. Moreover, he wanted to do it in a way that made his presence unnecessary for the changes to endure. Not only did he have a clear vision of what he wanted, but he also knew that the road to achieving it was by engaging a change process based on 'really hard, structured yakka, where we know where we're going and we can put it into place and we can take it through step by step'. He confessed later that he thought my way of operating was 'a load of absolute rubbish… the last bloody thing we want'.

Somehow, I do not know how, David came to decide that he would work with me and that what we would do is put him, me and all his managers in aluminum boats and, starting at a small out-station in the centre of Australia, boat down the floodwaters of Cooper Creek (a normally dry riverbed that turned into a watercourse about once every 50 years) into Lake Eyre, Australia's notorious 'inland sea'. The trip was scheduled to take ten days, and we were to be accompanied by a film crew. The physical aspects of the expedition were to be organised by one of Australia's leading adventurers, Graham Joy, who had distinguished himself sea kayaking across Bass Strait and walking to the North Pole. And so our heroic adventure began.

I have written about this adventure elsewhere, but what is sufficient to say here is that, while David's sights were on an external goal, his heroic quest took him deep into himself. Amidst torrents of emotion David reviewed his war-torn childhood, his difficult years as a boarder in a Dickensian institution and his subsequent difficulties in relationships. David did nothing in halves, so the tears, rages, insights, joys and spells of inner peace came in waves, one after another. At the end of our ten days David had made a number of discoveries and decisions. First, he was committed to managing his temper; dumping his anger on others, he had realised, wasn't serving him or anyone else well. He also decided that if he was going to get the results he wanted 'from his people', he himself was going to have to lead the way. As he wrote in the introduction to my book *Peaceful Chaos: The Art of Leadership in Times of Rapid Change*:

> *...it's obvious to me now—it wasn't for many years—that the first individual that we need to work with is ourselves. As managers we've been exhorting others to change but at the same time, we've been fearful of letting go of the old ways on which we've based our authority, influence and self-esteem. If we are to be successful in the future, those old ways have to go because they are holding others back from realising their full potential. Admitting that we are the ones creating the blockage is the first step—and the most difficult.*

So David stopped being the blockage. He put his energies into better understanding himself, developing his own humanity and using that growth as a way of connecting more fully with the people and the environment around him. For the first time in his life, David invested time in deep self-reflection. He indulged his love of photography and spent extended periods in the Australian bush he loved so deeply. He put time and emotional effort into enriching his relationships with his partner, his friends, his colleagues, his bosses and his staff. He also led what has always been to me one of the most heartening transformation projects I have ever witnessed.

Before he died, David had overseen the participation of the majority of the township of Portland in a personal development program. He had sponsored the creation of a gym, a crèche and a medical centre for use by smelter staff and their families. His people had developed one of the most successful rehabilitation programs for street kids run in Australia. The smelter had sponsored one of Australia's leading jazz musicians, Don Burrows, to fly regularly to Portland to work with local school children. Managers from the smelter went onto the boards of the local schools, hospital and clubs. The smelter ran the Portland Speakers Circuit, which saw world-class speakers such as David Suzuki fly into town and lecture to local residents, thus broadening their horizons. Smelter staff had also regenerated a natural (later award-winning) wetlands around the plant.

In the business arena, Portland Aluminum Smelter became a pacesetter in terms of technical and cultural innovation. Their culture can be summarised in David's words: 'By addressing the needs of the individual, we're bringing greater productivity to the organisation and opening up a whole new dimension to our lives.' Portland Aluminum was named as the world benchmark culture for an aluminum smelter. During this period, the rates of industrial injury, staff turnover, absenteeism and solid waste were dramatically reduced. David had fulfilled his dream: his smelter was recognised as the best in the world in many areas. Planeloads of people arrived from around the world to discover Portland's secret. David travelled regularly to help smelters in other parts of the globe introduce the concepts that had led his smelter to world-class excellence. David was the first Australian named by *Industry Week* as an Unsung Hero of Industry. Shortly after this he passed away.

On the day of David's funeral, I was scheduled to run a seminar with the top team of a leading industrial organisation. For the first time in my career, I cancelled a workshop. I told them politely that I had a funeral to attend. I was not alone. Alcoa had hired a jet and flew in dignitaries from far and wide to pay homage to this great hero. As we filed into the church, the school children of Portland, conducted by Don Burrows, played David's favourite songs. The church was packed to overflowing. Speaker after speaker got up and told us how this courageous man had used his personal battle with cancer as a spur to make a difference not just for himself, but also for everyone around him. David had touched many lives, stretched many people's ideas of what was possible and provided us with a model of living every minute of life to the full, experiencing life's pains, joys, sorrows and challenges.

We had all seen David fight and lose his war with cancer. We had seen his physical strength wither before our eyes. And all this because he let us. He had made a decision to use his struggles for the benefit of others—we had, each of us, learnt more about the value of life through watching David fight to extend his.

As the funeral procession wove its way through Portland, the township stopped. The streets were lined with shopkeepers, housewives, school children and smelter staff, all saying their last goodbyes to an heroic man.

Like Ulysses, David's journey had taken him far away from known territory. Personal misfortune had triggered David's heroic quest, a quest that had compelled him to leave the certainty of the known and delve into parts of himself that he had previously ignored. What he discovered there empowered him to achieve highly ambitious worldly goals, and at the same time his growing sense of self, his confidence in his own being and his courage helped David achieve some deeply personal goals. When we were down Cooper's Creek, David had made it clear that his highest goal was to find within himself deep inner peace. Through much of his illness this eluded him. One day some weeks after he had become too ill to work, David phoned me. 'Margot,' he said, 'I am frightened.' I asked him what he feared. 'The black hole,' he replied. I asked what he feared about the black hole. His response was, 'Margot, I'm tired. I'm frightened that if I go into the black hole I will never get out.' David couldn't describe his black hole to me because he was avoiding it. He didn't know if it was depression, listlessness or some shadow of his approaching death. His black hole was a black box, the great and mysterious unknown, an unknown that he feared. The best thing, then, was to get to know it. I suggested that David set his alarm clock for five minutes ahead of the setting time and metaphorically climb into the black hole and explore it until the alarm rang. This would signal time to come back to the outer world. I suggested that he do this for a few days during small, closely timed periods. I indicated that if he wanted to he could increase the time as he felt more comfortable.

Some days later David rang back. 'Margot,' he said, 'I have for the first time in my life experienced real personal peace.' The next day David died.

A true heroic quester, David had found the courage to explore new territory—both deep within himself and in the outer world.

His quest had led him to bring his dreams to reality. While his journey had allowed David to extend his life past all medical prediction, it didn't stop him from going on the final journey into the unknown. It did, however, prepare him for all eventualities.

All these years later I am still telling David's story. This heroic man reminds us all of what is possible when we engage with life, when we choose to do the inner and outer work that is involved in the heroic journey.

Heroes, Warriors and Other Myths

Rollo May writes in *The Cry for Myth*:

> *Our powerful hunger for myth is a hunger for community. The person without a myth is a person without a home... to be a member of one's community is to share in its myths* (page 45).

The dominant myth in the world of business and government is the myth of the warrior. For so many people nowadays, life is a battle. How often do you hear, or perhaps even think, 'You don't get anywhere if you don't fight for it'? We all know of business leaders who run their firms as a battlefield. They must win at all costs, and almost everything takes the form of a contest. The warrior mythology is reflected in the highly militaristic language of business, where the highest respect is paid to corporate *strategy*. We run marketing and sales *campaigns,* and one even hears talk of *killing* the competition. The myth of contest is reinforced by the engagement of sporting champions as corporate motivational speakers, and the endless rhetoric of sporting analogies as warriors attempt to convince themselves and others that public life can be simplified to a competition with clear-cut rules, distinct winners and losers, and the legitimate and proper use of force, guile and skill to win the day.

Mythically, warriors are people with strong, active energy who can follow orders, push forward along set paths and engage in battle with the competition. David, of Goliath fame, is remembered as a warrior (he also played the harp and wrote love songs, but nobody taught me that in Sunday school). Warriors like Mark Antony are remembered in poem, story and film. The American Western provided today's leaders with a plethora of warrior role models. In surveys to determine the mythical models of American corporate leaders, the resounding favourite is the Lone Ranger. Jennifer James in *Thinking In The Future Tense* writes:

> *The concepts surrounding this myth are powerful: work alone, except for a trusted semi-servant who has no real status. Do not tell people what you are doing.*
> *Disguise yourself. Have no personal life. Ride a flashy horse. Believe you are exceptional, a crusader. Their ideal is of a strong moral man bringing security to others and asking nothing in return except total control (p.80).*

In *Care of the Soul* Thomas Moore tells us that warriors delight in using brute strength and tend to have a narrow, rationalist vision. They also have a strong instrumental view of relationships and life in general. Economics and business faculties have often pictured their disciplines as more like the sciences than the liberal arts. For warriors, concrete action that is measurable against a plan is far more important than poetry, art or love. It's not that warriors dismiss these things, just that they are an aside: something to do if, and only if, you have time. More than that, warrior public relations is invariably about measurable achievement—what is seen to be true. Warriors live largely on the surface of life, concentrating on image rather than the intrinsic value of heart and soul.

Times, however, are changing, and with that change the warrior myth is becoming outdated and irrelevant. If we are to keep up with the pace of change we need to notice when it is time to change our myths. People who hold on to yesterday's myths and role models can increasingly become an embarrassment. There are good reasons why it's time to recognise that warriordom has become redundant.

1. Unfettered warrior energy, even that channelled to meet the orders of superior officers, no longer fits the changing reality of the corporate marketplace. The warrior's style is fitted to the old-style organisation which asked its manager to 'control, order and predict'. Yesterday's organisations are based on models that came out of the Industrial Revolution and found their theoretical underpinning in Newtonian physics and, later, scientific management. Margaret Wheatley, in *Leadership and the New Science,* explains that scientific management and Newtonian principles describe how the world works through the use of machine imagery:

> *In the machine world, one must understand parts. Things can be taken apart, dissected literally or representationally (as we have done with business functions and academic disciplines) and then put back together without any significant loss. The assumption is that by comprehending the working of each piece the whole can be understood. The Newtonian model of the world is characterised by materialism and reductionism—a focus on things rather than relationships.*

Warrior relationships are instrumental cause-and-effect relationships based on past trends and tangible, observable, measurable 'facts'. Old-style organisations and the warrior management principles they support are best suited for stable environments, where things are predictable and knowledge and information are restricted. Such conditions breed old-style warrior managers, whose skills are their ability to:

- imitate, administer, maintain
- focus on structure
- rely on control
- have a short-range view
- accept the status quo
- be classic good soldiers

New-style organisations, however, are post-information age. In today's reality, change is the only constant; knowledge and information are open, plentiful and incomplete. The reality of the new-style organisation is characterised by chaos, complexity, uncertainty and paradox. The rate of change is such that we can no longer even pretend that we can know what is going to happen next. Whole industries come and go overnight. Mergers, takeovers and technological innovation revolutionise the industrial landscape daily.

The Father of Management, Peter Drucker, wrote:

> *The talk you hear about adapting to change is not just stupid, it's dangerous. The only way to manage change is to create it. By the time you have adapted to change the competition is ahead of you.*

This is particularly true because we are in a new era. The IT and communication explosion has signalled the death of capitalism as we know it as surely as the invention of the machine signalled the death of feudalism. Prior to the invention of the machine, we lived and worked in extended family units in rural communities. Power rested in the hands of feudal monarchs, feudal lords and the Church. Professions were passed down through families, and education was received at home and on the job. People even thought differently: they thought in terms of seasons, so their thinking processes were circular, encompassing the possibility of mysticism and fate. Ritual was a significant part of life.

With the invention of the machine, people moved to live near the factories, where towns and then cities grew. Increased mobility led to the breaking up of communities and extended families, and thus the nuclear family was born. Work once manual became automated. New learning was needed, so we saw the rise of mass education. As machines got smarter, we saw the rise of mass higher education as people were trained to handle the new technologies. Power shifted into the hands of industrialists, financiers, politicians and bureaucrats. And our thinking changed. It became mechanistic, linear and rationalistic.

The technology has now changed again, and this has changed every aspect of how we live, work and think. We are now in the post-capitalism age of the e-world (e-business, e-mail, e-motion, e-ducation, e-cology, e-nergy). The new technologies have thrown

us in to a global village. We are now competing and working globally. At the same time, we are cocooning, making our homes our castles and retreating into them. More than 75 per cent of people in the developed world now work in the service sector. We are changing careers so quickly that we now live in the age of life-learning, with many people having five or six careers in one lifetime. Power, too, is shifting, from the nation states to large global enterprises. It is time again for our thinking to change so that we can capitalise on the changes in the environment.
Leaders in this environment need to:

- innovate, originate, develop
- focus on people
- inspire trust
- have a long-range view
- challenge the status quo
- ask what and why

People in today's organisations are now being asked to be self-starters, creative and entrepreneurial, working in semi-autonomous teams on complex and rapidly changing issues and projects. People in corporate life are now implored to run the business as if it was their own, to think outside the rules and boxes, and to manage a highly complex web of relationships, both locally and globally.

Being competitive in today's world demands cooperation. When BP and Mobil Oil were merging their European operations I was asked to work with their European heads of manufacturing. The challenge was that while these two giants were merging their European operations they were remaining competitors elsewhere in the world. For some key personnel, this meant they were working simultaneously for two masters—the merged European entity, and the single and competitive entities elsewhere in the globe. Half the time they were colleagues, the rest of the time rivals.

The boundaries between competitor and ally are becoming blurred. This lack of clear definition—of who belongs where and whose loyalties are whose—produces dynamics very similar to those in blended families, when suddenly children have multiple parents, grandparents and a whole new set of siblings. Organisations and blended families no longer have clear-cut lines of command, nor discrete internal/external boundaries. They are characterised by a myriad of changing relationships. This is no longer the well-defined world of the old-time warrior. Fighting your way forward is no longer appropriate in today's organisational environment, which is characterised by strategic partnerships, joint ventures and relationship marketing. This is a world where communication, trust, a strong sense of self and expert relationship skills are paramount. These are not the skills of the warrior.

2. All this leads us to the second reason why warriors are reaching their use-by date: business is now being called on to be socially responsible. Over the past few decades there has been growing public awareness and concern over air, land and water pollution, and fierce lobbying against depletion of non-renewable resources. A *Business Week* survey found that 74 per cent of people surveyed believed that corporations have too much power, while 66 per cent thought that large profits are more important to big companies than developing safe, reliable, quality products for consumers (Bernstein 2000). Some corporations are rising to the challenge of corporate and social responsibility. At the 2002 World Economic Forum, a joint statement entitled 'Global corporate citizenship: the leadership challenge for CEOs and Boards' was drafted and signed by 36 chief executives from multinational giants including Coca-Cola, Siemens and Renault. The key message was that 'corporate social responsibility needs to be made a central component of business strategy'.

The strength of the international environmental lobby is too great for any business to ignore. More challenging, perhaps, are the calls for businesses to be accountable for their part in exacerbating world poverty, starvation and illiteracy. The rise of 'systems thinking' around the world makes it increasingly clear that nobody and nothing operates in isolation. Business is being called to account for how it operates. Just getting your head around the incredible maze of global interconnections—across industries, cultures, societies, governments and ecosystems—requires huge breadth of vision and intellectual acuity. Being able to face the reality of a world of such highly complex and dynamic relationships, and operating effectively within it, demands that we start looking at the world very differently. Today's executives need to see the world in which they operate as a set of 'possibilities, tendencies, interconnections and interactions, all aimed at increasing the organisation's ability to adapt' (Nevis, Lancourt and Vassallo in *Intentional Revolutions*). This requires expanding our attention to not only the tangible things, but also the dynamic interaction among and between things so that we can recognise shifting patterns.

An example of this complex web of relationships and interconnectedness is the argument that it is the world banks who are leading to deforestation in South America. The argument runs that many indigenous farmers have large banking debts—the pressure to repay these loans encourages the farmers to overuse their land, which quickly becomes depleted and infertile. The farmers then need new space to grow their cash crops, so they clear more forest in search of fertile land. Deforestation reduces the availability of oxygen and decreases the planet's capacity to deal with carbon monoxide overload. Therefore, the reasoning goes, one of the quickest and easiest ways of reducing pollution is to get world banks to forgive the debts of impoverished indigenous farmers. This is a whole new world view—one which demands new ways of thinking and being that are alien to the warrior.

3. The bursting of the IT bubble, the corporate collapses of the early 21st century and the global financial crises have highlighted the need for a level of ethical behaviour, transparent communication and honesty that is alien to the 'information is power' and control ethos of the warrior. A survey conducted by *Training Magazine* and the Center for Creative Leadership found that honesty and reliability from leaders was in high demand. The survey found that ethics, integrity and values rank highest across all managerial levels. The survey also showed that managers believed that leaders currently aren't performing highly on such standards (Scettler 2002).

This was echoed in a TMP worldwide survey which found that one third of males and a quarter of females had been pressured to engage in unethical and/or illegal activity in their workplace and had refused to do so. More shocking was the finding that 33 per cent of the people reporting misdemeanors or pressure to engage in unethical or illegal activity found that no action was taken. Worse still was the finding that 23 per cent of such employees were either disciplined or sacked for speaking up (TMP Worldwide 'Unethical/illegal activity not uncommon to the workplace', press release http:/autmp.com/press/october2001.asp).

Institutional and private shareholders are no longer prepared to sit back quietly and have their funds used to sponsor illegal and unethical behaviours. Nor are they prepared to support organisations that operate in ways that limit transparency of information and behaviour. Moreover, changing legal frameworks make directors personally liable for corporate misdemeanour. Shareholders, directors and executives alike stand to pay highly for clinging to old-style warrior behaviours.

4. Living as if on a battlefield is killing us on a personal level. According to the World Health Organization (WHO), 15 per cent of the population in developed countries suffers from severe depression. With one person in five having a depressive episode at some time in their life, WHO predicts that by 2020 depression will be the second largest killer (after heart disease). The estimated annual cost of this to US business is $44 billion in terms of productivity and absenteeism losses, and other indirect causes ('Disabled by Depression' news release, University of Michigan). In *Care of the Soul,* Jungian analyst Thomas Moore argues that depression is a symptom of us failing to care for and nurture our souls. 'When soul is neglected, it doesn't just go away, it appears symptomatically in obsessions, addictions, violence and loss of meaning. Our temptation is to isolate these symptoms and to try to eradicate them one by one, but the root of the problem is that we have lost our wisdom about the soul, even our interest in it.'

Warriors have little interest in soul. They are too busy working to maintain the status quo and their power therein. To do this in rapidly changing times is extremely hard, so warrior bosses are working harder, longer hours and faster, and insisting that everybody else does the same. Jack Beatty wrote in the *Atlantic Monthly*, 'Compared to their peers 30 years ago, America's 80 million white collar employees are working longer hours, for the same pay and fewer benefits, at jobs markedly less secure and for corporations that regard firing whole ranks of employees as a way to post paper gains and so win Wall Street's favour.' Studies across all developed countries reveal that workers are increasingly fatigued, stressed and concerned that they are losing balance between their private and work lives. Technology billed as saving us time invades our personal space—at home, on vacation, even in the bathroom.

The way we are working is causing an epidemic of depression, exhaustion, alienation, soullessness and relationship rupturing, and a plethora of accompanying stress-related diseases. Moreover, the restructuring of the job market has heightened its complexity, meaning that some people are exhausted from overwork, while others are exhausted from looking for work or having to please many masters.

Warrior ways negate self and soulfulness. 'When the soul's power is neglected, usurped or toyed with, then we fall into the truly problematic condition of sadomasochism which can range from being an extreme clinical syndrome to a dynamic at work in the most ordinary, simple transactions,' writes Thomas Moore (*Care of the Soul*, pp.129-30). When genuine power is in use, there are no tyrants or bullies, and no real victims. This is reversed in sadomasochism, where we find dichotomies of violence and victimisation, controller and subject. According to Moore, 'Sadomasochism, though it may look superficially like genuine strength, is a failure of power. Whenever one person victimises another, real power has been lost.'

The line between warriordom and sadomasochism is pretty fine. This can be hard to see in complicated relationships (such as those at work), where there are differentials in power. In these circumstances, 'weaklings puff themselves up and try to act strong; tough people hide their vulnerability; the rest of us fail to look past the surface.'

5. Warriors tend to be young and male. No one has much use for an ageing warrior. I heard a business commentator say that 'The executive job market is moving to 50, fit and fired.' For decades, women have had great difficulty breaking into the warrior culture, and have done so generally only when they have been prepared to sacrifice their femininity and adopt warrior behaviour.

This has robbed business and government of the kind of diversity that it needs if it is to understand fully the complexity of the world in which it operates. Moreover, the rising average age of the population in developed countries should encourage business and government, for both social and economic reasons, to find ways of capitalising on the expertise and experience of its older workers.

Unfortunately, old warriors can become an increasing burden and embarrassment if they are committed to old, ever more outdated behaviours, mind-sets and myths. Undermined by years of denying their emotions and spiritual wellbeing, old warriors can become a real liability. Age without wisdom is definitely not a good idea.

In short, warriors tend to see things in a linear means/ ends fashion, and then, without too much reflection or need for emotional maturity, engage in highly planned and instrumental action. The environment is saying that this is no longer good enough. Warriors, trapped as they are in their old mind-sets, do not understand that the way they think and the place in which they are searching for the answers are actually what is causing all their problems. They are creating their own exhaustion, depression and redundancy.

Heroes are Good for Business

Warriordom is bad for the environment, bad for the individual and out of date. It is also very bad for business. Studies into world's best business practice reveal that it is heroic leadership styles and practices that have companies out-compete their rivals over time. James Collins and Jerry Porras, who reviewed the practices of companies which were, over a period of 60 years, six times more successful than their nearest competitor and fifteen times more successful than the market, found that what led to outstanding success was values (*lived*, not those natty ones on laminated cards), heroic leadership (they called it 'level 5 leadership') and organisational cultures that fostered community. The researchers went so far as to say that when companies concentrate on product, profit or strategy ahead of building the community spirit and culture, they can expect to fail.

Jim Collins in *Good to Great* argues that outstanding success over time requires the presence of at least a few level 5 leaders. Level 5 leaders have strong self-efficacy, drive, the ability to accept responsibility for outcomes, and they apportion success to others. Level 5 leaders know what they want and get it through win-win-win relationships with other people. They have strong professional will and great personal humility.

Best-practice companies provide their level 5 leaders with staff who have the capacity for growth, self-discipline and relationship. Great people make great companies, so great companies seek to attract and keep the best people. Good people in these times of hyperkinetic change are not just good technically—that is a given. They must also have the capacity to develop emotionally, professionally and personally. They also need to be able, willing and excited about being part of a community. When people want to be part of the organisational community they are less attached to what the company actually does. This is essential, because all the world's best-practice companies are prepared to throw out what they do if it is no longer relevant to their changing environment. Collins and Porras found that great companies are prepared to change whatever is necessary to survive as a community. They were able to do this because the people they employed were flexible, intelligent, committed and easy to manage. In fact, they mostly self-managed, getting on with the things that mattered in line with their personal desires and the organisation's strategy (as it evolved and changed).

Level 5 leaders lead their companies to success because they are able to face reality. This makes sense. If you can't face and deal with the truth, if you don't have the courage and integrity to surface underlying problems, you can't prevent disasters, seize opportunities or adequately prepare for the future. This is in direct contradiction to the warrior strategy of avoidance, the wish to ignore problems, avoid conflict and maintain the status quo. World's best-practice companies and their heroic level 5 leaders realise that they live or die by the quality of their decisions, and that good decisions can only be made on true, full and accurate data. The capacity of individuals to deal with the truth is both a function of their personal maturity and the safety of the environment in which they work. The environment is largely a function of the quality of leadership. Level 5 leaders reward truth-telling over political correctness, and problem-solving ahead of sycophancy. Integrity/honesty is one of the key personal qualities that excellent leaders demonstrate. Level 5 leaders also have the courage to deal with conflict, chaos and the problems that emerge when the truth is spoken.

In short, the research tells us that success comes from putting leadership, people, values, goals, relationship, community and culture first. When good leaders live the values they espouse, empower the right people and promote a culture that encourages honesty, participation and innovation, profits and corporate longevity follow. It is in reversing the usual warrior mind-set that short-term and long-term success become compatible. The road to world's best business practice lies in encouraging people to change their thinking and relationships through going on the hero's journey.

World's best-practice companies are change masters. They maintain their competitive advantage by investing in people and creating leaders and cultures that live by humanly enhancing values. Corporations as communities are profitable, sustainable and exhibit outstanding success. They are able to combine increasing shareholder value with being exciting, rewarding places to work. They combine economic success with good corporate citizenship. They also combine a capacity to maintain the highest quality with a constant capacity for change and innovation. Obtaining such win-win outcomes demands that we reverse our thinking, putting people and community first and profits second.

What world's best-practice companies are *not* is comfortable. They build strong and robust cultures and community so that people can deal with ongoing challenge, continuous growth, unending reinvention, change and transformation. This makes them exciting and wonderful places to be, but uncomfortable and unsettling. This provides a big challenge for warrior leaders driven by avoidance and obsolete bottom-line focus. The research shows us, however, that the rewards for meeting this challenge are huge.

Recognising Heroes

Changing times require a change of myth. Rollo May writes in *The Cry For Myth*:

> *Our task as part of the discovery of contemporary myths, is to rediscover the fundamentals of heroism ... the rediscovery of heroism ... will suffice to inspire us to go beyond the cocaine, the heroin, the depression and the suicides, through the inspiration of myths that lift us above the purely mundane existence (pp 56–58).*

Heroic level 5 leaders are not easy to spot. In business life they tend to shun the limelight. In public life this is less easy. Nelson Mandela and Mother Teresa are wonderful examples of heroes. These are people who have marched to a different drum. They can both be considered visionaries. Mandela believes in relationships and has the intelligence and breadth of vision to see the congruence between purposeful action and the common good. This was also true of Mother Teresa.

Heroes have a strong sense of self. They know who they are and that for which they stand. They are their own people and are undaunted by the apparent obstacles presented by rigid systems and rules, and the irrational behaviour of others. Heroes decide where they are going and then find a way of getting there that is socially and culturally nurturing. Their integrity, deep sense of who they are and commitment to their vision make heroes true stayers. Twenty-seven years in prison didn't daunt Mandela's beliefs. The sheer and unending nature of her quest did not stop Mother Teresa working with the dying and poverty-stricken around the globe. The persistence of heroes is matched by their creativity and flexibility as they respectfully work their environment and artfully manage their relationships.

This isn't to say that heroes are easy to get on with. Being very much their own people, they follow their own lead and do things their own way. Heroes are uniquely themselves. They are very much in touch with their own hearts and souls, and constantly challenge other people's preconceptions and the status quo. Being at home with themselves, their calling, their inner demons, their strengths and their weaknesses, heroes are willing to accept other people's humanity as readily as they accept their own. Thus, in apparent contradiction, heroes appear as both magnetic, enlivening and fascinating people, and as challenging, threatening and downright uncomfortable to be around with their non-conformity and originality. Heroes can be male or female, of any race or creed, and they seem to get better, more effective, more powerful and more revered as they age. As Rollo May writes in *The Cry for Myth* (p. 54):

The hero carries our aspirations, our ideals, our beliefs. In the deepest sense the hero is created by us; he or she is born collectively as our own myth... heroism... reflects our own sense of identity and from this our own heroism is moulded.

Heroism, then, is qualitative, not quantitative. It reveals itself in human character and how that character is reflected in private and public places. The new challenge for organisations is to find heroic myths that inspire people to new forms of being, thought and action that are not only congruent with the changing needs of the environment, but also nourishing to the human spirit.

Currently the major carriers of our need for heroism are organisational and political leaders. Unfortunately, they usually serve this function unconsciously and, for the most part, remarkably badly. Freudian analyst and international professor of human resources Manfred Kets De Vries in *Fools and Imposters* (pp. 5-20) claims that we project our hopes, dreams and aspirations onto those who lead us. This gives the leader a mythical quality which mature, skillful leaders can use to further the common good.

The way leaders manage the mirroring process reflects their degree of maturity. The acid test is their ability to preserve their own hold on reality, to see things as they really are, in spite of the pressures from people around them to join their distorted mirroring game.

In other words, we are so keen to have heroes that we create them even when they do not exist, giving huge power to our corporate leaders who, if they are mature and personally aware, can skillfully manage our projections. Ironically, to do this well takes the skill of a hero.

So many warriors have let us down. We waver between our hope of finding heroic leadership and our cynicism that none will be forthcoming. As Rollo May puts it in *The Cry for Myth*, 'It is our fake heroes who give heroism such a bad name.'

Perhaps we are looking in the wrong places for our heroes. We have become so used to looking at external appearances that perhaps we do not see the hundreds of examples of everyday heroism that surround us. Moreover, on the outside, heroes do not look a whole lot different from anyone else. It is not how they look that makes heroes different, it is how they think and feel, as well as what they do. This is quite a radical concept in a society that idolises people on the basis of how they look and how much money, power and status they accumulate. As a society, we canonise the rich and famous regardless of their intrinsic value to themselves and to others. We have made a social decision to judge the book by the cover. We all want good times, wealth, endless happiness, eternal youth and status. The pages of popular magazines do not ring out with heartwarming stories of everyday heroism. No, they tell us that Madonna was caught getting off an aeroplane without her make-up or that yet another politician, businessman or film star was caught with his pants down. Rollo May in *The Cry For Myth* (p. 55) claims that we have confused heroes with celebrities. Celebrities are merely people who are known for being known. So how, then, do we recognise a true hero when we find one?

If heroism is about character, values and quality of thought, feeling and action, then we are most likely to detect it through relationships. Because heroes possess a deep sense of self, aliveness and emotional and spiritual presence, relationships with them are dynamic and enlivening experiences—we feel enriched, animated and challenged as a result of our association with a hero.

Everyday heroes are real. They are, however, rarely saints. In fact, it is often their acceptance of their own faults and flaws that make heroes approachable. To benefit from knowing or associating with a hero, you need to be a bit of a hero yourself. If you are to detect real heroism when you encounter it, you need the courage to see past the surface, to risk bringing some of yourself into relationships. Only when we are in touch with the seeds of heroism within ourselves are we in a position to not only see, but also encourage, heroism in others. When we get in touch with the hero within ourselves, we are able to recognise heroes and heroic acts everywhere. It is then that we will find that our lives are filled with awe and gratitude, as the heroism we perceive around us bolsters our belief in humanity and helps us to feel a little more optimistic about facing life's problems.

This, says Rollo May in *The Cry For Myth* (p. 53), is also the path to community, for 'the hero is typically the soul of the community. Heroes are necessary in order to enable the citizens to find their own ideals, courage and wisdom in society.' He quotes Ernest Becker, who said, 'Society has to contrive some way to allow its citizens to feel heroic.' We hunger for heroes as role models, as standards of action, as upholders of ethics—heroes who are flesh and bone just as we are. The paradox, of course, is that we need heroes to feel heroic, but until we sense our own heroism we will not recognise the heroes our hearts and souls so desperately crave.

Developing Heroes

Since it takes inner heroism to recognise a hero, and since this recognition comes through relationship, warriors, being out of touch with their own heroism and being notoriously superficial in their relationships, generally have great difficulty spotting heroes. It is hard for the unaware or untrained eye to discern a hero when what makes heroes different is largely inside their own psyche.

As warriors are externally focused, they are trained and disciplined to follow orders. They are therefore used to attributing blame and responsibility—in both their personal lives and their work lives—to others. Warrior training is very much about providing models, frameworks and exercises to help people learn the skills, thought patterns and responses seen to be appropriate by the hierarchy at any particular time. As long as they are shown concrete ways forward, warriors are quick and able learners.

In contrast, heroic development is almost the opposite to this. Heroic quests are journeys of self-discovery, inner expeditions led by the heroes themselves. Skilled and able guides are useful—in fact, essential—but the driving force for the heroic quest has to come from the hero as an individual. The seeds of destiny are within us all: the heroic quester is the person who acknowledges the presence of his or her own 'seeds of greatness' and invests the time and energy that it takes to nurture these seeds so that they will grow and flourish. To do this, individuals have to open to their hearts' desires and souls' yearnings, so that they can hear, see and smell the signs that lead to their own heroic roots. Nobody can force you to be a hero. Not only do you have to choose to go on the journey of your own volition, but you also have to possess the courage to keep going, even when the terrain gets rough. In our society, the road to heroism is rarely easy.

As a society, we more commonly follow the way of the warrior. This, suggest Anne Wilson Schaef and Diane Fassel in *The Addictive Organisation*, has us acting in ways that have closely come to resemble the behaviours associated with drug addicts and alcoholics. It seems that as a society we have got it horribly wrong. We claim we want trusting relationships, ongoing learning and creative problem-solving, but our actions reflect those of addicts.

Wilson Schaef and Fassel tell us that prestigious business magazines such as *Fortune* and *Forbes* are little more than testimonials to the wonders of workaholism, and that many books on leadership, which exhort the leader to work whatever hours it takes to be successful while being prepared to sacrifice health, family and peace of mind, are really manuals on how to live and work like an addict. As addictions are diseases that can become life-threatening, this is a very strong claim. However, it is one that Wilson Schaef and Fassel argue convincingly.

They write that the symptoms of addictive behaviour are:

Confusion... self-centredness... dishonesty... perfectionism and ethical deterioration along with crisis orientation, depression, stress, abnormal thinking processes, forgetfulness, dependency, negativism, defensiveness, projection, tunnel vision and fear.

These are the lived values of our society. Of course, we do not advertise it that way. Walk into any large corporation and reach into the pocket of any well-socialised staff member and there you will find a laminated card that tells you the organisation's values and vision. You will read that the organisation cares for its people, serves its clients and practices integrity to the highest order. Then walk down to the human resource department and peruse the results of the past few culture surveys. I have no doubt that you will find that the people in the organisation are saying loud and clear that leaders in the organisation do not 'walk their talk'. What the leaders say in official in-house communications (such as value statements) does not match the way they operate. This is so usual that we have come to think that there is no other way of operating. Hence, we bury our disillusionment in another lightweight magazine, mindless movie or 'fix' such as junk food, alcohol, tobacco, pornography or illicit sex.

Hypocrisy has become pervasive in our society. We have actually ceased to expect any better. Following Wilson Schaef and Fassel's line of reasoning, the ways of the warrior lead, over time, to ethical degeneration. Yet with constant distractions, such as those provided by the media, not only do we have plenty of opportunities to focus on external appearance, but this situation is also constantly reinforced. We thus avoid the need to acknowledge consciously the hollowness and duplicity that has become the social norm.

In my experience, most corporate training programs, fads and instant actions are the 'fixes' of the warrior. As with other addictive substances, these fixes make you feel good when you first use them. However, as reality sets in, you need another fix to keep going. What addicts overlook is that the fixes themselves undermine, and eventually destroy, their ability to cope with life. Almost all corporate training is warrior training. The skills and techniques used in this kind of training are becoming increasingly sophisticated; the really skillful trainers and facilitators are working at a subconscious level (similar to subliminal advertising), manipulating the emotions and actions of the participants and ensuring that warriors are getting enough of their fix to ensure their enthusiastic acceptance of prescribed skills and information. This could be seen as the addict being given their drug. Short-term satisfaction often leads to long-term damage.

Warren Bennis in *Behavior On Line Conversations* notes:

I've never seen anyone derailed from top leadership because of a lack of business literacy [read technical competence] or conceptual skills: It's ALWAYS because of lapses of judgment and questions of character. Always. The second interesting problem is that judgment and character tend to be ignored by those responsible for educating others and are arguably difficult or even impossible to 'teach'.

Heroic development is based in reality and on character. Heroes work with the reality of their thoughts, feelings and environment, going at their own pace on a journey of self-discovery, developing their inner self, growing in their courage to take risks, and building supportive and sustainable relationships. This is often an uncomfortable and energy-intensive process. For those hooked on the latest training methods, reality can seem very dull, boring and non-productive. Reflection and relationship building at a deep level can seem a complete waste of time to those addicted to warrior training.

Warrior training, unfortunately, will always produce warriors. How sad that we spend so much time and money training warriors when what the world needs is more heroes.

A Word on Passion, Energy and Assertive Action

Due to the remarkable ignorance about heroism in the business world, we have come to correlate the aggression of the warrior with action and achievement, while we consider self-knowledge, self-reflection, emotional awareness and intimacy to be unproductive— at best a luxury, at worst a waste of time, or even undermining to the effectiveness of the warrior.

Warriors tend to operate on pure adrenalin; this keeps them energised and able to charge forth like a dinosaur on a mission. This creates a natural high for the warrior, which many people mistake for a feeling of aliveness. Adrenalin may be the body's natural response to danger and crisis, but it is not the indicator of whether you are truly alive.

Warriors have cast their world as a battlefield and therefore live on a continuous adrenalin rush, which gives them spurts of energy and keeps them separated from their feelings and senses. This is why so many executives suddenly become critically ill without warning, and why people get sick on vacation and at retirement. It is only when our adrenalin level falls that we realise how our body actually feels; in other words, how sick or well we are. It's not that we weren't actually sick before, it's just that we didn't notice. Unless we do notice, we are not in a position to take appropriate preventative action. This is the clue to warrior behaviour. Warriors are so focused on their goals, so hyped up on adrenalin, that they rarely notice the subtleties of their actions, their physical responses or their environment until they are faced with a disaster. So, warriors charge from crisis to crisis.

There are other, much more effective ways of developing potent energy and harnessing it into action. The energies released from emotions such as love, passion, desire, jealousy, fear, grief, hope and strong spiritual belief can all become fuels for creation and achievement. Couple this with the will of an heroic spirit and you have a force with which to reckon. Unlike adrenalin surges, emotional and spiritual energy does not need to have detrimental physical and social effects.

As we will see in later chapters, the energy of the heart and soul is a sorely neglected key to effective action. Not only does it provide healthy sustenance for action and thought, but it also allows us to be strong, to stand our ground, to persist and deal effectively with the toughest opposition. Unlike the force of the warrior, however, emotional and spiritual energy, if used with skill and awareness, is immensely flexible and especially effective in relationships.

Studies such as those chronicled by Daniel Goleman in *Emotional Intelligence* show us that those who have learnt to work with their emotions are measurably more effective. Research shows that the more complex the task, the more important our emotional intelligence becomes. Results of a variety of studies provide us with some stunning figures. The top one per cent of programmers in the IT industry, for example, had a 1272 per cent higher productivity rating than their peers. While technical skills were necessary here, they were hardly sufficient. The differentiators were elements of emotional intelligence displayed through collaboration and teamwork.

Those with high emotional intelligence have been found to be motivated, self-disciplined, to aspire to excellence, to continually seek to reskill and learn, and to add value. They sustain long-term business development and build strong corporate cultures that promote high morale and prevent loss of talent. Warriors replace their lack of emotional intelligence with brute force, obsession and hard work. They create around them crises and busy work. Heroes, on the other hand, are constantly developing their emotional intelligence and work smarter, not harder. Heroes get things done through and with others and achieve their goals more effortlessly. In a warrior world, these skills are often seen as weaknesses, and heroes face discrimination in warrior cultures, despite (or perhaps because of) their obvious and measurable ability to perform at higher levels of productivity, complexity and ongoing success.

This is why heroes also need to have high spiritual intelligence. Danah Zohar and Ian Marshall in their book *SQ: Spiritual Intelligence, The Ultimate Intelligence* describe those high in spiritual intelligence as having the capacity to be flexible, to face and use suffering, to face and transcend pain and to be inspired by vision and values. Those with high spiritual intelligence are reluctant to cause unnecessary harm to others or their environment. They have a tendency to see the connections between diverse things (they are holistic), and have a marked tendency to ask 'Why?' or 'What if?' questions and seek fundamental answers. They also have the facility for working against convention. Thus those with high spiritual intelligence question, think creatively, change the rules, and work effectively in changing situations by playing with the boundaries, breaking through obstacles and innovating. Spiritual intelligence encourages us to see the bigger picture, to be co-creators of the world in which we live.

To succeed in the fast-changing world of post-capitalism, we need high emotional intelligence and high spiritual intelligence. Heroes have both. The path to heroic success is the heroic journey.

The Heroic Journey

Joseph Campbell, in the much quoted text *The Hero of a Thousand Faces*, sets out the three key stages of the hero's quest. They are:

1. separation or departure;
2. the trials and victories of the initiation;
3. the separation and reintegration into society.

Stage 1: Separation or Departure

This stage involves the recognition of a need to look beneath the surface, to go on the hero's journey. The impetus for stage one may come as the result of conscious intention—a decision to go after a dream or search out inner demons. We know this involves risk and yet we consciously move out of our comfort zones in search of something we intuitively feel to be there, even if, as yet, we have no tangible evidence that it is real, or even worth our interest. Alternatively, the call to the hero's quest may come after a crisis has been thrust upon us and we come to the realisation that a dramatic change of heart is needed. My friend Caroline Jones, an Australian journalist and broadcaster, told me that, after doing hundreds of in-depth interviews for her program 'The Search for Meaning', in which she encouraged people to reveal the intimate stories of their lives, she was convinced it was suffering that had led most of her interviewees to undertake the journey that led them to discover their own heroism. Napoleon Hill, in his classic *Think and Grow Rich*, studied the lives of hundreds of successful people and suggested, 'All who succeed in life get off to a bad start and pass through many heartbreaking struggles before they arrive.'

The turning point in the lives of those who succeed usually comes at the moment of some crisis, a crisis that encourages them to go on a journey to discover their other selves. Joseph Campbell tells us that this process is not without its false starts. It is only sensible to feel fear when embarking on an unknown voyage to an unknown destination. Those who move on from stage one, therefore, are those who are sufficiently determined to find the courage necessary to leave known territory and their own comfort zone for uncharted waters.

For some, the call to the hero's quest is so compelling that it feels as if they have no choice but to heed it. When we study the lives of the great heroes, we find that they often felt compelled to develop their own heart, spirit and personal gifts. Saint Ignatius, the founder of the Jesuit order, determined to change his life radically while recuperating after a painful operation. Hours of reading and quiet reflection brought him in touch with a deep calling to give up the wealth of his noble birth and go out into the world penniless.

For those who hear the summons to the quest less strongly, it is often easier to set out on stage one when they are in a sudden state of disaster. If known territory is suddenly unbearable, the unknown can seem a positive alternative. Some people, however, are so determined not to hear the heroic summons that even pain, disaster and hardship will not propel them onto a new path. Unfortunately, when discomfort, change or misery creep up on us, we can sometimes become victims of the boiled frog syndrome: while a frog thrown into boiling water will quickly jump out, paradoxically it will allow itself to be boiled alive if put into cold water which is then slowly heated. Slowly accumulating pain and hardship can trick us out of our ability to rebel.

Meeting With Your Mentor

Apart from inner drive and motivation, the factor most likely to help us to take the leap into the abyss that represents the hero's quest is the meeting of a mentor or guide, someone to accompany us on the journey. This person is likely to have been on his or her own heroic quest and can therefore understand our apprehension. The experience and wisdom this person has gained from his or her own searching can give us the heart we need to invest in our own development.

Historically, heroic mentors have commonly been priests and priestesses. Today, they include the spiritual masters and gurus who serve as inner guides for their flock. Perhaps the most common heroic guides today, however, are the psychologists, psychiatrists, analysts and psychotherapists who have made being at home with the inner world their life's work. This is not to say that everyone working in these fields knows how to be an heroic guide. Unfortunately, many spiritual leaders and psych professionals use their people skills and knowledge as a shield against the pain of growing and learning themselves. When this happens, they, in their own way, become warriors. They keep other people small and dependent, fitting into some predetermined model of spiritual or psychological wellbeing, rather than supporting people to follow their own inner calling and grow in their own way.

Heroic guides, in contrast, operate with a quite different agenda. They walk alongside the questing hero, asking questions rather than giving answers, empathising rather than directing. They encourage problem solving and reframe the heroic quester's inner and outer struggles in ways that open up possibilities for personal growth and socially responsible success. This doesn't mean that good guides help you conform to society. Their role is to help you find and develop your own unique character, styles, desires and gifts so that you can apply these in ways that enrich both your world and that of the people around you. Being heroic questers themselves, good guides are often somewhat eccentric and will certainly not help you to 'normalise' your behaviour or aim to achieve some predetermined standard of perfection. Their aim is transformation, not conformity.

As with any professional group, gurus, priests and psychology professionals are of varying quality. A poor guide can lead the quester down many blind alleys. Yet with luck, determination and Good-quality support, the heroic quester leaves stage one and finds him/herself in, to my mind, the most vital part of the hero's journey.

Stage 2: The Trials and the Victories of the Initiation
This stage of the journey will involve uncertainty. Although much preparation has preceded stage two, this phase requires the heroic searcher to trust in his or her heartfelt response and meet what they meet. Joseph Campbell in *The Hero With A Thousand Faces* presents this stage as being the battle with the dragon. Many have taken this as signifying the need to be a warrior. James Hillman in 'The great mother, her son, her hero and the puer', however, presents a different picture of the journey at this stage. There may be elements of an external, world-based battle present, but actually the major challenge is the unknown. When the dragon is actually the mysterious uncertainties of our inner and outer world, battle is nonsensical. No gain comes from battling the unknown—the unknown needs to be allowed (a painfully difficult achievement for an action-centred warrior).

The hero's journey is calm, cool and definite, involving no passionate thrusting after a known end (if we knew what the outcome would be, there would be no transformation). The transformation comes from learning to accept both the reality of life and ourselves at a different level, through learning to embrace the unknown, or at the very least the first step, on the path to the unknown. This learning often comes through inaction, stalemates and false turns. Here we can think of Nelson Mandela and his many years in gaol. Many heroes have had such periods of apparent hopelessness. Ulysses was lost for ten years before he was rescued and able to make the journey home. These times are like a small death: until the old passes, there is no room for the new. It is likely that in these trying periods, the 'dark nights of the soul', real compassion is learnt—for it is when we have the opportunity to feel our own pain, without defence and covers, that we are able to truly empathise with the pain of others.

It is only through, and because of, this second stage of crisis that the hero drops the defences and the facade that usually armour them against reality, the outside world and their inner world. Warriors are well trained, programmed really, always to wear their armour firmly in place—to go into battle without it would be suicide. Fighting the unknown is, however, pointless.

Holding up your guard against inner wisdom, emotional maturity and relationship is equally senseless. For most warriors, therefore, changing deeply ingrained habits of self-protection, aggression and domination takes a massive shift. Perhaps Mandela's time in jail was the preparation he needed for the great task that was ahead of him. Perhaps it was this period of incarceration—a period of incubation, if you like—that allowed him to develop in himself the qualities of greatness that have made him one of the few great heroes and statesmen of our time.

As with all mythical journeys, there are no prescribed routes. Stage two could last two seconds, two weeks, two months, two years or two decades. That is part of the not knowing. Yet life, surely, is unknown. Surrendering to the hero's quest is nothing more than surrendering to the process of life. This is anathema to the warrior, for whom surrender is weakness. For the hero, however, it is the tempering of the steel that ensures the quality of inner strength: a durable flexibility that accommodates life and change as it happens.

Isn't this exactly what the corporate world is seeking: people who are sufficiently emotionally robust and free of psychological blocks that they see life with minimal distortion and are thus capable of dealing with reality effectively, speedily and with wisdom? The answer is a resounding yes. We desperately need heroes, but developing heroes is an act of faith and courage—characteristics that are neither rewarded nor supported in most organisations.

Stage 3: Separation and Reintegration into Society
This is now the final test. The hero must integrate and consolidate the learning gained from the quest into his or her life. This can be seen as 'reality-testing' the gains made to date. Stage three is a trying time, an endeavour of real strength. I am reminded of the story of the monk sitting on a mountain top, engaging in years of deep meditation. Convinced that he has finally achieved inner peace, he returns to his village in the valley below. As he enters the village, a stray dog runs in front of him and the monk

falls, then picks himself up and shouts at the dog, his inner peace shattered.

All over the world, the monks and gurus are coming down from their mountains. The Dalai Lama is a wonderful example of a spiritual master who has dared publicly to reality-test his inner quest. In his dealings with those who have seized his country, Tibet, the Dalai Lama shows us a new way forward—not just in his teachings, but also in his actions. For him, his work on behalf of his country is as much a part of his spiritual practice as his hours of meditation and prayer. His campaign for a free Tibet is his chance to integrate his inner wisdom with worldly action in order to lead humanity forward in real and tangible ways.

For us more humble beings, integration of inner learning with worldly action can be no less exacting. Stage two involves real pain for the heroic quester. Facing our inner demons, dwelling in the unknown and surrendering to the process of living are all emotionally and spiritually exacting practices, wrought at a real cost. When, in stage three, we try to explain this learning to others, they are unlikely to understand unless they have been on their own heroic journey. We may then feel distanced from those we love; from those with whom we are or would like to be intimate. Expressing our truth may evoke conflict in those we meet. The returned hero is different, strange, a bringer of new myths. Like the sighted person in the land of the blind, the newly initiated hero has a wisdom and perspective that is not shared by those around him or her. Communication in such situations becomes an art form. The hero is constantly looking for a bridge between his or her knowledge and experience and the world view of those who are less heroic. So the hero must, as part of stage three, become a teacher, a guide and a mentor to others.

Heroes, unlike the Lone Ranger, do not go riding off into the sunset by themselves. Nor are they immediately cast into the mould of the conquering hero. Union, reunion, home and workplace are the daily realities of heroes. While all this may seem rather unspectacular and ordinary, it is in ordinary life that returning heroes can make their biggest contribution. Heroes are rarely showy; few boast celebrity status. They are simply more aware of the reality of their emotions, spirit and circumstances. They are ordinary people who have discovered within themselves the extraordinary wisdom of their deepest humanity. For the returning hero, the ordinary becomes beautiful. While the world itself may not have changed, the way in which the hero sees and relates to that world will have been transformed. This liberates the returning hero to a sense of joy, hope and soul where others see the humdrum and mundane. The heroic world view finds its greatest application in daily life. Real heroes are those who experience the extraordinary wonders and fullness of the ordinary and then share their intangible difference with those around them in ways that lift others' hopes, dreams and, above all, everyday experience.

The hope for a better world lies in those who can successfully bridge stages two and three. Theoretical heroes aren't going to make the difference that is needed—it is heroism in practice that is so necessary. Yet we give returning heroes so little support. In fact, because we sense their inner difference, heroes both attract and intimidate us. We want to learn their secrets, but we are afraid of their different perspective and their new myths. So, to achieve stage three successfully, heroes have to protect themselves by applying the skills of the warrior. To protect what they have gained, they have to be experts at what they have let go. It is in bridging this paradox that heroes distinguish themselves as leaders.

The returned hero has become master or mistress of two worlds. The worlds of outer worldly achievement and the inner world of personal peace, happiness, wisdom and fulfilment. For people who haven't been on the hero's journey, the accomplishments of the hero are often explained away as external skills. Viewing the hero from a superficial perspective, the warrior can only see the external accomplishments and competencies of the hero. The hero, however, knows that what he or she has gained is far, far deeper. But explaining this to a warrior is virtually impossible. Wise men keep quiet because explaining wisdom to a fool is not only a waste of time but invokes anger and attack. We can each only understand from our current level of knowledge, maturity and experience.

Heroes Are Only Human

Perhaps you are reading this thinking that heroes are somehow superhuman, that you could never be a hero because of your myriad failings. Well, that just makes you a perfect candidate. I haven't met a great person yet who wasn't laden with shortcomings. What makes a hero isn't being male or female, tall or short, strong or weak, black or white, well or sick, young or old. The only thing that makes a hero is desire: the desire to live life to the full and to do so in a way that enriches you, the people around you and your environment. Heroes are just normal people who have made an abnormal choice.

So why bother? Is it not hard enough just getting on with your own life? Why the great need to be heroic? This comes back to personal choice and values. We can, and most people do, choose to live out our lives as a mere shadow of what is possible. We usually convince ourselves that due to the circumstances of our lives we have no discretion to act in any other way. Yet we know in our heart of hearts that this isn't true. We read of amputees running great distances to raise money to help those less fortunate than themselves. We all know or know of someone who has exceeded their normal limits, whether it be a paraplegic driving a long distance, a mother fighting to save her children or a passer-by rescuing a stranger from a life-threatening situation. At these times, we are reminded that we are all capable of much more than we exhibit in daily life. By ignoring our inner flame, we somehow deaden our own self-respect; we let ourselves down by being less than we are capable of being, and all the whingeing or blaming other people or circumstances in the world doesn't make us feel any better. We cannot simply excuse our less-than-exciting lives by saying that we do not have the self-esteem or the skills or are lacking in some way.

The real joy and incentive in the hero's quest is that once you have embarked upon it, you begin to hold your head up high. You develop self-respect. You feel purposeful, empowered and motivated by life. This is enhanced by growing self-knowledge. As we come to know ourselves better, we are in an enhanced position to be true to who we know ourselves to be. We therefore begin to trust ourselves and our actions. As we do this, others come to trust us, too. Life becomes an exciting adventure. We enliven ourselves and in so doing we inspire those around us who, in turn, provide us with feedback to continue on our journey and to reach even higher. The cycle upwards becomes self-perpetuating—not just for the individual, but also for everybody in that person's life. This is a rewarding, interesting, stimulating way to live. It is not safe, not without risks, but it is one hell of a lot better than playing the victim to circumstances and accepting the dull superficiality that seems to be the alternative.

Can You Be a Hero?

Sure, if you choose to be… if you have the courage to make the decision to take charge of how you respond to the world in which you live and of everything that happens to you. It will require an investment of time, energy and thought. It will stretch your boundaries, take you to areas of knowing and insight that may right now seem foreign, even weird. However, if you are prepared to invest in your own aliveness, in enriching your life and in making a difference, you are definitely hero material.

Chapter 3

Letting Go

To attain knowledge, add things every day.
To attain wisdom, remove things every day.

LAO TSU

I recently met a consultant working in the field of organisational leadership who had sought me out because he had heard of my work, or, more particularly, of my financial success. After paying me several compliments he exclaimed, 'There are no accidents. Obviously our meeting was the will of Universal Energy—it is bound to lead to something.'

Well, in the short term, what it led to was me feeling manipulated, patronised, suspicious and angry. I meet thousands of people and have learnt that it is best to take people as I find them, to let them be who they are and to enjoy and learn from every interaction. Whether any particular meeting is the result of Divine Will I feel totally unqualified to decide. What I do know, however, is how I feel as I progress through each interaction. By paying attention to my emotional response to each person and each situation, I have learnt that I can empathise with others, share both my reality and theirs, and subsequently learn and notice the intentions and actions of the people I meet. 'Universal Energy' or not, in my meeting with the consultant I felt that my reality was being denied, my humanity was not being heard and that I was communicating with someone who wasn't being upfront about their agenda.

On reflection, I realised that during that meeting I had been told that I was (on the Myers-Briggs scale) an extrovert (which is no longer true), and that when people grow their primary relationships break down (which is quite contrary to my personal and professional experience). Whenever I revealed any of my own experience in a light that was less than 100 per cent positive (for example, when I suggested that, it being the end of the year, I was tired and needed a holiday), my comments were ignored. In contrast, whenever I said anything that was unshakably positive (like, I was happy to have attained the success I had), I was rewarded with a comment such as,

'That's excellent, wonderful.' In short, I felt I was unheard. We weren't having a conversation; I was simply being showered with New Age mind-sets and jargon that ignored my reality while keeping the other person in a position of control.

What was particularly worrisome is that this particular consultant has a successful international practice advising people on leadership. He is using sophisticated psychological techniques of group dynamics without any formal training or ongoing professional supervision. I wondered how many people's reality he had invalidated, how many he had harmed to date and how many more would be damaged by his well-intentioned ignorance and enthusiastic naivety.

Mental Maps

Master educator and psychologist Carl Rogers wrote, back in 1959, that movement to psychological health involves the individual moving:

...away from a state in which feelings are unrecognised, unowned, unexpressed. He moves towards becoming a flowing process in which ever-changing feelings are experienced in the moment, knowingly and acceptingly, and may be accurately expressed.

He went on to say that at the extreme end of the continuum is the individual who is not in touch with how he or she feels. 'An example would be the intellectualising client who talks only in abstractions, leaving one quite ignorant of what is actually going on within him.' The picture of the individual at this end of the continuum corresponds very closely with the people I see when I enter most organisations. We have been well schooled to separate our human emotions from the work we do. Unfortunately, the demarcation between our humanity and our work has become endemic. Most educational and employment institutions encourage us to discount our personal (emotional) experience of reality. Following Rogers's reasoning, this means we have come to institutionalise emotional ill-health. When we are distanced from our personal reality, we are cut off from our most effective medium for making sense of life and relationships as they happen, which of course means as they change.

How many times have you been in a meeting or a social situation and felt uneasy, as if somehow your needs or interests were not being respected? When we heed these intuitive senses and examine their source, we often find that they are valid. If we are experienced and adept, we can skillfully and quickly manage any situation based on the information that our emotions and intuition bring. We are biologically programmed for our intuitive senses—our emotions—to connect us on a deep level with the social and physical world around us. Hence, we feel a shiver up our spine when we are in danger (even before we become conscious of any threat); we know instinctively that some people are untrustworthy and others are 'good guys' even before we have developed a relationship. When we disconnect from these senses, we disconnect from our speediest, most effective means of sensing change as it happens. It is also our ability to feel emotions and make sense of them that allows us to develop meaningful relationships with others and to operate within those relationships above and beyond the most superficial level.

Unfortunately, most of us have been schooled in, and even rewarded for, ignoring our emotional reality and reproducing socially acceptable mental maps of how things should be. If we spend a moment reflecting on these mental maps, we know that they have very little to do with how things actually are, but we have been so well trained and so richly rewarded for conforming to accepted models that we avoid this reflection. Unfortunately, this means we become increasingly alienated from ourselves, each other and the reality of the world in which we live. We can even manage to avoid facing the folly of this situation by colluding in our behaviour and agreeing not to discuss it.

Psychological health, Carl Rogers tells us, demands 'loosening of the cognitive maps of experience. From construing experience in rigid ways that are perceived as external facts' the individual moves away from tightly held mind maps towards ways of perceiving and making sense of reality that are more fluid constructs which are reshaped and modified by each new experience. Research on the work of Rogers and others shows that the movement towards psychological health involves a shift:

> *...away from fixity, remoteness from feelings and experience, rigidity of self-concept, remoteness from people, impersonality of functioning. It moves towards fluidity, changingness, immediacy of feelings and experience, acceptance of feelings and experience, tentativeness of constructs, discovery of a changing self in one's changing experience, realness and closeness of relationship, a unity and integration of functioning.*

Despite the awkwardness of Rogers' words and the strangeness of many of his ideas, I reproduce them for you because they hold within them radical learning that makes most business, leadership and management books appear ludicrous and misguided. More than that, once we understand the message in Rogers' words we see that most leadership training and practice actually promotes mental ill-health and is completely inappropriate in the rapidly changing, multi-faceted, globalised world of business.

What Rogers is telling us is that we live in a fluid world. The more psychologically healthy we are, the more at home we are with this situation. We are able to be flexible in thinking and feeling. By being in touch with our feelings, we are able to reorientate ourselves to the world as it changes; through acknowledging and accepting our personal reality, we are able to make sense of and act appropriately in our changing environment. Moreover, by raising awareness and acceptance of our personal emotional experience, we are able to let go of rigid mental maps that keep us stuck in a fantasy world out of touch with the fluidity of real life.

Those of us who are aware of and can accept our own emotional reality have no difficulty extending the same courtesy to others. This builds and sustains relationships that are imbued with trust, honesty, acceptance and support, and are therefore capable of moving into deep levels of intimacy.

More on Mental Maps

As a society, we accept and applaud theory that can be scientifically tested. The majority of our education system is based on the study of researched material. We like concepts and theories that can be stated clearly, rigorously investigated and conclusively proved. As I watch my young friends study, I realise how highly rewarded they are for learning the 'facts' and presenting them convincingly.

This is why some educationalists claim we are building timed redundancy into our children. In many fields, especially science and computing, the half-life of knowledge is so short that most of what students at our educational institutions are currently learning will be obsolete within the next ten years. This demands a shift from teaching information (mind maps/theories we currently know and have tested) to teaching people how to learn, ie, how to process new, ever-changing masses of information and knowledge in ways that allow that knowledge to be applied before it is out of date.

This requires an entirely new way of learning, thinking and processing information—a way that demands more of our intellect, a way that demands more of our senses. Lateral-thinking guru Edward de Bono in *Six Thinking Hats* tells us that good thinking involves using our emotions and feelings as well as our minds. This expands both the depth and breadth of our thinking, allowing us to be more adept at processing information quickly, practically and laterally. Daniel Goleman in *Emotional Intelligence* tells us that our emotions not only affect our thinking capacity and strength, but also help us to manage our relationships, prepare us for forthcoming changes and keep us up to date with rapid change and the information revolution.

Biologist Umberto Maturana in *The Tree of Knowledge* informs us that emotions are simply body-felt senses. All animals, including humans, have emotions and these body senses have positive biological foundations. Fear, for example, leads to the fight-or-flight response that saves the lives of deer, lions and humans alike. Jealousy allows for survival of the fittest, and anger ensures self-protection. Love allows for human cooperation, survival and protection.

Emotions are a natural energy source that also provide us with a wealth of information about ourselves in relation to our environment. Emotions are neither good nor bad. They are simply our body's way of providing us with energy to act in a range of biologically important situations, such as threats to our safety, mating, survival of the species and our need to grow as individual adults.

When we reflect on our emotions and express them through language, they become feelings. So, feelings are a combination of our body-felt senses (emotions), our awareness of our emotions and the things we tell ourselves about our emotions. Feelings, therefore, are linked to expression. Imagine, for instance, that you are falling in love. Initially you have no notion of this. You may notice that you have lost your appetite, that the world looks brighter, that birds sing more sweetly and that you want to spend time with a certain person. All these are emotions, which scientists have increasingly studied and found to have real biological bases. It is not, however, until you reflect on these emotions and realise that they are the 'symptoms' of love that you are in touch with the feeling of being in love.

It is our ability to reflect on our emotions and express them as feelings through language that allows us to move into the realm of conversation which Maturana claims is the way we humans put our body-felt senses into words and thus communicate them consciously to others. The Latin *con versare* means we 'turn with the other'. This is the daily flow of life. We live in changing experiences and we explain them to ourselves and others through conversation.

Our skill in real conversation, 'turning with the other', depends on our ability to notice our emotions and then to express them. I have found that many people are completely out of touch with their emotions. This is so acute that many people don't even know words that describe how they feel. When teaching people to communicate emotions, most trainers give out lists of words describing emotions in order to extend people's vocabulary sufficiently to make even rudimentary conversation possible.

Unfortunately, emotions and feelings have gotten a bad name in business—not because they don't serve a useful function, but because we are very unskilled at noticing them, listening to the information they bring and using their energy to propel us into constructive action. We have come to see emotions as uncontrollable and irrational because of this lack of skill, and therefore perceive them as a problem.

In a work context, we have colluded to disallow meaningful conversation—turning with the other in the natural flow of life—frightened that we are too unskilled to handle what may transpire competently and 'professionally'. Emotions and feelings transgress our desire for scientific measurable theories. They are alive, human, messy, mysterious and ever changing. In business, we have decided, we need things to be measurable, testable, containable and controllable—best then, we have decided, to outlaw emotions and feelings in the workplace.

We have replaced the reality of life and humanity with testable, scientific mental maps—theories of how reality should be. The problem is emotions and feelings cannot be so easily dismissed. They can be forced into silence, hidden for fear of ridicule and punishment, and denied, but they don't go away. They merely go underground, from whence they pop up continuously, out of our conscious control and dressed in a manner acceptable to our marketplace—that is, intellectualised and presented as rigid mental maps.

Ironically, this has even happened to the human spirit and emotion. While it is very exciting to see the success of books such as Daniel Goleman's *Emotional Intelligence* and Danah Zohar and

Ian Marshall's *SQ: Spiritual Intelligence, The Ultimate Intelligence*, which legitimise emotion, soul and spirit, it is disappointing to see the authors argue their case in a mechanistic way, providing rigid mind maps to explain the sacredness and wonder of human emotion and spirit. By laying rational scientific theory over our humanness, we attempt to control ourselves, to manage our emotions and spirit. This is very different from befriending our humanness and bringing who we are into what we do.

Emotions are real; denying them or turning them into rational competencies and skills won't make them go away. In fact, trying to perfect who we are only makes our emotions and spirit less controllable, and business conversations, relationships and life harder to handle.

Keeping our emotions hidden beneath the surface and not dealing with them openly, or turning them into rigid mind maps, gives us little opportunity to become masters of our two worlds. Non-conversation centred on apparently 'rational facts' becomes the basis for business discussion, making rewarding relationships, emotional growth and quick effective business decisions incredibly difficult.

Yet, by learning to feel and acknowledge our personal response to life as it happens, and by being able to comfortably express our reality as we experience it, we increase our ability to adapt to the world as it changes. This means we can build and sustain the kind of relationships that ensure personal happiness, mental health and professional success. Moreover, by replacing rigid mental maps with knowledge gained through experience and modified as our experience changes, we are able to gain stability in and mastery of every situation. This comes not from a place of arrogance or control, but from the humility of acceptance and the strength of awareness of our own response and also that of the complex, changeable and ecologically fragile world around us. Thus it is by becoming increasingly aware of and accepting and acknowledging our personal experience that we gain the ability to deal with the complexity of our world and move into meaningful, appropriate action. This is the way of the hero. It is also the way of the twenty-first century.

Feeling Our Way into the Future

Maynard and Mehrtens in the *Fourth Wave* tell us that we can expect to see the emergence of seven trends:

TREND 1	Shift from the unconscious way of thinking to rising personal consciousness and accompanying commitment to making a personal difference.
TREND 2	Growing challenge to the scientific way of looking at the world and increased acceptance of the non-tangible (personal, intuitive) viewpoint.
TREND 3	Authority and power will be qualities that emerge from within the leader, not externally.
TREND 4	There will be a decline in materialism—greed will be far less fashionable than intangibles such as honesty, truth, courage and conviction.
TREND 5	There will be growing political democratisation and increased demand that business take more responsibility for environmental issues affecting air, water and soil.
TREND 6	The business world will continue to extend beyond individual nation states to the world. The borderless world will become reality.
TREND 7	Globalisation will mean more than organisations having branches in major regions of the world. It will mean that within these regions there will be a spin-off responsibility to take care of the environment in which these branches are located.

These trends are all evident. A percentage of people are raising their consciousness, and an ever-growing number of publications argue that there is more to life than that which can be seen, measured and scientifically proven. The message that leadership power comes from within is spreading. Values are changing. There are growing calls for business to be more responsible. The world is becoming increasingly borderless. At the same time, however, we are also seeing a trend towards increasing fundamentalism and conservatism, of people wanting to revert to known mind maps. This is leading to aggression, terrorism and war. We thus have simultaneously an heroic trend to grow emotionally, spiritually, intellectually and socially in ways that help us embrace and capitalise on change as it happens, and a fundamentalist trend to promote rigid mind maps over reality.

We live in a world in which each of us will need to find our way through a complicated maze of intangible, interconnecting changes on a global scale. Many will attempt to do this by battening down the hatches and, like the ostrich putting its head in the sand, hoping that if they pretend the world is static and they are in control, then it will be so. Other, wiser souls will know that survival in the 'new worldview' is no longer a matter of competition and relying on old formulae. Wise folk know that we need to cooperate locally, globally and as a species if we are to prosper.

In the future, relationships, acceptance of diversity and the ability to understand apparently alien viewpoints and cultures will all become increasingly important. To increase our ability to be effective citizens of the twenty-first century, we will need to understand Rogers' words about 'loosening of the cognitive maps of experience'. We will need to notice, acknowledge and differentiate between our personal experience of the world and socially agreed 'facts', thus bringing ourselves into relationship with ourselves, other people and life as it happens.

Now, just as an exercise, think back over the last two business books that you read. My guess is that they comprised page after page of mental maps, theories and models, masquerading as 'external facts'. It may not have passed your notice that this is to some extent largely true of this book. I have gone out and found 'cognitive maps of experience' that support my personal experience. I have chosen to write this book not as I would work with a client, but rather to provide you, the reader, with a range of models, theories, stories and myths that open up the possibility of difference. I have learnt that most people like mental maps. There is temporary comfort in being told how the world is—

even if this invalidates our own experience. Most people seek out authority figures to provide mental maps (theories and models to superimpose on reality) and will follow these mental maps even when their own experience has shown them numerous times in the past that mental maps have very short use-by dates. Large numbers of clients have made it very clear to me over the years that they don't want to experience their own reality: they want the latest and most sophisticated mental maps, and if I won't provide them they will find someone who will.

We invest so much in our mental maps. We spend years studying, developing and testing them. They become our friends, our power bases, the source of our income and the basis of our self-esteem. People will fight to protect their mental maps, even when these have become outdated.

James Gleick in *Chaos* uses Tolstoy's words to explain this:

> *I know that most men, including those at ease with problems of the greatest complexity, can seldom accept even the simplest and most obvious truth if it be such as would oblige them to admit the falsity of conclusions which they have delighted in explaining to colleagues, which they have proudly taught to others and which they have woven thread by thread into the fabric of their lives.*

Joel Barker, in his video *The Business of Paradigms*, explains that when we let go of our existing mental maps we can feel that we are letting go of everything. When the paradigm changes, Barker relates, everybody goes back to zero. What he means here is that if we let go of our mental maps, what we are left with is ourselves, our feelings, opinions, emotions, relationships and the reality of life as it happens. From this standpoint, we are all at an equal level of ignorance. Our power then comes not from what we purport to know, but from the strength of our character, our ability to relate and our skill at learning from every experience. For warriors, this can be terrifying. Better to hang on to outdated information—stale but currently accepted mind maps—than take the risk of being human, learning and growing in equal relationships with others through acknowledging the reality of life as it changes and modifying our knowledge and understanding as we go.

So the fads come and go. Remember Re-engineering, Value Based Management and the model for outstanding performance proffered in the international best-seller *In Search of Excellence*?

As Robert Quinn tells us in *Beyond Rational Management*:

- *the rules taught in textbooks are misleading;*
- *no one theory is inherently better than another;*
- *change is not inherently better than the status quo.*

In other words, life is, business is and change is. What is fascinating is that we try to lay formulae, mental maps and models over the reality and then talk in 'abstractions'—intellectualising rather than emotionally perceiving. By doing this, we leave people quite ignorant of what is really happening; we pretend to ourselves and others that our mental maps are actually external facts, such as claiming our actions are guided by 'Universal Energy' or that business and life work according to some particular formula or model.

The reality of the world in which we live is complicated enough without us confusing things by unconsciously putting a layer of theory over our own experience. After all, our experience is the only thing that we can ever truly know. (Remember when people knew for sure that the world was flat, that the atom was the smallest unit of matter, that time was linear and that European and American history were both largely about the doings of white males?)

Of course, successful entrepreneurs intuitively know the value of experiencing, accepting and relying on their own reality. I was amused to read the *Marketing* account of a speech delivered to the UK-based Marketing Forum by Britain's most successful entrepreneur and marketer, Richard Branson, founder of Virgin Records, Virgin Atlantic Airways and Virgin Cola, to name just a few:

Somehow this 'marketing speak' was the least convincing aspect of Richard Branson. The vocabulary of marketing seemed unfamiliar and uncomfortable to him. His response to questions about branding were halting or non-existent. He laughingly admitted he had never read a marketing textbook. But this surely is the key. He had never had the time for marketing theory; he has been too busy marketing. His actions and beliefs are instinctive, they almost defy analysis. The fact that he finds it difficult to articulate the reasons for his success does not diminish it.

On the contrary, the people who study Branson's marketing success and put it in the next generation of textbooks will have no difficulty in turning his intuitive knowledge into models, theories and prototypes which by the time the books hit the shelves will be out of date. Branson didn't need the textbooks: he had the courage to listen to his own desires, feelings and intuitions. Of course, he got it wrong sometimes—in some cases, horribly wrong—but he just kept on believing in his own experience, validating his own reality, following his heart.

By now you may be thinking that I am anti-intellectual, which isn't the case. What I am saying is that we need flexible ways of experiencing the world and that our emotions provide the quickest route to making sense of changing reality. Unfortunately, those who are emotionally immature or suffering from psychological illness present as rigid in their thinking. They use models, theories and intellectual abstractions as a defence against growing emotionally and psychologically. The outcome of this is not just that they stay emotionally and psychologically stunted, but also that they greatly impair their thinking, which becomes narrow and inflexible. Thus fixed mental maps, while they purport to usher in change, can actually mitigate against change if they keep the mind rigid. Replacing one mental map with another does not free up and improve our thinking. Growing up emotionally does.

This is not to say that all great thinkers and creators have been emotionally mature. They have, however, listened to their intuition, their senses and their own inner knowing. How else could Columbus have discovered America, or women and members of minority groups have had their voices heard and entered into history?

Anita Roddick, founder and director of the Body Shop, was a powerful example of someone who combined intuitive knowing and a strong sense of reliance on her own instincts. Anita opened her first Body Shop in Brighton, England, in 1976. Today the Body Shop operates in 61 countries with over 2,400 outlets. The Body Shop was voted the second most trusted brand in the UK by the Consumers Association and a survey of international chief executives published by the *Financial Times* ranked the Body Shop the 27th most respected company in the world.

In an interview, Anita told me that, in bringing herself and her people to this level of success, she got no help. 'There are no books written,' she claimed, 'that tell you how to do it. You have to rely on your experiences.' And rely on her experiences is exactly what Anita did. She learned from her failures (a previous attempt at running a hotel and a restaurant) and her successes (each Body Shop outlet features a uniformity of decor, product and staff culture). The Body Shop's remarkable success also stems from Anita's reliance on her values and beliefs. 'Business,' she told me, 'should have human empathy attached. Those with humanity,' she continued, 'haven't been to business school.'

Anita, who was committed to sponsoring her own business courses rather than follow the traditional route, believed that business is about more than money. She was quoted as saying 'Business is about compassion and social justice,'. 'Businesses should not be judged on their balance sheet, but on how they look after the weak and frail.'

Anita Roddick was considered to be one the best-known businesswomen in the world. In 2003, Queen Elizabeth II appointed Roddick a Dame Commander of the Order of the British Empire. Some of her achievements included: Veuve Clicquot Business Woman of the Year; British Association of Industrial Editors Communicator of the Year; Mexican Environmental Achiever Award; Women's Center (USA) Leadership Award; Institute of Charitable Fundraising Managers (UK) Philanthropist of the Year; UNEP 25th Anniversary of Women Leaders in Action Award;

and the International Peace Prayer Day Organisation, Woman of Peace prize. Anita received no less than nine honorary degrees and was patron of seven organisations, including the Association of Creation Spirituality and Findhorn College of International Education. She was also a UK Ambassador for British Business.

Each branch of the Body Shop has its own community projects chosen and run by staff. These projects include: human rights campaigns; providing funding for community projects; corporate sponsorship and community trade programs (buying natural products from poor communities to use in beauty products, thus providing indigenous people from pre-industrial societies such as in Mexico and Ghana with the means of achieving economic independence). The Body Shop, inspired by Anita, is also famous for its strong stance on environmental issues and corporate responsibility. By being herself, following her own beliefs and encouraging her staff to follow their own principles and sense of compassion, Anita Roddick created a company with a distinctive, high-profile culture that is in tune with the feelings, beliefs and needs of its chosen market.

Anita claimed that her ability to stand up for what she believed in stemmed from 'being an outsider'. Her Italian parents were the 'only immigrants' in the small seaside town of Littlehampton where Anita grew up. She was never comfortable being 'part of the throng' and learnt to use her difference as a leverage point. Her commitment to human compassion and difference encouraged her to work hard on keeping the culture of the Body Shop 'small-scale, intimate and human. You've got to let people know that you bleed,' Anita told me. 'Let them know that you argue with your old man.' So the Body Shop encourages a culture of storytelling, hope and passion. It boasts workplace counsellors for staff, and a childcare centre, and concentrates on one-on-one staff development.

Anita herself loved talking about feelings and claimed that women bring feelings, family and community into the workplace. This, she believed, is essential, because 'you look for employees, but people come instead'. So as you have whole, full people turning up, you have a responsibility, according to Anita, to develop the whole human, including their emotions and their spirit. This is not only more fun and better for society, but makes good business sense. 'Business is a human endeavour,' Anita informed me. 'Everything is subject to change. So you have to develop relationships with people and encourage them to deal comfortably with paradox, chaos and revolution. We at the Body Shop love the anarchist in people. We love iconoclasts.'

This mirrors Anita's own personality. She was widely criticised for her outspoken views and her ability to use her stance on social and environmental issues to attract free publicity for her company. She shrugged this off. 'I know I'm right,' she declared. 'When I'm doing work, I know I'm right. What's more, it gives me pleasure, I get an incredible sense of achievement through my work and through using the Body Shop as a platform to talk about the issues that I believe in.'

'That's all right for you,' I remarked. 'You're independently rich and powerful. What about the employee stuck behind a desk with a warrior boss? How can they make a difference?'

'Get involved doing community work,' advised Anita. She encourages all her staff to do this, and has found that it has a big impact not just on the community but also on the individuals themselves. For Anita Roddick, 'Spirituality in the workplace is about doing service to the wider community.'

Desire

Anita Roddick was a woman who radiated passion for life and a desire to make a difference. James Hillman, in his challenging book *The Soul's Code* (I have difficulty reading Hillman's books, as I find they waver between blatantly challenging my reality, insulting my sense of propriety and providing brilliant and illuminating insights), introduces the idea of the 'daemon'. He suggests that we each come into the world as an acorn, which already contains so many of the elements that will be expressed as we grow. It's as though we are born with our heart's desire already in place. Mozart was born a musical genius, Michelangelo an artist and Shakespeare a writer. What time and growth allow is for each of us to grow down into the fullness of who we are—into our own daemons, into our own souls.

Those who are fully in touch with their daemon are filled with a passion for action. Unfortunately, most people have lost touch with their longings, their desires, themselves. As imagination, desire, the will to take action, enthusiasm and breadth of vision all seem to be intimately connected, those who have lost touch with their desires have lost a lot. Ambition, of course, is a powerful expression of desire. I love working with ambitious people. They are quick to learn—quick to take the risk of unfolding their own experience, of growing down into the skills, knowing and feelings that connect them to their richest potential, their daemon and their souls.

D.H. Lawrence wrote, 'desire is holy'. Related images come to mind: 'wings of desire', the desire that 'burns in the breast' and having 'fire in the belly'. These are powerful driving forces, expressions of longing, yearnings seeking expression, the gut-felt drives that can propel us forward on the hero's journey.

I find that ambitious people have the desire, the energy, the motivation to do whatever work is necessary to take on the challenge of following the hero's way. I guess this is not surprising, as that which blocks our desires is the same material with which we must work as we follow the hero's quest. Those who have lost sight of their own ambitions and desires have lost sight of what is possible, and generally lack the motivation to deal with their own fears, doubts, self-limiting beliefs and inner demons.

I remember receiving an angry response to my article "Achieving personal success: Standing tall against the odds":

> *How terribly confronting it is to most people to see someone who refuses to limit themselves to accepted mediocrity. Someone who dares to believe that they can be more, do more and go further stands out as a thorn in the side of those too timid, too dull and too lazy to risk living life to the full. Successful people aren't necessarily born with some great gift—they are merely people who believe they can make a difference and then can withstand the disempowering effect of those who try to bring them back to the accepted average. So many people settle for so*

much less than is possible because they don't have the courage to dream, the self-esteem to believe they can have their dream and the energy and perseverance to go after what they want.

The angry response came from a self-styled yogi who had decided that desire was unacceptable. Although it was hard to determine just what he was saying (through the rambling intellectualisations and platitudes), I caught the drift that he thought ambition was sinful, desire was harmful and evil, and that the only true way was to cut attachments to such things as worldly possessions and relationships. I felt a deep sense of pity for this man who had used a rigid mind map to justify his fear of life. By deadening his desires he could avoid failure; by caring for nothing he could avoid the pain of loss. The cost of doing this was that he was avoiding life.

Of course, not all ambition is heartfelt. Many people have internalised the expectations of their parents, partners or peers, and are ambitiously seeking to be successful in other people's eyes. This sort of ambition can be killing. And yet, I would rather this than nothing. In my experience, ambition (whatever its source) is a strong driving force that can be readily accessed for the good of the individual and society. Someone without fire in the belly is just plain draining—they seem to lack the energy to survive, let alone grow and contribute usefully to society.

Our ambition, our desires, can propel us into life. The beauty of the hero's journey is that it uses the energy and force of this propulsion to have us grow down into who we are, into our hearts and souls. This is no easy task.

Desire versus Addiction

Given the strong tendency towards addiction in the business world, it is important here to distinguish between heartfelt desire and compulsion. Anne Wilson Schaef and Diane Fassel in *The Addictive Organisation* tell us that:

...an addiction is any process or substance that begins to have control over us in such a way that we feel we must be dishonest with ourselves or others about it... an addiction is anything we feel we have to lie about. If there is something we are not willing

to give up in order to make our lives fuller and more healthy, it
probably can be classified as an addiction (pp. 68–73).

This raises interesting questions when it comes to organisations. How honest are we with ourselves, our colleagues or our bosses? How often do we agree to something in a meeting because it isn't worth the trouble of stating what we really think, or working out how we really feel? How often do we go along with an instruction, a group decision or some inane idea simply to keep the peace? We probably don't think of this as lying. We probably don't think that in sticking to the status quo we are avoiding making our lives fuller and more healthy. Most of us think that the deceit and compliance that go on in organisations are normal. We are probably right, but the genius that Wilson Schaef and Fassel bring to the table is that they let us know that normal, or accepted, isn't necessarily healthy. More than that, they encourage us to find another more life-giving way. In my work with executives and corporations around the world, I know that there is a better, more enriching and rewarding way forward. I also know that most people are yet to realise that honesty, emotional health and sustaining relationships are possible and extremely productive in a work context.

One of the insidious things about addiction is that addicts rarely realise that they have a problem. One of the reasons for this is that they congregate with other addicts (alcoholics, for example, rarely socialise with non-drinkers). More than this, addicts have a way of justifying their behaviour as normal, and anyone who has a problem with their behaviour as abnormal. Wilson Schaef and Fassel's point is that in business we are behaving in unhealthy ways which we feel obliged to lie about to ourselves and to each other. This constitutes an addiction. Individuals and societies can only cure addictions by first recognising they exist and then taking constructive action to do something about them.

Listening to our heartfelt desires is a strong motivating force to help us do this. These heartfelt desires lead us towards having 'fuller and more healthy' lives, while addictions drive us towards compulsive behaviour and deception that in turn leads us towards ill-health, personal and relationship breakdowns and, in many cases, death. Family therapist Robert Stubby in "Inside the chemically dependent marriage" gives us nine 'rules' of the dysfunctional family system. These are in fact the nine rules of addictive systems. We can tell how addictive our own and other people's behaviour is by noticing how closely they adhere to Stubby's nine rules. Wilson Schaef and Fassel claim that these nine rules apply in most organisations. The nine rules are as follows.

Rule 1: It is not okay to talk about problems
In *Reaching for the Stars: The Politics and Process of Bringing Vision to Reality* I list the problems that leadership teams of highly successful corporations have told me they avoid discussing. These 'off-agenda' items include:

- personal fears, disappointments, concerns, obstacles
- people and their performance
- succession planning
- staff movements
- personal goals, objectives, beliefs
- conflict within the group
- profit
- capital
- structure
- evaluation
- costs
- perceived business performance
- interpersonal relationships
- different methods of operation and major philosophical differences within the group
- examination of external business factors that appear to be out of the group's control

- disagreements about the validity of measurement practices used within the group in both financial and non-financial areas
- different industrial relations practices used by group members

Even highly intelligent, successful business leaders can, when operating within an addictive system, manage to avoid discussing any business or strategic issue (no matter how important) if such issues are considered a problem and are outside of the group's tolerance for discomfort, reality and conflict.

Those with heartfelt desires, on the other hand, openly table and deal with problems, simply because not to do so gets in the way of greater success. In his best-selling *The Road Less Traveled*, psychiatrist M. Scott Peck makes the point that:

Problems, depending upon their nature, evoke in us frustration or grief or sadness or loneliness or guilt or regret or anger or fear or anxiety or anguish or despair. These are uncomfortable feelings, often very uncomfortable... Yet it is in this whole process of meeting and solving problems that life has its meaning.

He tells us that 'Problems are the cutting edge that distinguish between success and failure.' As such, dealing with problems demands courage and wisdom. It also creates courage and wisdom. It is in dealing with problems that we grow mentally and spiritually. Warriors, unskilled at noticing and dealing with the emotions that problems induce, do their best to ignore, deny and repress problems. This not only means the problems don't get tabled and solved quickly and efficiently, but also that warriors are robbed of the emotional, spiritual and intellectual learning that comes from working through problems as they arise.

'The tendency to avoid problems and the emotional suffering inherent in them,' writes Peck, 'is the primary basis of all human mental illness.'

Heroes, realising the wins involved in dealing with conflicts, change, chaos, paradox, challenge and difficulty, quickly bring to the surface and work through problems as and when they occur. Thus heroes appear to have more problems than warriors, simply because heroes talk about and deal with difficult issues. Warriors strive to appear perfect, but are often sitting on a minefield of issues which are neither acknowledged nor resolved, and invariably cause hardship and pain to others and often lead to the unseating of the warrior when today's hidden problems eventually erupt.

Rule 2: Feelings should not be expressed openly
Those following the path of healthy desire have no difficulty in owning their emotional reality. As we have seen from Rogers, this allows them to flow with life as it happens—adapting, readjusting, capitalising on new situations as they arise. Addiction, however, keeps people locked in fixed patterns of thought, behaviour and response. When this is coupled with an inability to acknowledge and resolve problems, it is extremely debilitating both personally and organisationally.

Some years ago, a man (let's call him Jim Jones) was sent by his boss to my Camelot program (a nine-month program for corporate high-fliers). His boss felt guilty that Jim, having been a loyal and hardworking employee, really had no future in his present company. Jim was rigid and fixed in his ways and thinking, and wasn't keeping pace with the rapid changes happening around him. From the moment I met Jim, I liked him. He felt flattered that he had been sent on such a prestigious leadership program. He was keen to learn, but felt stuck in his current job and didn't know how to move forward. The more Jim spoke, however, the more bored I became. I pride myself on my exceptional listening skills, but it was all I could do to stay awake while Jim continued his monologue about his good fortune in his company sponsoring him to undertake a challenging leadership program.

Over the course of the Camelot program, Jim's ability to bore anyone within earshot to sods became a point of celebration. Jim gave me and the other members of Camelot permission to tell him when he was becoming too dull. This allowed us to sing out singly or in unison 'Boring!' before the paint started peeling off the walls. Through all this, Jim realised that he, too, was bored. At an early age, he had shut down his ability to notice and express his emotions, he had shut down his heartfelt desire. In order not to put us to sleep, he himself had to wake up—to his own emotional reality. He needed to grow down into the embers that could rekindle the fire in his own belly. When he did so, his life took off. He included his family in his own 'wings of fire'. He received feedback from his family, his colleagues and his boss that he had become a new man (an alive, exciting, purposeful one), and over a period of two years he received two big promotions.

What continues to amaze me is that no one had ever told Jim how boring he was. In fact, I find again and again that rarely are people told by the people who love them, employ them, live with them and work with them, what impact they are having. Unless we are in touch with and express our emotional reality, we undermine our own achievement, joy and aliveness, and that of those around us.

Rule 3: Communication is best if indirect, with one person acting as a messenger between two others.
Some years ago, while working with the top team of a large industrial company, I was told repeatedly by the managing director that he had great problems with one of his general managers. I knew and liked both men, and found it curious that the problems the managing director was having were in areas such as flexibility and learning, where the general manager had particular interest and was avidly pursuing further growth. When I discussed this with the general manager, he noted that his blocking of the MD had more to do with a variety of emotional issues and personal preferences than his dislike of change. Upon prompting, the general manager approached the MD and discussed his misgivings, fears and desires, and the two men developed a strong, workable and successful relationship. Some time later, the general manager (a man in his fifties) told me that this was the first time

in his professional career that he had had an open, self-revealing discussion with a boss about their mutual relationship.

While you may not find that amazing, it knocks me out. How can we work with people, live with people, coexist with people and not have open, direct communication? How can we expect our relationships to work if we pay them no attention? We wouldn't think of flying a plane that wasn't regularly serviced and maintained, and yet we fly through life without paying attention to the safety and health of even our most important relationships.

The difference between those with an addiction and those with healthy desire is that, once made aware of the need to work on relationships, the addict either ignores, denies or ridicules it, whereas those with healthy desire face up to the shortcomings in their relationships and do something constructive about them.

Rule 4: Be strong, good, right and perfect
One of the reasons people cling so strongly to fixed mental maps is that, if you know what the rules are (even if they are outdated, ludicrous, artificial and dysfunctional), you can learn how to follow them and you have more chances of being 'right'. This, of course, is the world of the warrior. There is a pervasive terror in the business world of showing any vulnerability. Heaven forbid that we let one person admit to human fallibility, because what would that say about the rest of us? Yet it simply isn't humanly possible to be strong, good, right or perfect all, or even most, of the time. Nor is it constructive.

Following your heart's desire means that you will be very vulnerable. As no two hearts beat to the same drum, acknowledging and admitting our heart's desire sets us apart and puts us on our own unique hero's journey. In an addictive system, only one reality is allowed, and that is the reality of the addict. Being strong, good, right and perfect actually means adhering to the addictive reality— in other words, being emotionally anaesthetised, mentally inflexible and unyielding in relationships. To do this is to deny our inner light. To deny our inner light is to deny ourselves and society of all we can be—our personal genius, imagination and spiritual fire. That all sounds pretty weak, bad, wrong and imperfect to me.

Rule 5: Make us proud

Now this is a heavy number. The difference between addiction and following your heart's desire is that the addict, because their entire system is based on deceit, control and denial, wants to manipulate the world around them so that no one will unmask their neurotic, sickly game. Those following their heart's desire are so fully themselves, so emotionally and spiritually alive, that they have no need to control others. They simply live and let live. More than that, being in touch with their own heroism means heroic questers see heroism and heroic behaviour everywhere they look and do their best to mentor, guide and develop anyone who seeks their help. Heroes encourage you to make yourself proud, not to dance to someone else's tune.

Rule 6: Don't be selfish

To the addict, this means 'give me what I want, conform to my dysfunctional reality'; to those following their heart's desire, 'don't be selfish' means share more of who you are, let the world see your inner light. Of course, it is very hard when operating in an addictive system to resist the addict's call.

I remember receiving a telephone call from an executive in a major company for which I was doing a lot of work at the time. He was working in another part of the organisation and was keen to arrange for me to meet with one of his colleagues. The problem was, I live in Sydney, the executive lived in London and his colleague lived in Boston. When they were both due to be in Australia, I was in Brussels. However, it did seem possible for us to meet up in London. They asked if we could all meet one evening. Knowing my own limits after days of working one-on-one, or in workshops with very senior executives, I pleaded that I would be too tired. 'What about on the weekend?' I was then asked.

Now you might remember that it was they who wanted to meet me. When I am away on business, I don't have my usual support systems and I work very hard to keep up my morale, energy levels and sense of self. Giving up my weekends is a big sacrifice anytime, but they were being so obliging that I agreed. Then they told me that they would be flying in from Australia on a flight arriving at Heathrow Airport at 5am. Now I know how I feel when I get off that 24-hour flight from Sydney to Europe. No way would I meet with anyone. The next request was for me to get up at 4am so that I could meet them at the airport. The implication was clear—just how selfish was I prepared to be?

What interested me about this incident was that this was not a particularly important meeting (for me, at least), but the pressure I felt to give up my personal time and space was immense. It helped me to understand how the other members of that organisation must feel. For me, this was a one-off event; for others, it was a regular thing. How many Sunday mornings had they missed with their family? How many times had they denied their own needs, each time deadening their heart's desire, all in the name of not being selfish?

Rule 7: Do as I say and not as I do

This rule is all about the difference between content (what I say) and process (what actually happens). To the hero, process is everything. Life is a process, business is a process, relating is a process. Process is fluid, multifaceted, uncontrollable, potent. Knowing this, accepting it in the depths of their being, heroes stay in the moment and get on with life as it happens. They ask no more or less than this of others. Those who follow their heart's desire give permission to others to do the same.

Ricardo Semler, owner and leader of one of the world's most revolutionary businesses, knows this. He has converted his manufacturing business into a worker-run enterprise, encouraging workers not only to run their sections and set their own agendas and salaries, but also to buy parts of the business and become entrepreneurs in their own right. Like Richard Branson of Virgin, Semler boasts that his encouragement of others to follow their heart's desire has led to the creation of many self-made millionaires.

To those with a vested interest in preserving an addictive system, giving away this amount of power would be lunacy. While kings and princes have always given land and wealth to their loyal knights, the sovereign always retained enough power to reclaim these gifts should the knight be anything less than loyal. Allowing people to set up their own businesses gives them enough power to be their own master, set their own rules and run their realm their own way. Those presiding over addictive systems have a vested interest in ensuring that the system remains intact. Their desire is not to optimise success, health, wealth or happiness, but rather to sustain the system that feeds their neurotic needs. This demands that control is maximised, free discussion is repressed and opinions and emotional responses are suppressed if they could challenge the unhealthiness of an addictive system and the behaviour it fosters. Thus, warrior kings only give away enough power to buy allegiance.

Rule 8: It is not okay to play or be playful
I love to play. As a trained educationalist, I know that laughter and play improve creativity, health and our ability to learn. So, for my job satisfaction and for effective results, I include fun, play and laughter in my work with clients whenever I can.

As a young consultant doing a lot of organisational facilitation, these techniques helped clients quickly and apparently effortlessly achieve their desired results. They also caused me a lot of problems. Repeatedly clients would be delighted at the end of workshops and personal sessions because they had achieved objectives that initially seemed very ambitious, even impossible. They would then completely discount what they had gained because it had all been 'too easy', 'too much fun' or 'too enjoyable'.

It took me many years to work out that in addictive systems how you do things is more important than the results obtained. This, of course, has less to do with success and more to do with the ongoing survival of the system. It also minimises the chances for radical transformation, especially for those in positions of power.

For those wishing to maintain addictive systems, work—and, in fact, life—are part of the same serious business where everything is controlled and rigid. They have to be. Play, on the other hand, is spontaneous. If play is allowed, creativity blossoms, truths are spoken and life is induced in both people and organisations. Aliveness, being hard to control, can be very threatening to warriors.

Dom was the managing director of a highly successful family company. He became my client after he took over control of the family business previously ruled by his now aged father-in-law. His father-in-law had ruled the company with an iron fist, strongly enforcing all the rules of addictive systems, ensuring that nobody spoke their truth and that his, the patriarch's reality, was the only one allowed. Despite this, it was Dom who had taken the business from a small family concern to the sizeable organisation it had become. The price to Dom, however, had been high. His health was suffering, he had completely lost touch with his own needs and desires, and he mourned the loss of his playfulness.

An expert marketeer, Dom had always played. He loved to joke and to laugh. While his father-in-law had been in the company, Dom had been punished for playing. His jokes and pranks had been frowned upon, his playfulness ridiculed. For Dom, one of the great delights in being released from an addictive system was being his 'old self again', playing and enjoying it.

Play, we now know, is a great source of creativity. Fun is a wonderful way of building productive, life-giving, growth-inducing relationships. Entrepreneurs such as Richard Branson and Ricardo Semler know this and do whatever they can to build environments in which play is fostered. Those who follow their heart's desire encourage playfulness in themselves and others.

Rule 9: Don't rock the boat
The precarious, dysfunctional, restrictive system of the addict and the addictive organisation is founded on very unstable ground. Those who support such systems, therefore, are very keen to ensure not too many questions are asked and that control is maintained at all times. It is ironic that the leaders of many organisations

often claim that they are seeking quantum change, when all their behaviour is aimed at ensuring that nothing different ever happens (Rule 7: Do as I say and not as I do). For many years, I have claimed that most major organisational change programs are set up to ensure that no real change actually occurs. This is achieved by concentrating on content—trying to replace one set of rigid mind maps with another, rather than working with the process to free up the emotional retardation that underlies restricted, limited thinking and action.

Those who follow their heart's desire, however, operate in exactly the opposite direction. They foster emotional aliveness, play, honesty and validation of personal reality—all the things that overturn boats that aren't seaworthy—fostering imagination, change and innovation while allowing problems to be brought to the surface and dealt with before they become crises.

How Did We End Up Here?

While writing about desire and addiction, I have been continually struck by how unhealthy, ludicrous and bad for business the current, largely addictive way of operating is. So the question arises again and again, why do we as individuals, businesses and as a society operate in such an unhealthy, counterproductive way? Why do we limit, undermine and sabotage our own wellbeing and success? Why do we settle for so much less than is possible?

If we accept James Hillman's theory that we are all born with our own daemon, our own acorn already intact, then our life's journey involves the playing out of our inner story through our growing down into the fullness of who we are. From this view, it is difficult to see what happens to us along the way as obstacles to personal fulfilment. Rather, our life's journey is simply our daemon playing itself out against a changing set of realities. It is this interaction between our own spirit and the world around us that creates who we are. When working with extraordinary people I can see this most clearly. It is as if they have a magnetic attraction, an irresistible urge, to be all that they can be. Their family history, genetic make-up and life experience intermingle to produce the will, calling, energy, persistence and application that lead to greatness. As Hillman tells us in *The Soul's Code* 'Perhaps they are extraordinary because their calling comes through so clearly and they are so loyal to it. They serve as exemplars of calling and its strength, and also of keeping faith with its signals.'

Family of Origin

All this seems very important to me because I have found, over the years, that we are so strongly influenced by our early childhood experiences. What is fascinating is the role of the individual in shaping themselves around what happens to them as they develop.

It is quite apparent that the first place we learn to relate to others (and to ourselves) is the home or institution in which we are raised. As has been discussed by so many great thinkers, such as Carl Jung and Laurens Van der Post, and as is acknowledged by worldwide religions, the original emotion is love. Love is both a state of being and an emotion. The key feeling associated with love is that of connection; a state of feeling connected with someone else. The other side of that is the sense or feeling of loss and loneliness—disconnection, being cut off, separated. All fears evolve from the original fear of loneliness, loss and separation from love. It can even be seen in the Bible—Adam being kicked out of the garden of Eden for following his desire. He was utterly rejected: he committed the original sin for which many people believe we all still carry the can. Separation, Jews and Christians believe, was the price of that original sin. The fear of rejection, which is manifested in the fear of separation, is very deeply ingrained in the human psyche. This goes beyond words and symbols, as exemplified by the failure-to-thrive syndrome in which normal, apparently healthy babies provided with adequate food and drink die through lack of being cuddled, spoken to and feeling nourished. In short, they die from lack of love.

So the story goes like this. Babies develop in the mother's womb in a state of total connection, total love. Assuming their mother is healthy, the baby's every need is met before they even know they have it. Baby and mother are one. Then comes birth and the first experience of disconnection—the first pangs of hunger, feelings of cold, feelings of isolation. No matter how caring, devoted and diligent the parents, babies begin to experience fear, rejection, separation and loss of love. As a result, as babies grow, they do whatever they can to get back the love they have lost and to avoid losing any more.

To understand this story properly, we need to remember that babies think like babies and adults think like adults. The human brain goes through several stages of development before it achieves adult maturity and the ability for rational thought that accompanies it. Let's, for the sake of argument, pretend that parents are perfect. They all love and adore their children and want nothing more than for their children to grow into healthy, well-functioning adults who fit happily and productively into their chosen community. Let's picture the baby much loved and cherished, full of curiosity and longing for reconnection with the eternal fountain of love and fulfilment—mother. Now let's imagine a scenario where baby is lying bare-bottomed on a sheepskin rug on the floor, catching the morning sun as a prevention against nappy rash, enjoying the delights of being alive on a sunny spring morning. At one moment, baby notices some interesting brown stuff on the rug. The stuff has an interesting odour so the baby picks some up, and wanting to know more is about to put the brown stuff in its mouth when all-loving, caring mum arrives, grasps the baby's arm and vigorously rubs the faeces off the baby's hands. From an adult point of view, that is the sensible, loving thing to do, but what about from baby's perspective? Baby was just minding his or her own business, learning about his or her world when the person who matters to them the most in the world appears for no obvious reason to be angry with them, threatening to withdraw more of that wonderful, so keenly desired love.

This story is played out again and again: baby tries to bite the cat, stick a fork in the electric socket, examine a knife or pull a pot off the stove. Every time the devoted parents race to baby's aid, grabbing baby away from the danger. Every time baby interprets this from the perspective of a baby. 'Perhaps,' reasons baby, 'I had better find out what I need to do to make myself more lovable.' Seems crazy, I know, but that's about the way it works. As loving parents, we try to keep our kids alive, have them grow up to be happy, healthy adults. As kids we feel reprimanded, rejected, cut off and judged for doing what comes naturally, so we start putting our natural instincts on hold and learning what we need to do to get and retain the love we crave.

Now all this may not work too badly if it weren't for the fact that parents aren't perfect. They have their own failings, prejudices and weaknesses. We know that a surprisingly high number of parents physically, emotionally and sexually abuse their children. Other children are abandoned by their parents, physically or through the parents being addicted to drugs (including alcohol), gambling, sex, work and overeating.

So the workings of the system mitigate against children growing up trusting their emotional reality, trusting their instincts, believing that they are lovable in and of themselves and therefore having the courage to explore the world as they find it. Children learn to look to authority figures such as parents to tell them what to do so that they can find the most appropriate way forward. Those children considered 'good' are usually those who have significantly dampened their own desires, curiosity and instincts and have conformed and fitted into their parents' world. This, of course, continues at school, where teachers do what they can to get children to fit a mould—not out of some malicious plot to dampen children's natural energy, but merely so that they, the teachers, can get through the day and instill some learning in those children who have some interest left in it.

The playground, too, serves as a harsh forum for instilling social conformity. Those who are different—whether it be exceptionally gifted or in some way physically, socially or mentally disabled— are made to suffer for standing out from the crowd. I have found, over the years, that one of the quickest ways to unleash emotion in senior executives is to talk about playground bullying.

As many executives are very bright, they were often the ones singled out for persecution. They were locked in cupboards, had their heads pushed down toilet bowls and were subjected to ongoing taunts. One of my clients, a highly intelligent and sensitive man who had attended a bush school in outback Australia, told me how he was tied in a hessian sack by his school 'chums' and left in a creek bed. The messages come loud and strong: don't be different, don't follow your heart's desire, suppress your emotions and survive.

What is amazing is that most people do live through their childhood. What is even more amazing is that, in the face of brutal or even loving socialisation, some people grow up determined to be themselves, to live life on their own terms, to feel life as it happens, to listen to and trust their instincts and senses, to follow their heart's desire—in short, to be heroes.

Most of us suppress who we are, disconnect from our inner selves and do whatever is necessary to cope. Nicholas de Castella suggests that we do this in three ways:

1. We detach, run away, physically, mentally or emotionally. Some may choose to live life like the self-styled yogi mentioned earlier, others develop mental illnesses, others shut down emotions and intellectualise, rationalise and generally lose touch with reality; and/or
2. We distract ourselves by becoming terribly busy, allowing ourselves no time or space to feel. We may try to 'think it all through', but many of us don't want to touch emotions in anything but an intellectual sense; and/or
3. We dampen our energy, especially our emotional energy, through the use of alcohol and drugs, eating disorders such as bulimia and anorexia, and through addictions such as sex and gambling.

Having gone through all this, we are fully socialised and ready for the world of work. Try as we might, however, there is no one we can blame for this. Even if our parents were the worst ones in town, they were only acting out their own life's tragedy. If our teachers were lazy and evil, and our classmates in training for the Mafia, they were still just doing what they knew. What is curious is how some people come through the most horrific childhoods, traumatic schooldays and street beatings and rapes to become leaders in their chosen field.

Josephine Baker, for instance, was born at St Louis Social Evil Hospital in 1906 into a life of starvation, poverty, neglect and abuse. As a child, she was hired out to work for a woman who made her share her bed and food with a flea-ridden dog. The woman for whom Josephine worked beat her and kept her naked because clothes were too expensive. While still a child, she was sold off to work for and sleep with a white-haired old man. That she survived at all was a miracle—contemporary records of the St Louis health department reveal that 60 per cent of children in that district died before they turned three. Married at the age of thirteen, Baker went on to become one of the great dancers/ entertainers of her time, performing before kings and princes the world over, showered with jewels and public acclaim. Later in her life, she became a campaigner for human rights and adopted eleven children from many nations and colours, fighting to keep them together and ensuring they were fed, housed and schooled. Rather than give in to the injustices of her youth, she grew past them and later returned to fight against them on behalf of others.

It seems that those who stay alive, emotionally and spiritually, those who hear and abide by their heart's desire, do so through strength of character. It is not their circumstances that shape them, but rather how they react to those circumstances, what they choose to do with the hand that is dealt them. Even as children we are constantly making choices. The choices we make in response to the world in which we grow are always our own. Two children in the same situation will make entirely different choices. The real liberation in all this is that, as we are created by the choices we have made, we are in control of the process. Unhappily, most people don't realise this. Because their choices have long since been repressed and become subconscious, most people think they are shaped by their environment, an environment they see through the filter of their personally programmed subconscious patterning. While we may feel like victims of circumstance, we are in fact merely victims of our own perception and choices. Liberation, therefore, comes not by changing the world and the people in it (a totally impossible task), but by bringing to the surface our subconscious choices, making our mental and emotional patterning conscious and rechoosing.

Of course, to do this we will have to reconnect with our feelings, take time and space to reflect on our innate responses and make choices about our present behaviour. This is exactly what our socialisation has taught most of us not to do, what addiction fights to avoid and what business has punished, ridiculed and avoided. Poses an interesting challenge, doesn't it?

Chapter 4

Heartfelt Relationships

'When one has no character, one has to apply method.'
ALBERT CAMUS, THE FALL

After twenty years living and working with Native Americans, Carl Hammerschlag in *The Dancing Healers* wrote that there is a 'great, universal power inherent in the stories we have told each other in all cultures throughout all of time. There are heroes, there are monsters. People die, they are reborn. And there are miracles.'

He goes on to say that there is a 'universal connection among all who have walked the earth... Stories [therefore] speak to each of us. Understanding this connection is crucial if we are to be able to live together and to live with ourselves.'

Tom Chappell, founder and chief executive of Tom's of Maine, a manufacturer of natural personal care products, claims that through sharing his story with his people and having them share their stories with each other, he is working to develop the soul of his business:

> *When people share stories about their own lives, you get to know them as human beings and not only as secretary or supervisor or salesman. All of a sudden that person moves from the professional role into something bigger, and his or her story makes you more tolerant, more understanding and more appreciative of who that person is.*

Story, he claims, 'moves communication from the heads of the company to the hearts of the company.'

There is a growing movement of experts around the world who are shedding their professional armour and moving into relationships with their clients. These people, all leaders in their various fields, are replacing their professional jargon with stories—stories about their own lives; stories about other cultures, other times; stories about heroes and stories about monsters. Anne Wilson Schaef, who calls herself a 'recovering therapist', is one of these people; so is community psychiatrist Carl Hammerschlag. Stanford Professor of Psychiatry, Irvin Yalom, has turned personal storytelling into a fine art in his book *Love's Executioner and Other Tales of Psychotherapy.*

Wilson Schaef is pioneering a form of emotional healing that she calls 'living in process'. Hammerschlag is a pioneer in the field of psychoneuroimmunology (PNI) or mind/body/spirit medicine. What these leaders are saying in their own fields, in their own ways, is that abundant emotional, physical and spiritual wellbeing are attainable through relationship with yourself and others. This involves being with and noticing life as it happens *and* your emotional response to life as it happens, using the energy of your emotions to empower purposeful action and keep you full of enlivening good health.

Reading through the work of these pioneers, I recognise that what they are saying is revolutionary: the newness of their insights are ahead of contemporary thinking. I empathise with the communication challenge these pioneers face. It is not easy to explain rich, complex insights and understanding that has been discovered though experience, intuition and emotional awareness. We often restrict experts in the communication of their work by demanding tangible 'facts' presented scientifically.

Trying to describe the bliss, blinding flashes and paradigm shifts of the heroic quest to a warrior audience can seem as impossible as trying to describe an orgasm to someone who has never had sex. You can detail the physiological and scientific data, you can go through a description of the mechanics involved, but none of this gives you any real sense at all of the intensity and joy of the actual experience. Ironically, what these experts are saying is so simple, so obvious, so human, it is easy for people to overlook their profound insights and go in search of cures that use jargon and mental maps to sound authoritative.

This 'seeking the guru' behaviour is a sure sign of an absolute beginner in the field of healing, heartfelt relationships for there are no more powerful tools of positive social and personal transformation than storytelling and relationships. Sharing our stories is one way of sending a message that contains universal truth so that individuals can receive it in their own way, make sense of it in their own space and reject or use it as suits their individual needs. If our stories are spontaneous and real, if they reveal who we are from a place of sharing and searching (as against a place of wanting to maintain the upper hand), they can go a long way towards helping us form the kind of relationships that heal our hearts, our souls and our bodies.

People that really know this never stop growing and learning. They know that the more they know themselves, the more insightful and powerful will be their stories. The more they tell their stories, the more they grow. More than that, they know that the more they hear the stories of other people, the more they will learn about life, the world around them and other people. (This point has been brought out again and again in leadership literature, where leaders are constantly implored to listen, listen, listen.) Carl Rogers made the point that in the area of human consciousness and relationships, many people simply don't realise how much they don't know. They are 'unconsciously unknowing' and 'unconsciously unskilled'.

Whenever I see someone being less than respectful of another person's story, I know they are unconsciously unskilled, so oblivious to their ignorance that they don't even feel embarrassed. Unfortunately, due to the wonderfully effective socialisation process most business people have been through, the majority of people in business are unconsciously unknowing about their own and other people's psychological states and therefore are very unconsciously unskilled in relationships. Most warriors and warrior trainers are in this category. They may have a few convincing cognitive maps which they use to overlay and obscure their ignorance, but all this does is keep them stuck in an addictive system that actually undermines the success they claim to seek.

The first step out of this unknowingness, the first step on the hero's quest, is to start noticing and finding out just how much you don't know. While becoming conscious of how unknowing and unskilled we are can initially be a rather depressing thing (we will go on uncovering our ignorance forever, but somehow it becomes more enjoyable), until we admit our lack of knowledge, we won't put in the necessary time, effort and emotion to learn. Therefore, becoming 'consciously unknowing' and 'consciously unskilled' is a necessary stage on the path to healthy living and relating.

Once we get an inkling of what we don't know, of how unskilled we really are, we are ready to learn. That's where storytelling comes in. Storytelling allows us to take instruction from other people's lives, cultures and experiences, and integrate as much or as little of it as we want into our own. This way we don't just learn, we grow. We become bigger people. This third stage of learning is becoming 'consciously knowing' and 'consciously skilled'.

When we become very consciously knowing and skilled, when we are real experts, we become 'unconsciously knowing' and 'unconsciously skilled'. We come to realise just how little we can ever know or even need to know. Wilson Schaef in *Beyond Therapy, Beyond Science* illustrated this point wonderfully in the following: 'It's an occupational hazard to try to be wise.… I don't have to know what is going on; I don't have to have the answers; I don't have to be in control (or think I am). I only have to be present and participate by sharing what is going on with me.'

Surely this not having to be the guru, boss or know-it-all, this not having to be in control (which is impossible anyway), is what we call humility. Unfortunately, humility is in rather short supply in business. All those warriors just keep on pretending they know, that they have the answers, that they are in control and can therefore win the battle. The problem is they are fighting an imaginary war, in which the enemy is their own ignorance and limitations which they have unconsciously projected onto the world around them. It saves so much time and energy when we just admit our vulnerability and get on with raising our self-awareness.

These two steps may seem rather trivial, but don't be fooled. The most powerful social movement I have experienced in my lifetime has been the feminist movement. Like it or not, feminism has reshaped the face of Western society. It was not so long ago that women could not vote. Until quite recently, women were denied proper education. At the end of World War II, women were expected to give up jobs to their rightful owners, the returning men. Today, women can be judges, senators, professors, company CEOs—the list is endless—and play significant roles in all major aspects of modern life. There are still traces of discrimination, but these are gradually being eroded.

The integration of women into public life has had a huge impact on family relationships and social attitudes. Many attribute the big changes in business culture, sometimes dubbed as the feminisation of business, to these attitudes. The women's movement started with women getting together and telling their stories. Their slogan was 'Personal is Political'. By finding out that the personal reality of their lives was not greatly dissimilar from that of other females, women gained the confidence, the strength and the support to have their voices heard. When many voices speak at once, the noise can be impossible to ignore, a fact that was also used to great effect by the civil rights movement.

However, telling stories does not simply change society, it also heals lives. The programs based on the Twelve Steps of Alcoholics Anonymous place great store on the telling of stories. Through telling their own stories and hearing those of others with similar problems, alcoholics, workaholics, sexaholics and those with just about every addiction you can think of work to achieve their own wellbeing, aliveness and independence from the substances or obsessions that have been ruling their lives. Wilson Schaef claims that as business (in fact, society) is highly addicted, everybody should be working to heal themselves, their organisation and society by telling their story and listening to the experiences of others. Now, I think Wilson Schaef takes things a bit far in suggesting that the whole society and everybody in it is addicted and, therefore, sick. However, I have to agree that sharing our humanity with those who are prepared to listen with respect has a radically healing, enlivening and liberating effect. I have seen individuals and businesses revolutionised when people started speaking their truth and listening, really listening, to the personal reality of their peers.

Walking and Talking

When I am working with leadership teams, I often take them for a walk. I have walked with senior executives through the Australian wilderness, the desert, the cow pastures of the Netherlands and the cobblestone streets of St Paul de Vence (a medieval French town perched on a hillside overlooking the Mediterranean). The leaders walk in pairs; sometimes if there is an odd number of executives I take my place in the couplings. The pairs rotate so that by the end of the one or two days involved everybody has had a chance to walk and talk with everybody else. And walk and talk are exactly what we do. The set task is that executives share their personal stories. This is framed by asking that people both give and receive feedback that is about them and that the other person is unlikely to have heard before. Conversations usually last for about an hour.

Before being involved in these kinds of activities, most executives are very sceptical. They have better things to do than walk around some beautiful place chatting. After they have experienced the value of sharing their stories, they are nonplussed by the results. As one executive put it, 'When you get to our position, it can be very lonely. Sharing at a personal level helps you to feel more human. It also helps you to solve problems that you thought were only faced by you.' After realising their human connection, executives who have been 'walking and talking' start to open up to each other as human beings. They start to acknowledge and value their common problems, goals, doubts and fears. They put on the agenda and discuss sensitive personal, strategic, business and political issues that have previously been 'too hot to handle'.

After one of our little walks, executives start to admit what they don't know, and begin to ask for help and readily support each other to learn and grow. They swap resources, ideas, time and effort. They start to operate like a functional family system. It's as though someone has opened up the windows and let in the fresh air. The air allows people to breathe. The oxygen in the breath lifts their thinking and energy levels to such a degree that people's heartfelt desires start poking their miraculous heads through the stale carapace of rigid cognitive maps, social restriction and organisational cultures that were previously their way of being. Life-giving success becomes possible.

All this is very different from traditional 'outdoor training', where executives are put through a series of team-based exercises aimed at teaching them the skills of leadership and team cooperation. As it was originally designed to train military officers, it is hardly surprising to find that traditional outdoor training is very much about being a warrior, playing within the rules, pitting yourself against the elements and operating within a stable (if unknown) environment. The whole system is set up and controlled by the trainers.

When people go walking and talking they, the participants, set the agenda. I have no control over where we go, how long we are there and what people choose to say to each other. I make suggestions, of course, but all key decisions are made by the clients themselves. If people choose to reveal only superficial things about themselves and to give only nondescript feedback, then that is their decision. No bad report is sent back to head office. Conformists and blockers are not counselled to lift their game. I do point out that their time is very valuable and advise that taking risks is a good way of maximising their return, but I make no attempt to check up on people or pressure them into 'spilling their guts'. I am working with adults who are big enough to make their own decisions. My role is to help, to guide and to act as a resource, not to impose my way of being on anyone else. However, as people begin to experience the benefit in walking and telling their stories, they reveal more and more of themselves and become increasingly empathetic listeners.

Recently, while making up the numbers in one of these sessions, I was amazed by the huge shift I made during the course of a day. Each conversation opened up new avenues of insight and personal learning. Each listener asked different questions and provided feedback from a different perspective. By the end of the day, I had not only raised and solved a problem to which I had previously been blind, but I had an explanation about some rather unusual behaviour I had exhibited some months before. More than that, I had seen a path forward, a way to act more appropriately in the future. When the group members debriefed after their day's learning, it seemed that I, the teacher, was as much the learner as anyone else.

Learning on the Job

Relationships are great teachers. We learn by telling our story and by listening to other people's stories, but we also learn by doing and by noticing how we are affected by the actions of others. This is practical learning—on-the-job relationship training. This training is rarely straightforward, it does not come in a textbook, with clear subheadings and seven points to remember. Often the greatest learning comes when our expectations are confounded. Sometimes it comes from behaviour of which we may not even approve. The secret is in the learning. If we are lucky, we will have teachers who know this and use it to our benefit. Sometimes we will have to work it out for ourselves.

As part of my training in psychotherapy, I attended therapy for several years. My strongest memory out of what must have been hundreds of sessions was the day my therapist charged me for sleeping for one hour on her floor. It happened like this. At the time, I was working very hard to rebuild my business and nurse my daughter back to health. Life was hectic—being both mother and father to two small children, staying up all night when my daughter was ill, earning the money, all took their toll. Therapy was something I did every week for me. I turned down work, organised babysitters and did whatever was necessary to ensure that I turned up regularly at my sessions. One day as we sat down to begin a session, my therapist commented that I looked tired. I affirmed her insight and was about to launch into a description of why I was tired when she said. 'You need a rest, why don't you lie down?' Stunned, I did as I was told while she went to another room and returned with a blanket and a pillow. Before I knew it, she was rocking me gently, the hour was up. She asked me for her fee. I paid her and walked out into the street.

I can't tell you how much I learnt from that little nap. What I had experienced was someone who had enough belief in their own being to charge for two minutes advice. What's more, I had paid and had every intention of coming back. I had paid not for an hour of having an expert listen to me, empathise and put me in touch with my emotions. No, I had paid for participation in a relationship with someone with enough courage to believe in their own judgment and enough nerve to charge me for it.

Now, you may think that a con man could have pulled off the same trick, but this was different. You see, I really did need a rest. All the talking in the world wouldn't have helped me as much at that time as did an hour's nap. However, I was so used to following a routine, so comfortable with the same pattern, that I hadn't had the sense to cancel my appointment and do what I most needed, which was to sleep. By convincing me to catnap, my therapist had persuaded me to invest in my own best interests. The other side of the equation was that she had made no apologies for collecting her dues, even though at the time I could ill afford her fee. In a single action, she had shattered all my beliefs about the necessity of meeting other people's expectations. A whole lifetime of believing that to be accepted and rewarded I had to fit in, live up to a certain code of behaviour and be nice dissolved the second I handed over the money. I had experienced first-hand one of the most important lessons about self-esteem, courage and relationships that I have ever had. It happened not while pouring out my heart about my parents' neglect, not commiserating about my failed marriage, my daughter's illness or my father's death; it came through a real, adult-to-adult, present moment interaction. It came through relationship. I have since learned that that is where the best learning happens.

My therapist prided herself on her ability to stay present. I guess from her perspective what happened that day was that she saw sitting in front of her a woman who was so overtired that no amount of talking was going to help. The obvious solution for exhaustion is rest. However, by suggesting this and by charging me for the floor space, she took my thinking and our relationship outside of the circle. She taught me that the obvious and most simple solution is always the best—that healing does not have to follow a formula, that time invested is less important than outcome achieved—and that is an insight for which it is worth paying.

How grateful I am for that lesson. As a society, we greatly undervalue wisdom and human kindness. These are things you are supposed to do for free, while we are happy to pay highly for answers presented as rigid mental maps. If my therapist had not charged me for my little rest, she would not have been rewarded for being wise and I would have learnt that wisdom does not pay. If she had gone ahead with the session despite my obvious exhaustion, I would have learnt nothing (and so she would have been paid under false pretences). By charging me for common sense, she earned her fee a hundredfold. Today, I have an international practice built on my ability to value my insights, my ability to work wisely with the human psyche, state the obvious, believe in my own judgment and operate from a position of unconditional positive regard for others.

From that one-hour sleep, I learnt that a single action can be a more memorable lesson than hundreds of hours of talking. To learn this, I had to overcome my disbelief that I had been charged for what under other circumstance would be a simple act of human kindness. I made a conscious choice to see the learning and to believe that my therapist's intentions were honourable. These concessions, along with the money I paid, were cheap in comparison to the lesson I received.

A friend pointed out to me recently how easy it would have been for me to miss that learning. I could, my friend suggested, have descended into righteous anger and indignation, building up walls of defence and resentment. That I chose to remain vulnerable and open to the learning is what endowed the experience with its great value. My friend was kind enough to suggest that it took quite some humility on my part for me to receive the lesson that

I had been given. This made me wonder how often I had missed rich learning by closing down, shutting out and retreating into pain, anger and shock which I covered up with a plethora of rigid mind maps, thus avoiding the opportunity for reflection, growth and forward movement because I didn't like the way the gift of experience had been packaged and presented to me.

The problem with people is that they are hard to get on with. They lie and cheat, and do things the way they want, which is rarely the way I would have them behave. People put their own meaning on events, actions and situations. They make their own decisions, have their own value sets and their own agendas. They live life to their own standards and relate in their own ways. People have their own weaknesses and their own strengths. They perceive me and my actions their way, not the way I would have them do so. People insistently, steadfastly and uncompromisingly go on being themselves. I have learnt that when I can give myself permission to be me and allow other people to be themselves, amazing and wonderful things happen.

Not Knowing

I am reluctant to run workshops within organisations unless I have worked with the leader of that organisation for some time. This is because I work from a place of reality and aliveness, not a place of addiction. I have found that if I attempt to do this in addictive environments, people resist my work strongly and I have no desire to fight them. I feel no need at all to preach, convert or convince. So, I choose to work only with people who want to work with me—people who are prepared to work with process, to be challenged, to work with relationships and to own their feelings, responses and intuitions. If, however, I have built a relationship with a leader and he or she asks me to, I will come and work with their leadership team in the role of catalyst.

Some time ago, I was working with a client's leadership team, the members of which were on the threshold of committing to work in a non-addicted, heartfelt way. They had experienced the value of noticing and expressing their emotional reality, sharing their differing insights, surfacing and resolving problems, acknowledging and allowing individual difference and working on their relationships. They liked the results and were on the verge of asking for more. This meant an ongoing commitment from me as well as from them. There was, however, one person in the group who was more reticent than the others; one person who was asking more defensive questions, hedging his bets.

During a break, the leader took me aside and asked my advice about whether this man should be forced to participate if the group decided to continue their work with me. As he looked at me, trusting my judgment because it had taken both of us so far in the past, I heard passing my lips the words, 'Buggered if I know!'

My client complained, 'I haven't flown you from the other side of the world to pay you at great expense to tell me "Buggered if I know!".'

'But I don't know,' I protested. 'We both know that if I did, I would be the first to tell you.'

It was true, I didn't know. When forced to search for an answer, I shared my experience that in the past people who were slow to continue working at a deeper level with their colleagues had often surprised me by becoming the informal leaders as the process moved on. Others, however, had been a pain—resisting, undermining and blocking at every turn. At this stage in the process, I was completely unable to tell whether an individual's reticence was simply a display of his strong respect for his privacy, an early premonition that he could uncover something that would be difficult to deal with in front of his colleagues or whether the individual in question was strongly committed to not growing, to staying the same, perhaps unwilling to reveal some hidden agenda or let go of addictive behaviour.

The answer to those questions lay deeply buried in the psyche of the individual himself. It was he who would decide whether or not to participate and he would do so for his own reasons in his own time. As I have no crystal ball, all this is beyond my ken. Moreover, I have found that when some people choose not to work in groups with their colleagues, they can still go through a major shift because their daily relationships with their colleagues change so dramatically *due to the changes in those who do participate.*

On one occasion when I took a leadership team on an extended outdoor team building exercise, one of the managers in that team didn't join us. He had been away a lot on business and his wife complained. So he decided to stay home and mind the 'shop' on behalf of his colleagues. He later reported that when his colleagues returned from their expedition, one by one they had approached him and shared their experiences and learning. 'It was,' he told me, 'the first time in my working life I haven't felt lonely.' This man's non-participation changed his life. On other occasions, however, non-participation has led to programs being undermined further down the track.

The third reason why I had no idea what we should do about someone who might not want to participate is that I have a personal belief that it is unethical to force people to do personal and relationship work if they don't want to or feel unready for it. However, I can understand that some leaders, when they commit to lead in non-addictive ways, don't want people in their team who are not prepared to try new ways of operating. If the price for not participating was dismissal or loss of esteem in the eyes of the leader, then perhaps it was unethical not to force participation.

Having expressed all this to my client, he decided that the choice should be left up to each individual, and each individual did choose, entirely of his or her own volition, to participate. The reluctant team member had both the courage and the integrity to make his ongoing involvement conditional on his experience over time. This reinforced my growing respect for him. He was respecting his fear and doubts.

When it comes to people there are no right answers. Wilson Schaef writes in *Beyond Therapy Beyond Science* (p. 148):

...we have whole areas of psychology built on... 'if-then' theories, which are too simplistic to be applied to the human organism. [These theories allow professionals to] believe they are the experts, hold the

power and be essential. Working the way I do with people now has taught me how little I know and how little I need to know.

As nobody really knows what is happening inside another person, any relationship worth having has to be based on respect for each person's individuality at the deepest level. This includes respecting those parts of their behaviour, attitudes and personalities we dislike and with which we strongly disagree. I have found that these nemeses often have wonderful messages for us and valuable lessons to teach.

This does not mean we should allow people to bully, intimidate, control, dominate or wilfully harm us. On the contrary, poor behaviour on the part of others challenges us to find ways of dealing respectfully with our own need for physical and psychological safety. What it does mean, however, is respecting each person's right to be his or herself and then giving him or her appropriate feedback (through words and/or actions) on the impact that his or her behaviour is having. This invites people to be themselves on the other side of the boundaries and limits we set up because we deeply respect who we are. This idea is most simply expressed as *I matter, you matter, we matter*. In short, because I value me, I trust myself to handle our relationship in a way that enhances my respect for myself and you; because of this, my respect for our relationship grows.

The Magic of Relationships

Relationships are worth respecting. It is hard to find any worthwhile book on business, psychology, sociology or economics these days that does not make reference to the new science. This is because with the wonderful innovations in technology, particularly computers, scientists around the world have found that things aren't what we thought they were. Great thinkers already knew that.

The studies of both Albert Einstein and Werner Heisenberg led them to the discomfiting idea that there may be no constants in life. Einstein found that the fluidity of 'reality' left him with no firm ground on which to stand. Heisenberg in *Physics and Philosophy* (p.107) wrote that in the world of quantum physics everything 'appears as a complicated tissue of events in which connection of different kinds alternate or overlap or combine and thereby determine the texture of the whole.' It turns out that not only is everything related to everything else and in a constant state of flux, but also that as one thing changes it triggers subsequent changes in the things to which it is connected (i.e. everything). Moreover, relationship systems are so highly sensitive they are changed simply by someone observing them or even one part of them. This is the magic of relationships. They both embody and engender change.

Margaret Wheatley in *Leadership and the New Science* writes that reality is made up of a 'constant weaving of relationships, of energies that merge and change, of constant ripples that occur within a seamless fabric'. If we learn how to work effectively with relationships, we open up the possibility of quantum change through minimalist intervention and the art of skilful observation. 'In the quantum world,' says Wheatley, 'relationships are not just interesting: to many physicists, they are all there is to reality.'

This is also true in the human world, where the emotions, thoughts, physical senses and spirit are all interrelated and in a constant state of flux. A smell can evoke a memory that leads to a certain thought and an accompanying feeling. The way one person looks (or even does not look) at another person can lead to a passionate set of feelings, thoughts and actions that may appear to have nothing to do with the present situation and everything to do with an unconscious memory of something that happened perhaps decades before.

In his delightful tale 'Two Smiles', Irvin Yalom tells of a consultation that he and a colleague Mike had with a particular client, Marie. At two strategic points during that meeting, Marie smiled, signalling a deep movement in her thoughts and response. The tale traces the session and Yalom's, Mike's and Marie's interpretation of the smiles. What transpired was that what Marie was thinking and feeling when she smiled sent a message to Mike and Yalom, who interpreted that message in their own ways. There was, in review, very little apparent relationship between Marie's actual response, the message sent and the way it was interpreted by the two doctors. Yet all three people had been affected by the interaction, had deepened their relationships, raised awareness and thus moved forward. The smiles led to change. They were part of the seamless fabric of relationships, the flow of life, the interchanging energies and constant ripples of ever changing reality.

Unless we are extraordinarily arrogant, particularly stupid or so unconsciously unknowing that we slide off the scale, how can we possibly believe that we can understand, know or control the wonderfully fluid physical, social and psychological realm that makes up our world? What we can do, however, is raise our awareness and learn to enjoy and embrace reality on every level, increasing our skill in working with relationships in ways that maximise our happiness, wellbeing and success, individually, organisationally and as a society.

The wonder of relationships is that this can all be done apparently without effort. Once we let go of our rigid mind maps, raise our awareness and immerse ourselves in the sea of life, we appear, like the skilful conjurer, to make magic happen through sleight of hand. The something–nothing of relationships, once we learn their mysteries, can transform our being, our life, our organisations and our world. The secret, however, is that we have to learn in radically new ways.

We have to let go of our need for certainty, control and knowledge, opening our minds, hearts and spirits to the dance of life and moving through the stages of consciousness and unconsciousness that allow us to perceive and operate in the world in new, enlivening and transforming ways that defy description and understanding. This way of being is reached through experience: emotional, physical and spiritual. Umberto Maturana in *The Tree of Knowledge* defines this as 'cognition'.

To Maturana, cognition is not 'the operation of neural information processing. It refers to the total biological interaction of the living organism in its domain of operation.' Moreover, cognition is a process whereby an organism maintains its identity in a changing world by altering its awareness through its interaction. There we have it again: everything comes back to awareness and relationships, awareness and relationships, awareness, relationships and change.

Heroic Relationships

Having done my best to convince you to challenge mental maps and to embrace experience, I am now going to provide you with a range of maps that I encourage you to review and then put aside. The maps I provide here are, like most maps, two-dimensional. They represent enough of the landscape to help you avoid getting lost, but they provide no real sense of what lies ahead, and none of the smells, tastes, sights or sounds of the territory in question. They provide you with no sense of the experiences that await you or how these may differ from what could happen to someone else. Unlike reality, maps are flat, dull representations. What makes the difference, what builds wisdom and creates pleasure, is going on the journey. Sitting in an armchair studying the map bears no correlation to actually exploring.

We human beings are complicated creatures. We are much more than flesh and blood. As if our physical make-up isn't complicated and intriguing enough, we also have highly complex and sophisticated inner worlds that are beyond the observation of even the most highly trained eye. When I work with groups, I often bring a troupe of actors along with me. A picture saves a thousand words and I have found that actors can show more about the nuances of relationships in a few minutes than I would otherwise be able to communicate in several hours.

In one of the skits the actors perform, a husband and wife are sitting together discussing the woeful state of their union. At one stage the wife remarks: 'I'm lonely in this marriage. I want to be close to you.'

Her husband looks at her in disbelief and replies, 'But I'm sitting right next to you.'

He is happy with a relationship that operates on a much shallower level than satisfies his wife. He is physically close, what more could she want? They are talking. How could she ask for more?

Relationships are possible on many different levels. The more skilful we are at each level, the more satisfying, life giving and success enhancing our relationships are likely to be, even if the people with whom we relate are unaware of the breadth and depth of our awareness and skill, and even if they are themselves incapable of operating at a similar depth or at as many levels. Those who know how to relate can relate to anybody. They can do this on many different levels.

People with fixed cognitive maps generally restrict their relationships to a narrow field of play. Their relationships are like a board game in which people cover and re-cover the same ground, varying the moves but within known limits and rules. When the ground shifts, when someone wants to introduce a new move or a new rule, there is generally conflict while the other person explores, checks out and gets used to the change. This is the usual model for organisational change programs. Because of the pervasive narrowness and inflexibility of mental maps in business, we all just go on playing the same old game, even when it has become completely irrelevant, redundant and stultifying. We limit our concept of life, relationships and business, and then learn skills to help us get better within the confines of our own thinking. Meanwhile, we let life, possibility, joy and wellbeing pass us by. What I see constantly in business is warriors getting better and better at playing war games because they can't even envisage peace, let alone comprehend the huge benefits that it carries. So the warriors become increasingly expert at playing the old game even though it undermines the possibility of peace, success and happiness. They may know a lot, but there is doubt as to the quality and appropriateness of what they know. Even more worrying is the quality and inflexibility of their thinking. The best data put into a poor-quality or ill-functioning computer won't get you very far.

As our mental maps loosen, as our cognition (à la Maturana) expands, we open up to life and experience on many planes. Scott Peck in *Further Along The Road Less Traveled* provides an interesting model of what he calls 'spiritual growth' which could just as easily be called the path to wisdom and aliveness. It fits nicely with Carl Rogers's model of conscious knowing and skilling, and mirrors the road to growing cognition and increasing flexibility of mental maps.

Stage one, which Peck believes encompasses about 20 per cent of the population, is labelled 'chaotic/antisocial'. People in this stage have no connection with their innate spirituality. They totally lack consciousness. Peck sees these people as being 'utterly unprincipled'. They may pretend to do the 'right' things—for example, attend church and follow a socially acceptable doctrine. They may even rise to positions of authority and status within their community. However, their motives, despite appearances, are always self serving and covertly, if not overtly, manipulative. Their lack of inner meaning is a constant threat to their psychological stability, which can change quickly and dramatically.

Peck calls stage two 'formal/institutional', because people at this stage are dependent upon an institution for their governance. In extreme forms, this presents as cultism. People at stage two are characterised by the desire for there to be one right answer, one way, one master, one path, one truth. Those at stage two in their spiritual growth will find, and then follow with vehemence, any guru, leader or teacher who is prepared to set themselves up as having the answers. This is the world of the warriors. It is also the place of unconscious unknowing, where doctrines, dogmas, models, theories and rules are used to protect the individual from awareness of their own ignorance, and from awareness of the fluid reality of life. Those at stage two value and will fiercely fight for the 'facts', which are external projections of their rigid cognitive maps of experience. Of course, the motivation behind a lot of this rigidity is fear. If one lets go of one's certainties (no matter how flimsy and artificial they are), what would happen to the cornerstone of one's life? How would one make important decisions and know how to behave appropriately? It is thus fear of the unknown that keeps people stuck in stage two.

While a growing percentage of people are moving past stage two, the majority don't. People at stage two make up what is known as the mass market. Those wishing to make a lot of money through mass marketing have a vested interest in supplying the demand for directive leadership, expert advice and formulae for success that arises from people at this level. Of course, the more this need (addiction) is filled, the more it undermines people's ability to grow and maintains the power base of those who set themselves up as the authorities. This is the stage of the warrior.

Stage three in Peck's model is about questioning and even rejection of previously accepted truths. Peck calls this stage 'sceptical/individual'. This is a stage of testing belief, pushing away from dogma, gurus and apparent certainty as individuals search for their own answers and the appropriate path for them. These are the people who are beginning to explore their inner world, to rely more heavily upon and explore more actively their personal experience and response to life. This is the first stage of deep reflection, deep analysis and deep experience, as the individual rejects externally imposed certitude and begins to understand the fluidity of life, the personal nature of experience and the complexity of reality. It is at this stage that people move into conscious unknowing. They start to let go of rigid mind maps and seek out truth at a deeper, more personal level. Stage three is the beginning of the hero's quest.

Peck calls stage four 'mystical/communal'. He writes of people at this stage:

They are people who have seen a kind of cohesion beneath the surface of things. Throughout the ages, mystics have seen connections between men and women, between humans and other creatures, between people walking the earth and those who aren't even here. Seeing that kind of interconnectedness beneath the surface, mystics of all cultures and religions have spoken of things in terms of unity and community. They also have always spoken in terms of paradox... Mystics are people who love mystery. They love to solve mysteries, and yet at the same time, they know the more they solve, the more mystery they are going to encounter. But they are very comfortable living in a world of mystery whereas people in stage two are most uncomfortable when things aren't cut-and-dried... People at stage two are not particularly threatened by the stage one people: the sinners. They love the sinners, seeing them as fertile ground for their ministrations. But they tend to be threatened by the sceptical individualists of stage three, and more than anything by the stage four people who seem to believe in the same things they believe in and yet believe them with a kind of freedom they find absolutely terrifying.

This is the fate of the returning hero and why stage three of the hero's quest is such a challenge. The paradox is that the mystical/communal insights and skills of the hero are both attractive and frightening to those who haven't yet left on the hero's quest. The returning hero's wisdom, depth of perception and vision enable powerful transformation. Yet the very things that make this possible engender fear in those who haven't travelled very far down the road of life, into their own soul.

Bridging this paradox requires great emotional strength and maturity on the part of the hero. It should not be taken for granted that those who have reached stage four on Peck's scale of spiritual growth necessarily have the emotional wherewithal to bring their wisdom into the everyday world.

In *Peaceful Chaos*, I lay out a model of human personality which helps me to explain this. At the most shallow level of our psychological make-up lies our defence system. I call it 'defended you'. This is both the 'social/political' face that we show to the world and the psychological tricks we have learned to play so that we can cope with life. Our defended you, therefore, contains defences such as playing the victim, trying to control others, the whole range of addictions (alcohol, work, overeating), dependence on external power bases, denying reality, being obsessively 'nice', repressing emotion and psychosomatic illness. Our defended you plays a very important role in keeping us psychologically intact, in protecting us from the irreparable damage that can be caused by emotional and psychological abuse and in helping us to operate in a society where superficial gestures, rules and etiquette are necessary for social acceptance and political survival.

The problem is that our defended you can be too effective. If we are unconscious, we can stay protected all the time, thus distancing ourselves from others, even those with whom we would like to be close. Perhaps more distressingly, an overefficient defended you can distance us from ourselves—from our inner knowing, from our hero's journey and from the kind of growth that will liberate our spirits, nourish our hearts and develop our souls.

Lying behind our defended you are our 'wounded you' and our 'essential you'. To grow emotionally, to be able to move successfully into stage three of the hero's quest, we need to raise our awareness of both our wounded you and our essential you and learn to deal with them in quite different ways. Our wounded you contains the psychological wounds we received as part of the socialisation process outlined in chapter 3. It presents as self-limiting beliefs, negative self-judgments and denied parts of our spirit, soul and emotional wholeness. It feels awful. A large part of the function of defended you is to protect us from feeling the emotional pain harboured by our wounded you.

Our essential you contains our spirit, our soul, our psyche. It presents as our ability to be spontaneous and child-like, have a rich, full spiritual life, enjoy intimacy within ourselves and with those we hold dear. Our essential you contains our natural creativity, innate aliveness and inner knowing. When we reach the mystical/communal stage on Peck's scale of spiritual growth, it means that we have developed a strong and real connection with our essential you.

Unfortunately, this is not, in itself, enough. Unless we bring to the surface and deal with the painful limitations of our wounded you, we may not be able to bring our spiritual growth into relationships. Hence, we have examples of religious leaders around the world (advanced spiritual beings) engaging in sadomasochism, paedophilia and corruption. Unless we deal with our wounds (by necessity, a painful process), they work subconsciously to undermine the value of our spiritual development.

Our defended you, too, needs our attention. We need to be aware of and manage it, or it controls us. The rule of thumb is:

- Raise your awareness of and manage your defended you.
- Raise your awareness of and heal your wounded you.
- Raise your awareness of and develop your essential you.

I find this way of looking at things much more effective than the traditional axiom of spiritual, emotional and physical balance which is about juggling the present—attempting to control a conflicting set of contingencies in order to manage stress. I find this axiom static, defensive and rather linear. Raising your awareness so that you can better manage your defended you, heal your wounded you and develop your essential you is about growth on the spiritual, emotional and cognitive levels. What's more, it enables you to do all these things in relationship to the people and the world around you. This helps integrate your mystical self with your social, political and emotional selves; it allows you to walk your talk and bridge the gap between the returning hero and the people who have not yet started their hero's journey or are at an earlier stage of their quest.

In other words, when we are healed emotionally, developed spiritually, adept at defending only when it is necessary and at peace with ourselves and the world around us, when we can accept ourselves and others for who we are, and respect the difference, we will be in a position to enjoy the fruits of our hero's journey, and put ourselves at the service of others. To me, this is one of life's great privileges. You could say it is the heart of the matter of living. It is also the essence of heroic relationships.

Relating Heroically

We are all responsible for 50 per cent of every relationship in which we are involved. When people have problems with a relationship, they usually set out to change 50 per cent of that relationship. Unfortunately, the 50 per cent they try to change is the half over which they are not responsible and over which they have no control—the other person's 50 per cent. Not only is this a total waste of time (because it simply does not work), but it actually aggravates the problems. If there is one thing people hate, it is others trying to change them. When we attempt to coerce another person to change, we trigger their wounded you and encourage their defended you to come out and do its thing big time. Hurting, defensive people are very hard to deal with; they are impossible to change.

If, however, we reverse this situation and decide to take full responsibility for our 50 per cent and exactly what it is that we want from each of our relationships, we are then in a position to see which of our wounds and defences is stopping us from getting it. Moreover, we can then work on our essential you, wounded you and defended you in order to get our psychological sore spots out of the way, develop our wisdom, insight, good humour and wellbeing, and use our defences skilfully to help the other person understand our needs and feel sufficiently positive about us that they want to help. I'm sure you'll agree that it is much easier to help a happy, grateful, approachable person than a blaming, defensive one.

However, it goes further than that. Once we have moved a significant way along the hero's journey, we start to send out vibes (those into the new science would call them 'fields') that have an apparently mystical impact on the world in which we live. People start coming into our lives just as we decide we need their help. Just the right opportunities appear apparently from nowhere at precisely the moment we are ready to capitalise on them. We somehow know to prepare for a big challenge before it occurs. The further along the hero's journey we are, the shorter the distance between when we decide we want something and it arriving. It is almost as if reality becomes like plasticine and all you have to do is mould it into the shape you want. This is when effortless, sleight-of-hand transformation becomes possible.

Heroic individuals who have dealt with their wounds, have developed their essence and manage their defences have an uncanny ability to catalyse the most dramatic personal, organisational and social transformations. In my experience, when you meet such people they present as being amazingly humble and extraordinarily ordinary, yet you feel better just from having been in their space. A famous example of someone who had reached this state of being was Mahatma Gandhi, whose own personal transformation metamorphosed an entire nation as he encouraged Indians to overthrow their British overlords peacefully. I guess if you keep at it long enough (and have the right parents), the end state along the path is that of Christ, Buddha and Mohammed, whose enlightenment changed the world.

There is no need when we grow to leave the people we love (or even the ones we hate) behind. If our growth is multidimensional and real, we will simply take people with us. I'm not promising it's easy, but boy is it exciting, rewarding, heartening, enlivening and soul enriching. Life really was meant to be this good.

Non-Heroic Relationships

This takes me back to warriors and their trainers. I have degrees in education and business. I have spent twenty years training and being professionally supervised in psychotherapy, and spend about two weeks a year in spiritual retreat. I meet and hear of thousands of business consultants, leadership consultants, organisational change consultants and executive coaches, very few of whom have regular, ongoing professional supervision. This scares me.

The human organism is fragile, complex, valuable and, to my mind, sacred. In the fields of medicine, psychiatry and psychology, it is normal practice for a professional to have their work (and, in many cases, their own psychological health) continually checked by their peers and those ahead of them in knowledge and experience. This practice of mentoring is also characteristic of many religions, where it is the role of the elder to guide individuals in their growth. Supervision helps us see past our own shortcomings and it provides feedback on our blind spots. A good supervisor brings another perspective and broadens our vision; they also keep us honest by gently pointing out where we could improve and encouraging us to go back and mop up when it is necessary. In addition to this professional guidance, a top supervisor will support our emotional and spiritual growth.

Any professional who is working at any depth with human beings, individually or in groups, should be professionally supervised by someone trained and experienced in working in depth with the human psyche. If people are not properly supervised, they are probably putting others at risk. We would not think of going to a doctor who was not properly trained or did not adhere to safety practices, yet we unthinkingly subject our psyches to all kinds of quacks. My experience as a participant in a good number of personal and organisational change programs has taught me that unsupervised trainers, facilitators, mentors and coaches create more problems than they solve. Their lack of personal awareness, egoic defensiveness and shallow insight when seen from a professional perspective are just plain frightening. To make things worse, highly sophisticated tools (such as neurolinguistic programming (NLP)) are increasingly used by those with little personal growth, appallingly low self-awareness and no, or inappropriate, psychological, therapeutic or educational training.

These are the people who make up the army of warrior trainers out there teaching our business leaders the new way forward. Unfortunately, due to the widespread nature of appalling ignorance in business about people and how they function on the many levels of their being, these totally ill-equipped and to my mind dangerous warrior trainers are serving as guides, mentors and coaches to our business leaders. Some trainers are obviously better than others and are making progress, but what about the failures and those individuals who suffer at the hands of ill-trained, unsupervised, self-proclaimed experts?

This is not to say that warrior trainers don't have university degrees; many are diligent and committed to their ongoing acquisition of skills and knowledge. This is very different, however, from growing personally, learning about themselves as human beings and increasing their knowledge, insight and ability to work safely and competently with the human psyche. The analogy I use is that of an axeman. An axeman may search out and find the best axe in the world. He may practise every day until he is expertly skilled at his craft. Yet if he has no knowledge of or care for the fragility of the natural environment in which he works, if he uses his axe to intimidate, to maim or to kill animals or people (even if the implications are not recognised for some time afterwards), then to my mind the time he has put into his training and finding the best tools is worse than wasted—it is out and out dangerous. It would be more beneficial if he worked in depth on his character—even if he were a little less skilled as an axeman, he would contribute more to society and the wellbeing of the planet. Constantly running after skills and knowledge may help us to feel competent, but without growing down into who we are as human beings, without growing down into our wisdom, we may inadvertently be using our technical competence in a way that puts people at risk psychologically.

It is by continuing our own growth that we help others to heal. If you take the concept of heroic relationships to its ultimate conclusion, this has to be true. As we grow, we magnify our ability to, through skilful means, change our 50 per cent of each of our relationships. By changing our 50 per cent, the relationship changes. As the relationship changes, both the people involved in the relationship change. The more we grow and the more unconsciously skilled we become, the more beneficially and effortlessly we affect those around us. This has absolutely everything do with our own growth and absolutely nothing to do with techniques, models, theories, dogmas, doctrines, manipulation and control.

Chapter 5

Unlocking Your Heart's Desire

...who am I to be brilliant, gorgeous, talented, fabulous?
Actually, who are you not to be? You are a child of God.
Your playing small does not serve the world.

NELSON MANDELA (INAUGURAL SP EECH)

Making your life work, with all its complexity, interconnected relationships and challenges, is far from easy. Making your life work in a way that maximises your wellbeing and contributes positively to the world around you takes time, energy, thought, imagination and commitment. Why, you may ask, would you bother? There are plenty of examples of world-class business leaders who seem to be interested only in money, power, status and personal aggrandisement. They appear to have achieved all of these things by being warriors. When it is hard enough to succeed in the rat-race of life and business, why would you go the extra mile and invest your scarce personal resources in enhancing the world? Surely that is idealistic or perhaps even grandiose?

It is certainly not compulsory to be a hero. Yes, people have risen to the top on the backs of others. Rape, murder, greed and exploitation are as old as humanity itself, but so are love, sharing, mutual support and community. Primitive humans (like most animals) cooperated to ensure the survival of the species. There were always threats from external predators and natural forces— there were also threats from other humans—but it was by huddling together that early *Homo sapiens* kept warm and safe. It was by hunting together that they increased their chances of success, and it was by combining the hunting of some with the food gathering of others that they survived the four seasons of the year and the natural cycles of nature.

Today, as never before, we are becoming aware of how the great intelligence, inventiveness and strength of human organisation and action bring their own problems. With the fragility of the ecosystem, the threat of new viruses, concerns over nuclear weapons, ongoing wars and civil unrest, and the unending problems of poverty and starvation, we have to ask if we have been using our intelligence to best effect. Have we been putting our inventiveness to maximum use and could we organise and act in ways that are more nurturing to the planet on which we live and the people in it?

On top of wider social, economic, political and environmental problems, there is widespread personal discontent. Even those of us who are lucky enough to live in peaceful countries where our human rights are protected—those who have the privilege of work, housing and adequate sustenance—even we crave for more as we become increasingly aware that man cannot live by bread alone. There is a growing hue and cry for soulfulness—intimate connection with ourselves, our fellow humans and the world in which we live. We want to be more, we want to make a difference, to connect. Playing small no longer satisfies our spirit.

Soul at Work

'The most miserable people I have known,' writes psychotherapist David Reynolds in *Constructive Living* 'have been self-focused', whereas the happiest have 'given themselves away' to others. The secret of life, he claims, is thinking past our own petty ego and working for the good of the whole. For those who follow this path, there will be 'moments of misery, times of sickness and grief, periods of doubt and worry. But soon they are back again at the business of adding to the lives of others. Then they sparkle.'

The selflessness of which Reynolds speaks does not involve the denial of self, emotion or our own needs. On the contrary, he claims that awareness of our inner theatre (especially our emotions) and taking responsibility for self-care and our actions are paramount. He simply claims that by 'investing ourselves in the world instead of wishing that others would save us', we build self-confidence, accomplish things, develop relationships and improve the social and physical world rather than sitting around wallowing in our feelings or being paralysed by emotions we are trying to suppress, ignore or deny. Through our own actions, we come to know that we can make a difference. This sentiment of 'investing ourselves in the world' is reiterated by the emerging cadre of experts writing in the field of sacred psychology, which focuses on the interconnection of emotional health and soulfulness. 'The soul,' writes Thomas Moore in *Care of the Soul* (p. 25) 'prospers in an environment that is concrete, particular and vernacular. It feeds on the details of life, on its variety, its quirks and its idiosyncrasies.' Soul is built not by shutting ourselves away from life, work, difficult people and awkward situations, but rather from a reflective interaction between the individual and the world. On the level of soul, we are not isolated, discrete entities. The individual's soul, the souls of others and the world's soul cannot be separated.

Soul building happens when we stop blaming others, circumstance and history for those things in our lives, our society and ourselves that we don't like and get on with the heroic task of making our lives, our relationships and our world work. When we do this with awareness, making conscious choices, feeling our feelings and continuously learning about ourselves, life and humanity, the soul is constantly enriched regardless of whether we win or lose, have times that are difficult or easy, or find ourselves in comfortable or uncomfortable situations. Soul building involves a choice to be emotionally and physically present in the real world, working in constructive ways to improve not just our own wellbeing, but also that of the people and environment around us. In this way, we make our spirituality tangible. We are not just acknowledging our connection to a force or order greater than ourselves, but also working directly in function to that force. In short, by choosing to be part of the world—taking responsibility for making the world a better place and working with reflective consciousness—we continuously build our sense of soulfulness, actively counterbalancing the alienation, loneliness and spiritual emptiness that has become so endemic in our society. As Hillman tells us in *The Soul's Code* (p. 44) 'A person's involvement with the world gives evidence of the descent of the spirit.'

Jean Houston in *Search for the Beloved* develops this theme further:

> *It becomes increasingly apparent to me, after several decades of work with extending human capacities, that capacities evolve and change in response to the larger cultural and mythic patterns of which we are a part. We can only extend our capacities when we are conscious of these larger patterns and assume our role as their co-creator.*

The message comes from many places. If you want a healthy, soulful life, a life with meaning and joy, then you will need to come to terms with the reality of your emotional experience while enhancing the physical and social world in which you live. This necessitates being present, in the moment, with your emotions while noticing the needs of your environment and the people who inhabit it. You then need to take conscious, responsible action. This is the world of the hero.

The hero acknowledges and learns from both the night and day of life. Wisdom tells us that we all must suffer pain, loss, failure and death as part of our life's journey. The soul knows that if we stay open to self-reflection, growing wisdom, worldly learning and relationship building, it is life's sorrows as well as its joys that will build our inner strength.

While they may be dressed in shabby clothing in the eyes of today's fashion-conscious world, it is life's misfortunes, misadventures and problems that develop our character, deepen our soulfulness and teach us wisdom. From the soul's perspective, writes Thomas Moore in *Care of the Soul* 'every fall into ignorance and confusion is an opportunity to discover that the beast residing at the centre of the labyrinth is also an angel.'

When we look at things this way, work becomes the perfect place for the heroic development of soul. We rarely get consciously to choose the people with whom we work. To retain our jobs and achieve desired outcomes at work, we have to deal with a whole range of awkward, unpleasant and mundane situations, and a whole bevy of difficult people who at other times and under other circumstances we would seek to avoid. At work we can't. Moreover, our effectiveness and success demand that we find constructive ways of dealing with the realities of the people, situations and politics of the workplace.

What I find really exciting about this is we have a choice. We can deal with life at work by shutting down emotionally, armouring ourselves psychologically, learning to grin and bear it, or we can choose to see work as an ongoing, high-level personal development workshop where they pay you to attend. We can transform the reality of our world at work by transforming our way of perceiving and dealing with that world. The wonderful, exciting and unexpected outcome of all this is that when we operate this way, we increase our personal power and become much more effective at what we do. Our relationships improve, our objectives are reached more quickly and more easily, and we find that the world around us mysteriously improves in a plethora of very tangible ways.

This is the magical sleight of hand I referred to in chapter 4. Although it appears that the only change that has taken place is within us, this 'something–nothing' process can lead to apparently miraculous transformations in the system of which we are part. I see this time and again with clients, particularly those with whom I work over extended periods. While we appear to have done nothing but stay present with our emotional reality, walking and talking with our heartfelt desires, paying attention to the practical and political demands of the world in which we live and work, suddenly everything is different.

I remember being interviewed by a postgraduate student in business about my work at an international award-winning industrial plant. 'What,' she asked me 'changed?' I thought for a while and then laughed. 'Everything. The people, the culture, the systems, the strategy, the policies, the practices in industrial relationships, environmental protection, the way they organised their plant, thought about their issues, ran their meetings and related with each other all changed. Nothing remained the same.'

Other clients have put it this way: 'It's like a wave. It just builds over time,' and 'I could never have known when I started out that this is where I would be now. I didn't know that where I am now was possible.' Nobel Prize winning physicist Ilya Priognes in *Brain/Mind Bulletin* wrote:

> *The more complex the structure, the more energy it must dissipate to maintain all that complexity. This flux of energy makes the system highly unstable, subject to internal fluctuations—and sudden change. If these fluctuations or perturbations reach a critical size, they are amplified by the system's many connections and can drive the system into a new state, even more ordered, coherent and connected. The new state occurs as a sudden shift.*

Human beings are flesh and bone, but we are also energy systems. Our spirits, thoughts and emotions are perhaps the most potent form of energy we have. Our physical actions are a coarse embodiment of this high-powered inner, quite invisible energy. When we become aware of and learn how to use our inner energy skilfully, we can learn to transform not only our own lives, but also all the systems that we inhabit.

This is the power of heroes. By living close to their hearts and souls, by raising their consciousness of thought and by experiencing and working with their emotions, heroes can drive the systems with which they interact into new, more ordered, coherent and connected states. They do this with themselves, their integrity and their souls intact—transformed to a higher order, yes, but not destroyed, sold out, deadened or worn out by conforming to humanly crippling social and political norms. Heroes choose not simply to survive, but really to live their lives. They opt to become co-creators of the world in which they live and work. This is not easy, it is rarely comfortable, it takes time and energy, but it is an enlivening, productive, exciting way to be. It also makes sense. If we deaden our spirits, our emotions and thoughts in order to survive, we are actually killing our energy systems. No wonder we feel tired, alienated, alone and depressed.

I find it surprising that people who shut down to life, emotion and ongoing change get by at all. It has been a source of constant amazement to me for years that leaders of organisations that in their management, systems and politics seem to go out of their way to dull human spirit and emotion haven't seen that they are working against their own best interests. All that economic jargon about 'rational man' becomes laughable when you look at most organisational behaviour from a spiritual and humane perspective. The way in which most people treat themselves and each other at work is just plain silly; how most organisations are run makes no sense at all. At work, we have tended to regard ourselves and each other as intelligent machines, denying our human strengths of heart, soul and emotion, thus undermining all the creativity, energy and potential for transforming systems inherent in our humanity. We are, in fact, rather dumb machines, but we are wonderful humans. It's about time we started respecting that fact. We would all be happier, more spirited, more enlivened and more productive if we did.

It so happens that we are undergoing one of those periods in history when everything is changing. People call it a paradigm shift. Business and government leaders around the world declare that they are looking for transformational ways to work with social, political, economic, environmental and human issues on a global scale. At the same time, we have an emergence of theories, practice, ideas and experiences in fields as diverse as physics, medicine, psychology and spirituality that show us that there are powerful new ways of transformation available to us. This involves respecting the mystery of the human psyche, avoiding our compulsion to try to control reality, learning to live in a place of unknowing and choosing to raise our consciousness to our own emotional reality and the world around us, while taking responsibility for our actions and our part in co-creating the emerging patterns in society. In other words, the peace of mind, inner joy and wellbeing we seek, along with the transformation we say we want in the worlds of business, society and the environment, are all within our reach if we can raise our awareness high enough consciously to take total personal responsibility for our actions in a mysterious, unknowable world over which we have no control and about which we are consciously unknowing.

I know that this is easy to say and rather unsettling to live. Businesses run to schedules, plans and budgets. We run our own lives in accordance with our diaries, watches and calendars, all wanting to know what is next, when and why. However, just because that is the way we have become doesn't mean that it is the only way or that it is doing us any good.

As Robert Sardallo in *Love and the Soul* tells us: 'In the realm of soul logic, what is healthy is usually at first unsettling ... A sign of health is that more questions are raised than are answered.' When we decide to live and operate in a healthy, heartfelt, soulful way—a way that enables radical transformation of an holistic nature—we are taking an option that involves noticing and respecting process, change, pauses and the mysteries of life and transformation. When we attune to the reality of a fluid universe, to the mysteries of the human psyche, the power of systems and potency of relationships we can, as individuals, co-create a more human, life-sustaining world.

The paradox is that the healthy world of the soul, the realm of massive transformation, is the antithesis of how the business world currently operates. As we have seen, most organisations operate from the rules of addiction, which tend to wither, crush and anaesthetise the human spirit, heart and intuitive wisdom. As Tom Chappell of Tom's of Maine tells us: 'Business often tries to reduce commerce to controllable, identifiable, manageable transactions. And it's the elements of control and focus and measurability that strip the spirit out of an enterprise.'

More than that, the power dynamics that operate at work often strip the humanity, the heart, out of our relationships so that we end up interacting as role to role, rather than person to person. In such an environment our well-socialised psychological response is fear. So we keep our defensive shields in place, do what we think we need to do to keep the bosses off our backs and keep ourselves, with all our richness of emotion, soul, creativity and intuition, hidden. Building on our early socialisation, we become experts at sensing what will appease the power players and this is what we spend our time doing. To survive politically, we choose to ignore the messages from our own emotions and soul.

In other words, instead of giving ourselves away soulfully, we sell ourselves short defensively. If we do this often enough, it becomes normal. We become increasingly deaf to the messages from our heart and spirit until we cannot hear them at all. More sadly, we even begin to believe they don't exist. This is the norm in business and particularly so in the large number of organisations that operate as addictive systems reinforcing the patterns of denial, externalisation of focus and isolation developed during early socialisation.

When normality amounts to severe disconnection from ourselves, true relationships with others and with our environment become impossible. We start seeing the world as disconnected pieces and we search for disjointed answers from a plethora of sources. Enter the warrior trainers who provide piecemeal answers in the form of theories, models and other assorted mental maps. In our fearful need for certainty and haste to relieve the tensions of unknowing, we seize on the flavour-of-the-month management fad, thus losing the:

> *...occasion for soul work by leaping ahead to final solutions without pausing to savour the undertones... We think that power comes from understanding and unveiling But we should know from the story of Oedipus that this approach only goes so far. Oedipus solved the riddle of the sphinx but then he was blinded and only afterward slowly came to appreciate the mysteries that are beyond the scope of reason.* (*Care of the Soul* p. 125)

By blindly following the ways of the warrior, we kill our own heroism. By seeking to know, to control and to avoid the discomfort of soulful emotion, we thwart the powerful forces that could lead to our own health and ironically the massive transformation, the quantum leaps, that business leaders so enthusiastically declare they want. By putting our focus outside of ourselves, appeasing our political masters, ignoring our emotions and soul messages, we keep ourselves and our world stuck in the same place. We become co-creators of a world we claim to dislike, a world we rightly believe is stifling our humanity and crippling our human potential.

You—The Place To Start

Although it is obvious that we are all part of the problem, it still begs the question of what any one individual can do about it.

The answer is *everything*. The place to start is with yourself. The way to do it is:

- Decide to take the healthy, heartfelt, soulful choice in each situation.
- Raise your awareness about your needs, thoughts, feelings, environment and unconscious drivers.
- Feel your feelings.
- Choose your actions.

If you do this in your relationships with other people and your social and physical environment, you can enrich your inner and outer worlds beyond your imagination. Although this is easy to say, I recognise that it is far from easy to do. We have become so distanced from our own sense of personal power we think we are not in a position to make real choices. Our socialisation has been very effective in convincing us that we have to look outside of ourselves for power and approval. The less conscious we are of our psychological patterning, the more impact it has on our behaviour and response, and the less control we feel we have—which is true. Moreover, we have received so little support for listening to our inner messages that most of us have lost touch with ourselves and are shockingly self-ignorant. Most of us have forgotten to feel on a deep, natural human level and our lack of self-awareness has made our emotions seem like our enemies, not the friendly messengers and reservoirs of energy they actually are. We tell ourselves that we are victims of our circumstance and that even if we did choose our actions it couldn't make any difference to us, let alone anyone else. From this perspective, the thought of choosing heart and soul at work seems naïve. Our twisted thinking tells us that to feel at work would be suicidal. We feel done to and put upon. Individuals, however, can and do make a difference. When we get in touch with our inner power, we as individuals can change the world.

Abuse... Feeling... Liberation and Soul

But surely not at work? How can we take the healthy choice in an unhealthy environment that appears to punish us for being in touch with our heart and soul? Who really wants to feel what it is like fitting into a politically charged, inhuman system? How can you be responsible for your decisions and actions when you work in a large, bureaucratic or abusive organisation? Doesn't facing reality include accepting when you are beaten?

These were the questions that Kathy, a change agent in a large government agency, asked when I told her she could not only be effective at her job, but also simultaneously use the experience to improve her spiritual wellbeing and out-of-work life. I don't think it would be putting things too strongly to say that she thought I was mad. You'll remember that soul logic is usually unsettling. Yet the simple remedies of making the healthy choice, raising your awareness, feeling your feelings and choosing your actions have a well-proven track record in the most dire situations.

Sadly, as a society, we have an atrocious record of family violence. Although we like to think that homes are safe havens where people go to nourish their bodies, hearts and souls, in many cases this is more illusion than fact. Abused children have little choice about their situation—they have to find psychological coping mechanisms to endure what their parents dish out. Spouses, however, as responsible adults, do have real choice. So it is surprising to find out just how many abused wives choose repeatedly to return to their husbands even after life-threatening attacks. There are all sorts of rationales for this behaviour that revolve around economic support for the wife and her children, but when we realise that the level of abuse many women suffer actually endangers their health, sanity and even their lives, the economic arguments just don't stack up.

If, when working with survivors of domestic violence, one can get them to accept that perhaps their mental, physical, emotional and spiritual health and that of their children are worthwhile goals, you can begin to help those people to change. The first step is to help survivors feel what it feels like to be bashed, raped, put down and tormented by their husbands. The way most survivors tolerate abuse is by closing down their emotions and choosing to ignore the reality of their plight.

There is a strong tendency to downplay the severity, frequency and effects of domestic violence. Survivors can do this because they manage never to be psychologically around when they are assaulted. Being numbed to our problems, pains and sorrows doesn't make them go away; it simply disempowers us and robs us of the motivation and energy to do something about it. The challenge, then, is to get abuse survivors to feel what it feels like to be them, receiving the treatment they receive. This unleashes a huge energy and potential for change. Once we feel the righteous anger and outrage that results when we are conscious of others' inhumanity towards us, we become charged and ready for action. This is when choosing to act responsibly becomes very important. It would be extremely unwise for a short, slight woman to confront her abusive husband with angry words and accusations. This would surely incite violence. However, if the woman channels her anger into building up a group of supportive friends and professional help, if she finds ways of enlisting police and legal protection, if she locates a new (safe) place to live and perhaps embarks on improving her education or getting a job, she will indeed change her world.

We now know there is a cycle of violence. Children who grow up in abusive situations tend to find themselves in abusive situations as adults, either as the victim or the abuser. By becoming aware of their own patterns and choosing to break the cycle, women who move out of, or transform, abusive domestic situations don't just save their own lives, improve their own health and liberate their own souls. They actually give their children a chance of wellbeing and happiness.

More than that, when individual women share their stories, they give other women heart. By helping and supporting others, individual women have worked to change many lives other than their own. It is through the collective action of such women that we now have laws protecting the survivors of domestic violence and police trained and prepared to help. It is through women telling their stories and working together to help other women that awareness about family abuse has risen and we as a society are changing our ways of thinking, reacting and living. This doesn't mean that the problem is solved; women and children are still being abused all over the world. Others, however, have made the healthy choice, have had the courage to feel and to take appropriate action and, being lucky enough to find support, have made a new life for themselves and their children.

If unprotected women isolated in their own homes have been able to do this, why can't people work together in the workplace to improve their lot? It all starts with individuals choosing health, facing the reality of their lives, energising themselves with feelings and choosing to do something constructive about making a difference for themselves and others.

The Mysterious Process of Life

In the wonderful writings of Carl Hammerschlag we see the hero at work. A practising Jew, Hammerschlag went, as a new graduate in psychiatry, to work on a Native American reservation in the southwest of the USA. His idea (apart from avoiding being sent to Vietnam) was to 'help, to offer healing to the people'. He found, however, that the people weren't too keen to be 'helped' by a young, white, know-it-all, who apparently was ignorant to the sacred and important ways of those he strove to heal. Slowly and painfully, Hammerschlag began to learn from the people he had set out to teach. In the *Theft of the Spirit*, he tells of his first meeting with the Hopi holy man Herbert:

When he finally turned to me he asked, 'What do you know about the mind?' His tone was one of amazement, rather than contentiousness. And I was suddenly at a loss for words. In all my training, I had never before been asked that question.

I wanted to appear competent and knowledgeable—wanted him to like me. Should I launch into a lecture about the hypothalamus, the biological determinants of behaviour, neuropeptides? Somehow I did not think any of that would impress him. I could not think of a short, incisive answer.

'I guess,' I replied after a painful pause, 'I really don't know a whole lot about it, I mean, that can be answered briefly... in a short time.'

Herbert smiled and went back to his weaving. He appeared to be dismissing me with his silence. (In white society, we think something is happening when people are talking. In Indian country, they know something is happening when there is silence.)

I looked around the walls seeking some kind of solace for my awkwardness. I saw kachina carvings, pictures of children, assorted rattles. I had bungled this opportunity to become acquainted with a respected medicine man.

After what seemed to be a slice of eternity, Herbert turned to me and solemnly pronounced: 'If you cannot say what you know about the mind in a short time, then you know nothing of it.'

My immediate response was anger. This old man had just reduced all my years of education to inconsequence. 'What I know of the mind,' Herbert went on, 'I can tell you in one word.' He paused for a moment. 'Mysterious.'

Mysterious. The human mind was mysterious. Herbert had looked at the question of what is mind from another perspective, from the aspect of what we don't know. It was an important lesson for me. What I know about it, he was saying, is I don't know it.

I wanted to learn what Herbert could teach me. I was open to him, and happily he was willing to talk, then and many times

after. I call him my spiritual father. He would not make me a
Hopi medicine man but he could teach me some things about
Hopi ways so I could better understand them.

Hammerschlag serves as an awe-inspiring example of how to
function as a healthy human being in the workplace. He demon-
strates that it is possible to work with heart and soul. To do this we
need to notice, to learn from every interaction, to experience our
anger, our *awkwardness.* The pain of our bungled moments opens
our hearts, minds and souls to the learning that is so abundantly
around us. When we stop trying to control the moment, we cease
trying to force our lives and the world to be a certain way, we can
be present with the reality of what is. Then the knocks, insults,
jars, rebuffs, and apparent dead ends become sources of great
learning. They become the teachers that put us in touch with our
own wisdom. By committing to live a hearty, soulful life, we give
ourselves permission to notice our emotional reality and allow it to
push us up against the boundaries of the social and physical world
we inhabit. This is how wisdom is gained. Not in the teaching,
but in the learning; not in the talking, but in the silences, in the
reflection, in the feeling, in the noticing and in the action.

What is remarkable about Hammerschlag's tales is that they
show that it is in the very parts of our work, the painful, awkward,
difficult parts, that the best learning happens. It is in the dark
nights of the soul that our hearts learn their truest calling, our
spirits their greatest depths and our emotions their finest texture,
their widest breadth, their brightest colours. Yes, it is in the
mundane and the ordinary, the normal course of life and work,
that the best heroic training is Obtained—once we decide to see
things differently.

This is a hard lesson to learn. We want there to be more. We
want there to be clear answers, five-point action plans and helpful
techniques. How can we possibly survive in the rough and tumble
of business and government by choosing a life with heart and
soul, by raising our awareness, feeling our feelings and deciding
to take responsible constructive action in relationship to the world
around us? There has to be more to it than that, doesn't there?

Well, there isn't. Hammerschlag shows us that. Herbert knew it. And anthropologist Carlos Castaneda found it out by questioning Yaqui Indian, Don Juan, who claimed that modern Western man thinks and talks too much. He explained that we fill our heads with ceaseless inner chatter, as we tell ourselves how the world should be (in function of our childhood patterning and belief systems), repeating our inner choices (which we don't own) over and over, thus staying always on the same paths. Don Juan explained to his student Carlos that radical change happens when we listen to the world and thus allow change to take place. We get in our own way, unconsciously making impossible the changes we say we want.

Priest, theologian and psychologist Henri J. M. Nouwen agrees. Nouwen tells us in *Reaching Out* that we have become afraid of silent solitude and fill our heads with ideas, opinions, judgments and values that we hang on to and guard like precious objects. All this keeps us from experiencing life, as we cling to our familiar ways even if these are unhealthy and personally destructive to our hearts, bodies and souls. He writes:

> *Preoccupations are our fearful ways of keeping things the same, and it often seems that we prefer a bad certainty to a good uncertainty. Our preoccupations help us to maintain the personal world we have created over the years and block the way to revolutionary change… Instead of facing the challenge of new worlds opening themselves for us, and struggling in the open field, we hide behind the walls of our concerns holding on to the familiar life items we have collected in the past.*

So, instead of committing to our own and our society's wellbeing, raising our awareness, experiencing life as if happens and choosing to act as a co-creator of the world in which we are a part, we search for answers, certainties, mind maps, prescribed ways forward, all the while clinging on to our well-socialised certitude, beliefs and behaviours, which we project out and see as the external reality of the world.

In other words, we don't see straight. We see what we think, believe and tell ourselves is what is happening, because we have lost the ability to rest in a place of inner emptiness, unknowing and openness to whatever comes—terrified that it might be something we don't like or can't control, or with which we will not be able to deal. We search for external answers which do little but keep us stuck where we are. Put another way, unconscious of our inner theatre, we project it onto everything we see in the world—every situation and every interaction we think that the world is imposing on us—when in fact (because of our blindness) the world is simply serving as a screen reflecting our inner movies.

When, however, we free up our rigid mental maps and let them flow with the reality of life, when we empty our heads of inner chatter; when we raise our awareness of our own inner response, we actually begin to see the world and the people in it as they are, not as we would imagine them to be. This is the place of radical transformation.

When I work with clients, I do little else but help them stay with the reality of what is, in the moment. This means slowing down enough to notice what is real and what is their own projection onto reality. This process demands feeling. Feelings are the link between the unconscious inner world and our external environment. It is only when we can notice what is inside us and what is outside, and when we can stay present with our emotional reality, that we are in a position to make informed, powerful decisions as to our actions. It is only when we begin to see and think straight that we can act with maximum effectiveness. To do this, we need to be able to feel how it is for us, in the here and now. So I ask my clients how they feel. I have them reflect on their lives and share their stories, I share how I see the world, I provide feedback from my perspective and we muddle through all this information, getting to know more about ourselves, each other, the world and what is possible.

From this very simple process, this 'something–nothing', I see an invisible letting go of preoccupation and a freeing up of rigid mental maps which allows people to stay with their present moment reality, to see things as they are—not distorted by theories, models and outdated personal patterns of psychological response. This process translates into radical shifts in perception, action and outcome. In short, people change. Their relationships change and their world changes. All this starts with us letting go of our preconceptions, staying open to our emotions and trusting that our responses are genuine, valuable and sufficient. This has been the way of the medicine men across the ages, it is the way of the shaman, it is also the way of a growing number of experts in the mysteries of the human heart, mind and soul.

What is disconcerting is that the 'recipe' to having a full healthy, heartfelt, soulful life, amounts to little more than relearning what we forgot as babies, when we already knew how to be present, to feel and seek connection with others. Put another way, bringing about massive positive transformation in our lives and in our world is more about unlearning, letting go and dwelling in silence and emptiness than it is about answers, formulae and mental maps. This level of simplicity is almost totally unknown to today's modern, sophisticated worker and citizen, and yet it is little more than reclaiming our birthright. How do you teach able-bodied people to walk down the path that is before them when what is involved is their first deciding to move and then putting one foot in front of the other? It is all so basic and yet those of us living in 'advanced civilisation' have become so refined that we have devalued what is natural.

Our cravings for what is possible, however, have not gone away. Although our minds seem to have forgotten, we still have some distant bodily, heartfelt soul memories of a more fulfilling, enriching life, a life for which we yearn. To fulfil these cravings, we search incessantly for rational, modern, New Age answers rather than accepting that the simple things we have given away, forgotten and devalued are the most important and revolutionary things we could have. They will provide us with the sanest, safest and most valuable answers.

We don't need substitutes, we simply need to quieten down our inner chatter, let go of our sophisticated mental models and relearn to experience life as it happens. This is what Wilson Schaef calls 'living in process'. To live in process involves a leap of faith, a decision that feels no less terrifying than leaping into an apparently bottomless dark hole. You either jump or you don't. It is your decision and you are the one who has to leap—no one can or will push you. It's your life, your heart, your soul, your body, your emotions, your choice.

Following Your Heart's Desire

When we start living in process, when we give ourselves permission to be present and feel, our feelings, our hearts' desires and souls' longings start bubbling their way into our consciousness. This can be rather disconcerting because, as we have seen, the heart and soul have their own logic. This logic doesn't always coincide with what we think we 'should' want.

When working with clients, I very often ask them to tell me what they want not from their heads, but from their bellies. I call it their gut feeling or gut response. I have found that if I want to help people get in touch with their hearts' desires so that they can do what makes sense for them individually and as part of the wider systems that they inhabit, I need to help them feel the answers, not just think them. In saying this, I am mindful that my clients are all executives who are very good at using their heads. Sometimes too good.

Sam was the managing director of the European division of a highly respected multinational. His highly profitable firm became successful by keeping close to their market and tailoring their products to the needs of their clients. By staying flexible and client centred, they had come up with a formula that worked for them, but was taking them further and further away from the parent company's strategic direction. Sam came to see me not because of this strategic divergence, but because he was disgusted by what he saw as the incompetence and lack of leadership skills of the new global CEO.

Sam had been asked to take the CEO's job, but had declined for personal reasons. Now he was having second thoughts—not because he wanted the job, but because he couldn't bear the new incumbent. As Sam started talking through his personal difficulties with the new CEO and the several occasions he had clashed with his boss, I was struck that Sam, normally logical and cluey, just wasn't making sense.

'What,' I asked him, 'is your heart's desire in this situation?'

'Funny you should ask that,' he replied. 'I was only telling my wife on the weekend that what we need is a new parent company with a better strategic fit.'

Ironically, such a company had approached Sam on this matter within the past few months. I was amused that Sam was clashing with his boss in the existing parent company when what he wanted was to orchestrate a buy-out for strategic reasons. Why wasn't he putting his energies into selling his strategic intentions to the necessary power players and building whatever relationships he needed to get his division out of a company in which it no longer belonged?

As we worked through these questions, it turned out that Sam didn't believe that he could have his heart's desire. A man who had built up one of the most successful businesses in their global niche, a self-made multi-millionaire, could not believe that he had the skill and power to do what was obviously the best thing for all involved. By adhering to what he thought was the 'right thing to do', he was actually undermining his success and wellbeing, and that of his staff, his boss and all the shareholders. By daring to listen to, believe in and follow his heart's desire, he was in a position to orchestrate a strategic change that could lead to everybody winning.

In my experience, people's hearts' desires usually make a lot more sense than their logically thought through objectives and goals. Moreover, when we bring to the surface, acknowledge and commit to following our hearts' desires, we bring the power of our heart and soul into our actions. This frees up our energy and our thinking, and we find lateral, intuitive ways forward, flexibly working our way through issues and challenges as they arise.

When we work this way, people want to be part of the future we are creating.

More than that, should we fail for some unforeseen reason, we simply provide ourselves with soulful learning. Never having sold out our heart and soul in the first place, we just keep growing and learning, and enriching our lives.

Living in Process

'Repression of the life force,' writes Thomas Moore in *Care of the Soul*, 'is a diagnosis I believe would fit most of the emotional problems people present in therapy.' How can this be—can we really be suppressing our own energy, our own aliveness?

Yes, writes bodywork guru and psychiatrist Alexander Lowen in *Fear of Life*, who claims we are afraid of life, which we constantly seek to control and master. Acting out the role we think we should, as a person, perform is very different from relaxing into life with all its unseen mysteries, changes and challenges. Lowen suggests really living, actually 'being' a person rather than going through the motions requires 'that we stop our frantic business, that we take time out to breathe and to feel. In the process we may feel our pain, but if we have the courage to accept it, we will also have pleasure. If we can face our inner emptiness, we will discover joy. In this therapeutic undertaking we may need help.'

The help we need is that of an heroic guide, someone who has been down the path before us. Someone like Carl Hammerschlag, who can model living and working a different way. Good heroic guides have no need to maintain a position of power imbalance, of 'I know the answers and you don't', over others. Good heroic guides know that the answers, while being remarkably simple, demand that we have the courage to look at ourselves and life differently and take the time to notice, to feel and to act with purpose.

Good heroic guides (as we will see in chapter 6) are remarkably difficult to find, but are well worth the search. A good heroic guide will help us to re-experience the connection between our minds, bodies, spirits and emotions. They do this not by talking at us, not by explaining acres of theory, but through listening to our stories and sharing their own, encouraging us to listen to the messages from our hearts, souls, minds and bodies and do the simplest, most life-giving things such as breathing and getting enough rest. By failing to pay attention to our bodies and emotions, Lowen in *The Spirituality of the Body* tells us, we are killing ourselves, our aliveness, our relationships, our physical environment and our spirits. Human beings, he notes, are the only creatures who drive themselves so hard they lose their natural connection with life, nature and their own spirit.

Ironically, writes Lowen, this senseless, driven behaviour stems from our displaced need for love. Our lack of consciousness has led us to confuse success and power with our desire for love. We harbour the juvenile misconception that if we are powerful and successful we will be lovable. However, while success may attract attention, it will never bring genuine love. According to Lowen:

> *To be lovable, one needs to be lovable—that is, able to love. To be lovable one needs to be humble, to reach out, to open one's heart and be vulnerable. But the wilful person is proud. Having been hurt as a child when he was open and vulnerable, he is determined not to suffer that pain and humiliation again. He will command love by his power and position. He will prove his superiority, but he will not cry or ask for love. The intensity of his drive is in direct proportion to his hunger for love, but it serves only to frustrate that desire.*

This is the neurotic script that drives the business world. We are trying to solve an emotional problem by force of will. The pain of socialisation is so strong that it distorts our thinking, our perception and therefore our actions, our lives and our society. Thus the personal has become political, economic and social. Families, teams, organisations and societies are nothing but individuals living and working together. When we can reclaim the health of our hearts, souls, bodies and minds as individuals, we will heal the relationships and the systems of which we, as individuals, are a part.

The irony, the thing that is so hard to believe, is that it comes back to such simple things, such 'something–nothings', the things we take for granted, ignore, deny and repress. The great paradox of today's world and the people in it is that we already have everything that is necessary for our wellbeing and the health of all our human systems. Yet the problem is we have chosen to ignore, undervalue or deny the keys to our own liberation, wellbeing and global transformation. So when someone like me says it comes back to making personal choices, to feeling your feelings and choosing your actions, it all sounds so banal. Entreaties to tell our stories and choose to reconnect with others sound like platitudes. Advice, such as that of Lowen, to relearn how to breathe sounds inane when we are faced with world poverty, demanding shareholders, clients, a sick child and a pile of unpaid bills. But let's follow through this reasoning.

Lowen in *The Spirituality of the Body* tells us that as children we each react differently to the process of socialisation through which we pass. Our individual responses have a huge impact on how our bodies form as we are growing. Our emotional responses actually become programmed into our bodies. We each build up a repertoire of personal tensions in our musculature that determine how we hold ourselves and this becomes our body structure.

As babies, we have flexible bodies filled with energy. As we get older, our bodies become more structured and consequently our energy levels fall and we become more rigid. Lowen writes:

> *Eventually an older person becomes so set in his ways that he can barely move at all. I cannot recall ever seeing an older person jump for joy the way a young child can. Infants have the most spirited bodies of all because they are far more sensitive than the rest of us to their environment and to the people around them… A lack of aliveness is always the result of suppressing feelings.*

Wilhelm Reich, Lowen's mentor, noticed that when people held back an expression of thought or feeling they also held their breath. Conversely, by encouraging people to breathe deeply Reich found that thoughts and feelings would pour out, thus enabling people to let go of tensions in their bodies, become less rigid in their thinking and therefore take more constructive action in their lives.

I can tell you that when clients come to see me and I suggest that they can enrich their lives and reach their business objectives by breathing, they are rather sceptical. However, unless they breathe, they won't feel; unless they feel, they will cling to their rigid mind maps and body tensions; unless they let go of their rigid mind maps and body tensions, they will go on operating out of will, staying disconnected from their hearts and souls. Their fear of being vulnerable (and vulnerable is exactly what they need to be to attain the love and connection they desperately seek) will compel them to stay stuck in the same old patterns of thought, emotional response and behaviour. If I can just get them to breathe, they will begin to change. They will be more in touch with the world they inhabit and start to make decisions that are more centred on the reality of their environment and the needs of the people who inhabit it (we call this being strategic).

More than that, when we breathe we are able to be present and therefore to know what is the appropriate behaviour in each situation. So their thinking becomes more strategic, their behaviour more appropriate and their energy levels rise. Their growing freedom of thought and interconnection bring them more into personal relationship with the individuals in their world. Things start to change. All this from breathing. It sounds fantastic I know—some dream from on high. But look at it this way: how effective can a person be if they aren't breathing?

It seems important here to develop this notion of breathing a little further. As Lowen points out, we are constantly looking for techniques, so when someone says breathing is important we want a technique so we can get it right. The answer from the expert himself is: 'The body knows how to react appropriately and can be trusted to do so if the person will only let it.' There we have it again, no prescription. Just deciding, noticing, feeling and choosing to act appropriately by trusting our own inner messages.

I'm not suggesting that you spend your day in some form of yogic meditation concentrating on your breathing. Although that may help you relax and operate from a place of deep wisdom, it can also serve to keep you out of the cut and thrust of life. Moreover, someone who is spending their time concentrating on their breathing is less than exciting company. However, we can choose from time to time to notice how we are breathing. We can consciously choose to take deep breaths before going into or during a stressful situation. Moreover, we can spend time when we are alone listening to our bodies' need for breath and consciously learning to meet that need. To do this may involve breathing techniques from disciplines such as yoga or bioenergetics, but these are simply aids until we can trust our bodies to take deep, full breaths on their own, even in stressful or frightening situations (which is when we most need our breath so that we can think straight). So, starting from a place of being unconsciously unskilled at breathing, we can become consciously aware that we don't breathe well. This then gives us incentive to relearn how to breathe (i.e. become consciously skilled). In time we no longer need to think about when and how to breathe because with awareness and practice we can reprogram our subconscious to do it for us. By this stage, we will be breathing from a place of unconscious skilling.

Due to our lopsided thinking, constant self-denial and ongoing external focus, even something as simple as breathing turns out not to be easy. To illustrate this point, I sometimes get a group of actors to perform a skit in which people in a sales meeting are discussing the figures. I ask the audience to tell me what is happening in the meeting. People notice that the actors are tense, their relationships are strained and they are obviously discussing a big problem. I then get the actors to change one predetermined thing. They run through the same skit, sitting in the same chairs, repeating the same words. But something dramatic has changed. They appear more relaxed, they are easier to hear, their relationships are closer and the communication is more free flowing.

I then ask the audience to tell me what was the one thing that made all the difference. To date no one has noticed that the one single change that so radically transformed this meeting was that in the first instance the actors were deliberately breathing shallowly, in the second they were breathing deeply. Why has no one ever guessed the secret ingredient, breathing? This is because in most offices most people breathe shallowly all the time. Not breathing well is so normal we no longer notice.

Just in case you think that none of this applies to you because you run regular marathons, swim five miles a day or are a master in some martial art, forget it. I have worked with leading athletes and as soon as it comes to a situation in which they feel uncomfortable, out of control or stressed, they forget all those breathing exercises they've done for their sport and shallowly pant like everybody else. Isn't it startling that we are so sophisticated we have forgotten how to breathe? As we are about to see, however, there is a very good reason why this is so.

What Happens When We Feel

Reich was right. When we breathe, we begin to feel more deeply. Oxygen enlivens our body and we feel our emotions more strongly. This is exactly what most people in business want to avoid. They just don't want to feel what it is actually like to be them living their life and working in their organisation. Organisations run in such inhuman, senseless ways, we feel vulnerable, powerless and threatened. We are frightened that if we experience these feelings, we will not be able to function, to do our jobs, to earn our salaries and support ourselves and our families. We unconsciously decide that survival demands not feeling.

This is the same decision most people made to survive their socialisation as children. The difference was that as children we had very limited choices and, although it might not always feel that way, this is not true for adults. As adults, we are more powerful and have more choices than most of us ever dare to imagine. We miss this truth because our early programming is so strong, so pervasive and so unconscious, yet it drives our lives in a myriad of unseen ways. This is exactly why we need to relearn how to experience, notice and work with our emotions.

Our feelings are the connecting force between our body and our minds (our 'walk the talk' conduit), between our spirit and our body (our in-built ethics monitor), and between us and our environment. As such, they bring with them a huge amount of information to which most of us are largely deaf, blind and insensitive. Learning to notice, work with and decipher this information enables us to take our thinking to a whole new level, become radically more effective in our behaviour, dramatically increase our awareness of our environment, improve our relationships out of sight and take our intuition to a higher realm. Let's look how.

When we experience emotion, we become aware of physical senses, which through our mental processes can be articulated as feelings. Some of what we perceive is conscious, some is unconscious; some is about us, some about our environment; some is here and now, some is old childhood patterns. With practice, we can learn to make sense of and decipher these messages. To do so is to free up our actions, thoughts and possibilities for constructive action.

Jim (not his real name) is the head of an influential government agency. He has an impeccable track record for honesty, efficiency and performance. He came to see me because he was under a lot of public and political pressure to transform his organisation. However, it seemed that whenever he tried to bring about any changes someone somewhere objected and tried to stop him. He felt frustrated, annoyed and cramped. He was constantly under public scrutiny and he complained, 'I feel like I'm living in a goldfish bowl.'

So let's look at the information Jim has to hand.

First, there is some relationship information. He is receiving verbal, written and non-verbal information from the public and politicians that they want change. This is amplified by media calls for his bureau to reach certain targets within a certain time frame. There is also information from his staff. While they work well for Jim when things stay the same, his staff seem to resist change and let Jim know about it verbally as well as through their actions and their personal responses to him. Jim has good logical ideas about what is needed and how to accomplish his desired goals. What is interesting is that Jim feels frustrated, annoyed, cramped and like he is 'living in a gold fish bowl'. Another person may respond to the same situation by feeling excited about his ideas, challenged by the thought of working through the objections to the changes and delighted that both the public and politicians are calling for change, thus giving him extra power and leverage to push through a transformation that would be harder to achieve without high-level political support. Another person may also see the high level of public visibility as a tool for raising the profile of the changes and selling them to those involved. That Jim, a highly intelligent, optimistic man, didn't see it that way was curious. So let's learn a little more about Jim.

Jim grew up in a poor family. He, his older sister, his mother, his father and his mother's parents all shared a two-bedroom house. Jim reports feeling loved, but also remembers feeling like he was 'living in a gold fish bowl' because there was always an older person around monitoring his behaviour, watching him. Jim remembers feeling most powerful and free when he was on his own, away from the eyes of his sister and the adults. Then he became a high achiever, building his own winning racing car, becoming a champion sailor and earning high acclaim for his academic success. As long as he could do it on his own, away from the 'big people', Jim felt powerful. When it came to working in cooperation with authority figures, Jim felt cramped, trapped, watched and constrained. Jim's emotional response to changing his organisation brought with it information on many levels:

- his present moment response to the challenge of the situation he faced (there was no way this was going to be easy);
- the emotional response of the other people involved in this situation;

- insights into Jim's emotional history, which are important because when it comes to historical psychological patterns of thought and response, they don't remain history but shape the way we see the world in which we live.

Jim's lack of awareness actually increased the powerful effect that his childhood experiences were having on his present moment adult behaviour. It was only by becoming conscious of his own patterns (through learning to work with his emotional response) that Jim could take control of his present moment behaviour. He could then see the huge power he actually had to bring about change and harness his own energy and the energy of the people around him to achieve the result so keenly desired by all involved.

Transforming Reality by Transforming Awareness

In my work with executives, I use the information provided by my emotions all the time—to build relationships, to make sense of situations, to understand what is getting in people's way and to solve problems. In doing this, I am continually provided with information on my own subconscious patterns through which I continually have to work.

When we are not aware of our own programming, it rules us. More than that, we project it onto others. In psychotherapy, this is called counter-transference and results in a leader, trainer, therapist or guide seeing their own weaknesses, problems and fears in the client or person they are leading and then working not with that person's issues, but with their own. This is why the best leadership and support comes from those who are themselves growing, building their awareness and learning. These people invite ongoing feedback because they know that they cannot see their own blind spots. Feedback can be a great help in making sense of our own behaviour and responses.

As I work with senior executives, who traditionally have been predominantly male, the majority of my clients has always been men. For many years, when I did have a woman client I felt awkward and unskilled, far less relaxed than normal. As I learnt more about myself, none of this was surprising. I have always had a far more enjoyable relationship with my father than with my mother or sister. I decided early in my life that I got on much better with men than women. I liked men and they liked me. Women were much harder to handle and, to my unconscious mind, best avoided.

This situation began to affect me when I decided that I wanted more female friends and chose to look at the early childhood decisions that I had made about women. I noticed how I felt when I was with different women and reviewed what my response told me about them and about me. At this same time, my daughter was growing up and becoming a woman, so I had daily practice at relating to an adult member of my own sex. One of my professional advisers was a woman and my long-standing relationship with her helped me to learn different ways of relating to adult females. I then made a strategic decision towards affirmative action. I chose to restrict my client base to company directors, chief executives and women. I now have a growing number of female clients whose company I enjoy. By working with women, I learn more about myself. The work I do with my female clients is now one of the most enjoyable aspects of my job.

If any one had asked me five years ago why I had so few women clients, I would have been ready with a strong logical argument (supported by statistics) that anyone working at the upper reaches of organisations had very little chance of having a high percentage of female clients. I would have told you that executive women were harder to get on with and that I would gladly work with women if only they were available. All this would have been a rationalisation for the fact that I felt unskilled and incompetent around powerful women and was therefore threatened and intimidated by them. All this had more to do with my unresolved issues with my mother and sister than with the executive women I met. Today, I would tell you that the executive women I know are a sheer delight—they are open to learning, intelligent, funny and a great mirror into myself.

Over the past five years, there has been no significant increase in the percentage of executive women in the organisations with which I work. The tangible change that has taken place in my work (I now work with more women) came about because I listened to my emotions. My heart's desire was for more female company. I noticed that when I was with women, my emotional response seemed to bear little relationship to what was actually happening in our interaction. Hence I started to ask questions of myself, to listen more closely to my emotions and to notice my varying responses. What I learnt from this led to a change in my strategic decision making and my behaviour. All of this has positively affected every aspect of my life.

Managing Defended You, Healing Wounded You and Building up Essential You

By not working with women I was reflecting an aspect of my defended you. I have a great ability to avoid situations in which I feel awkward and unskilled, and a wonderful ability to rationalise any behaviour that I don't want to face. My awkwardness and feelings of incompetence with women came from the wounded you beliefs and repressed emotions I had collected from childhood experiences with females. My ability to alter my behaviour came from noticing my patterns, feeling my emotional response and remaking my decisions. The energy to do so came from listening to my heart's desire and my soulful need for quality female companionship. I believe this came from my essential you.

I have found that when I notice, listen to and sense the reality of my inner and outer worlds, I constantly receive information on many levels. I can then take action on many fronts. In this case, I noticed my defences and chose to manage them by consciously putting myself into relationships with women and learning from the relationships I already had. I chose to look at decisions I had made in childhood about my ability to sustain workable relationships with women and decided that, while I may have been burnt in this area as a child, as an adult I was totally capable of building nourishing relationships with members of my own sex. I am also very aware that my ability to listen to and heed my own soulful yearnings is greatly enhanced by building up my essential you through years of practice in personal reflection, yoga, meditation and prayer. Above all, I know that the whole process was messy, ill defined, painful, joyous, personal and uniquely my own.

This is what I find with each and every one of my clients. There are no proven routes, no definite answers and no universal techniques. In fact, I have found that prescribed routes and clear answers and techniques actually get in the way as they have an insidious habit of taking centre stage, of magically creating a means–ends inversion, with people using their worry about getting it right, knowing the correct steps and following the procedure to avoid staying with the elusive, baffling, intangible process of life, feeling, learning, growth and transformation. In the matters of life, heart and soul, it is our own unique journey that proves the most effective. Our own way forward, even if it isn't textbook perfect, is the way most likely to work for us. We each have within us all the knowledge, skill, wisdom, energy and resources we need to effect the lives we want. The trick is to learn to listen to our inner messages, to practise understanding their lessons and to use this learning as the basis of our actions.

This is a very courageous path forward in a society that values externalities above all else, a society where numbers are used to convince us that our own way is statistically not on. In a world that is reduced to 'controllable, identifiable, measurable transactions', having the courage to follow your heart, care for your soul and choose to connect on a deep level with yourself and your environment, through feeling and action, is very heroic indeed. It is also a sign of health, sanity and wisdom. However, because of the appalling ignorance about the essence of the human heart and spirit, and because of the endemic nature of addiction in our organisations, it is wise to ensure that your heroic quest is well supported. We may have to make our hero's journey ourselves, but we don't have to do it alone. In fact, as we shall see in the following chapter, one of the great joys of the hero's quest is learning to give and receive support. This is the key to bridging our inner and outer worlds. Support is the cornerstone of healing the individual; it is the key to the hero's quest. Support is the way to approach the corporate heart.

Supporting Your Heroic Quest

*Behind every successful woman there
is a well-developed support system.*

Many years ago, I copied the words above out of a newspaper article on mothers who held executive positions in large companies. The older and more experienced I become, the more I know that the wisdom in this quotation holds true for both men and women. If we want successful, healthy, heartfelt, soulful lives, we need to understand support, know where to get it, how to give it and how to use it. Support is the invisible process through which dreams come true.

What Is Support?

Support comes in many guises—practical, emotional, spiritual and political, to name just a few. I am convinced that the more types of support that you know and use, the easier it will be for you to embark on, stay with and successfully traverse all stages of the hero's quest.

Warriors don't go much for support. They think that they have to do everything for themselves. That archetypal warrior, the Lone Ranger, had no true friends and no home. He denied all his emotional needs and had little use for intellectual challenge and growth. He lived out of community, out of relationship and without material comfort. He was, however, smart enough to know that he needed more than his own ego to get him through, so he kept his horse and his selfless manservant close at hand. Like most warriors, however, the Lone Ranger undervalued the support he had and treated those who provided it with far less respect and affection than was their due.

Warriors see support as weakness. They see nurturing of the body, mind, emotions and soul as a sign of vulnerability. Hence they drive themselves and everybody else to the limit and then retreat into indulgence in some form of physical or psychological addiction to compensate for their self-generated exhaustion, depletion, inner emptiness and lack of aliveness. That anyone can possibly see this as strength is a source of great amazement to me.

Any sensible person would know that if you want to maintain something, a car for example, you keep it regularly serviced and maintained. If you want your car to last, be efficient in its functioning and retain its resale value, you take it to the best mechanic you can afford, someone who is trained to keep your car in top working order. You don't have to be too smart to know that if you don't put fuel, oil and water in your car, it just won't go and can end up costing you a lot more time and money than looking after it properly in the first place.

While this all seems pretty obvious and straightforward when applied to machinery, we are slow to transfer this wisdom to our own bodies, emotions, souls and relationships. Knowing our need for, obtaining and valuing good support are signs of intelligence and wisdom; failing to do so is just plain dumb.

Supporting Yourself

Different people find different things supportive. I love the story of the couple who, after thirty years of marriage, find themselves at relationship counselling, their marriage in tatters. 'Tell me, Mrs Smith' the therapist asks, 'what is it about your husband that has led you to believe that you can no longer live with him.'

'Well, there are lots of things,' the woman replies, 'but the worst thing, the very worst thing, is that every morning when he brought me breakfast in bed, he gave me tea and toasted crust. I hate crusts.'

'But my dear,' protests her distressed husband, 'I love the crusts. I saved them for you because they are the best part.'

Often what is sent as support is received as rebuke. One person's sacrifice is another's indulgence. Luckily, we are all different. We have different personal needs, different heart's desires and a different perspective. Our souls crave for different things. Spending the day cooking up a delicious meat meal for a vegetarian is a waste of time and likely to cause conflict and pain. More than that, as we all project our inner theatre onto the world around us (especially the actions of others), how things are received may have nothing to do with the intentions of the donor.

The first step towards being supported is that you have to work out what you find supportive. This is a surprisingly hard thing to do and takes quite a lot of reflection and self-knowledge. In large part, socialisation is about learning to put our needs on hold, to fit in to the overall needs of the family, school class or friendship group. Most people actually believe that taking account of your own needs is selfish. The Dalai Lama agrees.

He tells us, however, that there is selfishness and wise selfishness. Selfishness is about living your life in function to your ego, wanting to be the centre of attention, to be noticed and have other people make you feel good. This is the juvenile practice of giving responsibility for your feelings, wellbeing and comfort to others, whom you then beguile, manipulate or coerce into meeting your needs. This all leads to an incredible variety of games, whereby people do what they think they need to do to get other people to meet their needs, which they refuse to bring to the surface, name or request to have met. The main game goes like this:

If you really loved me/cared/were so smart/knew how to lead/ etc., you would know what I needed and what to do to meet my expectations. If you don't know and/or don't do what I want, then you obviously don't love me/don't care/are stupid/ don't know how to be a leader. You therefore are wrong and should change.

As a society, we are all so used to playing this game that we actually think it is what relationships are all about. We write books on etiquette and influencing skills. We do courses to get better at finding ways of having other people meet our needs without us having to know what those needs are or asking to have them met. This is not wise behaviour.

Wise-selfishness, on the other hand, is about starting at the beginning and becoming very aware of our needs. These will include our unique desires and requirements for physical health, emotional nourishment, spiritual wellbeing and intellectual challenge. Awareness is the first step in taking responsibility for our needs.

The second step is taking appropriate action to have our needs met. This will necessitate ordering our priorities of time, effort and financial resources to ensure we get such things as the rest, exercise and appropriate nourishment that our bodies require. On top of that, wise-selfishness is taking time to nourish our souls, listen to our hearts' desires and do those things that build our inner resources.

If this involves another person, wise selfishness entails asking for their help in ways that they are able to hear. As we are responsible for 50 per cent of every relationship of which we are part, wise selfishness means taking responsibility for the wellbeing and health of our side of each and every one of our relationships. It doesn't mean waiting for the other person to somehow guess our needs and meet them.

I am always amazed at how powerless most people feel when it comes to relationships. Many of us have spent a lifetime trying to change the people with whom we relate and, finding this impossible, decide that we cannot change our relationships. This is a false conclusion. While each person has to decide to change him or herself and how he or she relates to us, we can definitely change our relationships by changing how we operate in those relationships. When we act from wise-selfishness, we come from a place of personal awareness and strength. This gives us a kind of radical self-confidence and intuitive insight which we can use to work on our relationships in ways that are nourishing to all involved.

Roger was an executive in a large company. His boss was a high-achieving warrior type who worked eighty-hour weeks and had the habit of ringing Roger at home early in the morning and late at night to ask him to undertake extra, always urgent work. Not only was this interfering with Roger's need for privacy and rest, but he also noticed that the boss often rapidly changed his mind about what was needed, sometimes even before Roger had finished fulfilling the boss's latest request. Acting from a place of wise-selfishness, Roger decided how many hours a week he was prepared to work. He made an appointment with the boss and had the boss agree to these hours. After that, whenever the boss rang with a request, Roger would give him a choice. 'I am happy,' Roger would say, 'to do as you ask, but as you know I am also working for you on several other projects [which he would name]. If I do what you have just asked which of the other projects would you like me to put aside?'

Faced with responsible choices, the boss started to take responsibility for his requests and they became less erratic, more thoughtful and more appropriately delivered. More than that, some months later the boss actually thanked Roger for helping him to clarify his priorities. He, too, had decided that he could achieve more by working shorter, more effective hours. To achieve this outcome, Roger had to work out what his needs were. In this case, they were for time with his family, a restricted number of working hours and clear priorities from his supervisor. He then found a way of expressing his needs that his boss could hear (in this case, offering a logical choice) and took the risk of requesting what he wanted. He didn't try to change the boss, merely to change his relationship with the boss in a way that respected the needs, power positions and personalities of both parties.

I have seen wise-selfishness lead to people renegotiating all kinds of relationships for all kinds of reasons. It all starts with clarity, reflection, mutual respect and courage.

Political Support

If you are in a highly addictive system, it may seem like la-la land to think that you will be anything but punished for setting your personal limits. Here again, it all comes back to you. Nobody promised this was going to be easy. We all have much more power in every situation we are in than we think. Wise-selfishness involves knowing what you want, determining your power bases in each situation and then skilfully using them.

Belinda approached me just after she was appointed the marketing manager of a large public utility. She was excited at her appointment, but knew that she faced a challenge. Marketing in her organisation had traditionally been seen as public and community relations, operating to convince the public that they should be happy with the service they received regardless of its quality. As the utility held a monopoly position in the market, the aim of marketing had generally been to ensure that the organisation warded off any adverse media or public criticism that might embarrass or anger the politicians who were the public custodians of the organisation. That this situation didn't work was evidenced by ongoing media attacks against the organisation and the short-lived tenure of the people who had been marketing managers before Belinda.

An expert in marketing, Belinda realised that if she was to change this situation she was going to have to change the way the people in the organisation thought about their customers by making client service a central part of everybody's work. This was a radical shift in an organisation that cared little for its customers. Staff preferred to focus on the technical aspects of their jobs, which involved building and maintaining a massive engineering infrastructure. Belinda realised that if organisational members didn't focus on their clients, she would constantly be trying to cover up the damage done through the ongoing neglect of customer needs.

Belinda's problem was that she appeared to be the only person in the organisation who saw marketing as a way of operating rather than as a cover-up for organisational blunders. She knew that to do her job in a way that gave the results demanded, she had to mount an organisational change program—her bosses thought that marketing amounted to keeping the minister briefed, issuing a few press releases and, when things looked really bad, running an image-enhancing publicity campaign. The staff Belinda inherited had no skills in organisational change, community management or internal communication. They knew how to issue a press release, but were totally unskilled for the job Belinda needed them to do.

Being several levels below the CEO, Belinda didn't have the power to have her viewpoint heard and taken seriously by the key decision makers. When I met her, she had a huge job, an inappropriately trained staff and an inadequate budget. To make matters worse, her organisation had recently been through a massive downsizing exercise and most people in the organisation were scared. This had the unfortunate effect of encouraging erratic behaviour, workaholism and less than logical discussion and decision making.

Belinda asked me to help her because she knew what needed to be done, but just couldn't see how she could do it. She also believed I could help her find a way of doing her job successfully without her working any longer hours than the substantial fifty to sixty hours she already invested at work. Belinda was committed to her own personal development and quality of life in and out of work. She wanted to create a solution to her work-based challenge in a way that contributed to her growth as both a professional and as a human being. So, Belinda founded the Marketing Support Network.

To do this, Belinda and I sat down with two lists of names. One list was of the opinion shapers and power brokers in key strategic divisions across the organisation. The other list was of the people in every division that Belinda liked and with whom she wanted to develop a closer relationship. It turned out that there were twelve people on Belinda's 'like' list who also appeared on her 'movers and shakers' list. These twelve people were invited to join the network. Membership involved each individual spending one hour per month in a personal session with me and all network members (as a group) working with me for one day a month over a period of twelve months. The network had two clear objectives. One was to develop the corporation into a marketing-driven organisation, the other was to provide personal support and growth for network members.

For twelve months, the members of the network met and shared their stories; they discussed their hearts' desires, their dreams, problems and feelings. They talked about how they related to each other, to their organisation and to the political dynamic within the organisation. Occasionally, we talked about marketing. Over time, a high level of trust developed within the group. When people had a problem during and between network meetings, they asked their network colleagues to help them think through the issues, support their emotional response to what was ahead and help them look for lateral, creative, market-driven answers. One of the network members commented that the pooling of information that happened within the network was like putting together the 'pieces of a huge jigsaw, allowing gaps to be closed in knowledge of events, shifts, movements and feelings within the organisation'. This sharing of information, ideas and resources helped network members to increase their power in their own areas of influence.

In time, the feeling of camaraderie that grew within the network spread across the organisation. Because of the strategic positioning of network members, any meeting to discuss major organisational issues usually involved at least two network members. Without having overtly agreed to do so, network members found themselves supporting each other's ideas and issues at meetings. As their ideas usually involved some marketing content, they were also supporting marketing.

Over the period of a year, marketing was restructured, its staff was upgraded and its influence began to grow. A number of organisational presentations and publications began citing marketing achievements, and throughout the organisation marketing became a much discussed and well-respected issue. A number of senior managers signed up to do postgraduate degrees in marketing. Belinda was achieving the job she had been set.

What was interesting was that Belinda had faced but refused to be defeated by the difficulties of her situation. She was wisely selfish in bringing to the surface her personal needs for success, collegiate support and a manageable working week, and then finding ways of building and maintaining relationships that nourished her and the other network members. Keeping her eye on her desire to achieve strategically, she used her relationships to change a whole organisation. To do this, Belinda used her years of experience as an organisational player to understand how the system worked and then used that understanding to work within the system to achieve her desired outcomes. That she was able to employ me at all was due to her ability to market my services internally in a way that was acceptable to key decision makers. One of the reasons that the network was so successful was due to the intelligence, experience and political acumen of its members, proving that Belinda had chosen them wisely.

When you meet enough people like Belinda, when you see the impossible achieved enough times, it becomes very hard to accept the excuses people put forward for not having their lives work, not going after their hearts' desires and not being successful in humanly nourishing ways. Once we accept that it is not easy, but that we do, if we choose, have the power to make the most of every situation we are in, we can build around us sufficient support to achieve what may otherwise be impossible.

Of course, we won't always get exactly what we want. Sometimes we find ourselves working for people who are vindictive, malicious and abusive, and such folk sure pose a challenge. However, in my experience, every political challenge is best faced by building up your support bases and using them to best effect. Even if we fail to meet our objectives, we will have support to find other ways around or out of any situation.

Political networks are helpful whether they are inside your organisation or out of it. They are useful whether you work for a large organisation or a small one. Internal political networks help you to get a fuller picture of what is happening across the business. They help you to canvass support for changes, new ideas and having your needs better understood and resourced. External political networks not only link you into key areas of external influence such as professional and industry associations, media and pools of expertise, knowledge and skills, but if used wisely can also increase your power base within your own organisation. If you are well connected in ways that are helpful to key players in your organisation and you skilfully help them to understand and use the assistance you can offer, your political stakes will rise, making it easier for you to do the job that you are employed to do. If, like Belinda, you choose to do this heroically, you can actually combine your growing success with your personal emotional and spiritual development.

Unfortunately, most people think politics in organisations is a dirty business and best avoided. In adopting this attitude, they greatly undermine their own success and peace of mind. Organisations are systems with strong power dynamics. Part of operating effectively at work involves understanding these dynamics and learning to work with them skilfully. This means building up relationships with key players, building political support systems and learning to network with individuals and in groups.

It all comes back to understanding how people think and act. For example, most people are slow to accept new ideas and behaviours. If the first time we are made aware of changes we are in a group, we are likely to feel remote from and unskilled in the new ways. Should we be asked to make decisions concerning the changes, we are highly likely to reject newness, even if there are all sorts of logical reasons why the changes are in our own long- or short-term best interests. Recognising this, it makes sense if you want to get change through a committee or team, that you approach each person in that group individually, well in advance of any group decision making, and give each person hands-on experience of the new ideas and proposals. This gives people a chance to work through their objections in private and learn enough that they feel confident to discuss the issues without embarrassing themselves. It gives *you* a chance to sell the individual benefits to each person. Although this takes time and effort, it is worth it if you can get something dear to your heart accepted by the necessary people. Being 'right' and 'good at what you do' is of little use unless you can get your work accepted and implemented. To do this, you will have to build political support. This is a substantial and mostly ignored part of any job.

Although building up and using political support may seem difficult if you do not have a lot of power attached to the position you hold, it isn't as hard as you think. The skill comes in knowing what you want, observing and getting to know the political/ relationship dynamic that operates in your environment and then using your knowledge of that environment, the people in it and of humanity in general to manage your relationships constructively. I realise in writing this that an ability to manage relationships well demands that we understand ourselves.

It is so easy to project our inner theatre onto our environment and react not to our current reality, but to our perception of that reality. We so easily slip into disempowered childhood patterns, robbing ourselves of our capacity to bring about positive outcomes. This is where having quality emotional support is so important. When we are personally involved in a situation, it is easy to lose true perspective. A caring outsider, particularly if they are well down their own heroic path, can help us see things more clearly, think more constructively and act more effectively. In my experience, a person who really wants to create positive outcomes and who is supported can turn around the most difficult situation regardless of their apparent lack of position power. When we tap into our internal power and link up with supportive others we can figuratively move mountains. As we will see later, our ability to act truly powerfully at work is greatly assisted by having a personal heroic guide and being part of an heroic support group.

The political support provided by heroic companions is particularly effective because it recognises that every individual, situation and issue is unique, then works with the reality of issues, relationships and goals in the here and now, taking into account our personalities and needs. When we feel heard, supported and encouraged, we better face the reality of a fluid world. We therefore think more clearly, are more decisive and risk taking bold, appropriate action. When we feel alone and unsupported, we search for and often grab the rather flimsy support of mental mind maps, seven-point action plans or off-the-shelf cure-alls. While having something 'tangible' to cling to may give us short-term direction and confidence, following a formula for action can distract us from the reality of the situation we are in, how we feel about that situation and therefore how we can work with our own perception and relationships to create the most effective outcome. One unexpected result of having supportive people around you in a political context is that support helps us to feel powerful enough to stay in the moment, avoid becoming defensive, take effective, appropriate action and learn about ourselves, life and others in the process.

Heroes know that building political support is a crucial part of making their work life happy and successful, and making the maximum contribution to their workmates, clients and employers. This has nothing to do with being Machiavellian and everything to do with being maximally effective by working constructively on the relationships that impact upon you and your ability to produce results.

Group Support

Political support helps you get things done. On top of this, by working with like-minded others, we feel less alone, less vulnerable, stronger and more powerful. This fact has been used by successful people for centuries. Henry Ford, the pioneer of the mass-produced automobile and founder of Ford Motors, was born into poverty. He received very little formal education, yet by the time he died he had achieved his dream of making motor transport widely available and was undoubtedly one of the richest men in America. Ford's qualities of imagination, determination and hard work all helped him to achieve his heart's desire, but his greatest achievements happened after he had formed strong, supportive relationships with some other very great men.

The first of these was Thomas Edison, a fellow visionary and inventor. Later Ford met and formed links with Harvey Firestone, John Burroughs and Luther Burbank (each pioneers and leaders in their own fields). Napoleon Hill in *Think and Grow Rich* tells us that Henry Ford's astronomical rise to riches, fame and fortune came when he 'added to his own brain power the sum and substance of the intelligence, experience, knowledge and spiritual forces of these four men.'

Anthropologist Margaret Mead wrote: 'Never doubt that a small group of thoughtful, committed citizens can change the world. Indeed, it is the only thing that ever has.' Individuals make a difference; supported individuals change everything.

Simon was a young executive being groomed by his multinational employer as a key leader of the future. He enrolled in my Camelot program along with three of his colleagues. As the program progressed, Simon found that when he had a difficult problem or some issue about which his thinking was unclear, he would call on one of his Camelot colleagues and 'shoot the breeze'. Because of the rapport and intimacy he had built within Camelot with his co-workers, Simon found that he could open up to them back in the workplace.

Operating from a place of honest inquiry, he was able to resolve issues both more quickly and more effectively. Obviously adding more than one person's brain power to each dilemma was helpful, as was the different perspective and wider insights brought by his colleagues, but Simon noticed that there was more. After discussing things with people he respected and trusted, and having come to his own conclusions, Simon found that he felt stronger, more courageous and less afraid of taking risks. He felt supported not just in the strength of his decisions, but also on some deeper emotional level. He felt that there were people who believed in him, people who knew he could decisively and effectively see any issue through and overcome any obstacle. More than that, he knew that even if he failed or slipped up, his colleagues would not judge him harshly. They would be there, ready to accept him for who he was, and work with him to help him remedy any trouble that may arise.

This allowed Simon to tackle situations constructively that had previously been left unattended for years. He was able to make bold and necessary strategic moves and to take himself and his people to new heights of achievement. Because of the support he was getting Simon had no difficulty passing his sponsorship, compassion and understanding on to his staff, who in turn started taking bolder decisions and wiser actions.

It is the principles of emotional support and sharing of information, ideas, insights and perspective that underlie such organisations as The Executive Committee and The Young Presidents Organisation. These global networks for chief executives operate to overcome the loneliness and isolation of leaders by having them meet regularly with peers to share their burdens of leadership. It is well known that those smart and lucky enough to make use of these organisations have at their disposal not only an international network of high-powered champions in just about every industry and country, but also have access to some of the best business brains in the world.

Napoleon Hill in *Think and Grow Rich* calls this kind of grouping a 'master mind group'. He claims that being part of such a group gives people access to a great universal storehouse of intelligence and power through which all genius, achievement and wellbeing can be accessed. Marketing trendspotter Faith Popcorn in *The Popcorn Report* sings the praises of what she calls 'BrainReserves', which she claims allow you to harness and channel the energy, brainpower and perspective of a group behind the personal heartfelt desires of individuals.

I guess mentoring is a more individual version of the same process. Organisations around the world are now encouraging their senior executives to take a personal interest in promising younger folk, showing them the political and systemic ropes of their organisation and helping them work through their problems and think through their challenges. The idea of mentoring is also being used in a wide variety of training programs whose organisers have grasped the notions that two heads are better than one and that people who feel supported gain courage, commitment and persistence.

While these forms of group support are useful, their true effectiveness actually depends on the quality of intelligence, insight and character of the person or people giving the support. If your mentors or the people in your master mind or BrainReserve group are warriors, they will give you the kind of support that will help you to be a better warrior. This is my biggest concern about such groups—not that they aren't in principle a great idea, but that because of the way they are run they can empower people to do the wrong things. In other words, while they are a very effective way of helping people move forward, how constructive they are depends on the quality of their membership and the way the meetings are run. Hitler, a warrior of the worst kind, was very effective at utilising support. Unfortunately, the way he used that support and the people he chose to give it to him supported catastrophic destruction and mass murder.

If you want to be a hero, you will need to find and use support of a very different kind. You will need to find and nurture safe people and learn how to create safe environments.

Safe People and Groups

In *Peaceful Chaos*, I outline the features of a safe environment, which is a relationship space wherein you can relax, safely put aside your defences and open to spiritual and emotional growth on a deep level. It is in safe spaces that our stories can be told with feeling and heard with respect. Safe environments are those conditions under which each person's humanity is heard, validated and honoured.

A safe environment is one in which:

- you are accepted for being yourself;
- your emotions are heard and validated;
- people listen to you at the intimate level of heart and soul;
- people choose to be real, to reveal who they are and elect to take responsibility for their 50 per cent of relationships;
- people know where they stand because there are clear, appropriate boundaries;
- communication is direct and open;
- your heroism is seen, respected and supported;

- people are honest with themselves and each other—this means people seek and accept feedback and consciously build their self-awareness;
- agendas are open, not hidden;
- expectations are clearly expressed;
- confidences are respected; and
- people mean what they say.

Safe environments are created around safe people, people who are well advanced in their own heroic quest and therefore have the awareness, sensitivity, wisdom and compassion to value, respect and be with the mysteries of the human psyche.

As warriors are focused on externalities, lacking in self-awareness and locked into a mind-set of battle, they are not safe people. To see another's soul, genius and potential for heroism requires, says Hillman in *The Soul's Code*, 'an eye for the image, an eye for the show and the language to say what we see'. These things are learnt on our own heroic quest.

Safe people can see and respect the best in themselves. Therefore, they can see and respect the best in others. Because they know and accept their own hearts' desires, they can foster other people to do the same. Being in touch with their emotions, safe people can help other people to feel deeply. Being practised at making sense of emotionally transmitted messages and having found ways of channelling their emotional energy, safe people have an uncanny ability to help others accept, make sense of and utilise their own feelings.

Safe people, however, are not door mats. While they are exceptionally good listeners, their strong self-respect and robust soulfulness give them a powerful presence. This comes not as a function of their position in society or their success at work, but directly from their own essence. Safe people have no trouble letting you see who they are—being so at home with every facet of their characters, they have nothing to hide. They accept their physical, emotional and spiritual needs, and easily set and express their personal boundaries. They do this clearly, cleanly and directly.

Support from a safe person is an enriching and valuable gift. Simply being around safe people facilitates you getting in touch with your emotional reality and being emotionally and spiritually present. In fact, it is the quickest, most effective way there is. People can read books on emotion endlessly but they are still not able to do anything more than think about it. Being in the presence of a safe person, however, makes it very hard to escape being present with your own life force.

Warriors don't always find this comfortable. They have a vested interest in staying psychologically armoured. Safe people have a knack of getting through our defences and therefore making us engage with our own feelings. When this happens to a warrior, it is not uncommon for them to attack. The ferocity of these assaults is quite surprising until you realise just how terribly alone, frightened and empty warriors feel. Rather than bring to the surface and deal with these emotions, they will belittle, undermine, insult and abuse anyone who inadvertently puts them in touch with the reality of their inner world.

If, however, you have decided to have a healthy, soulful life and to follow your heart's desire, a safe person is exactly the person you need to help you. The problem is there aren't all that many safe people around—especially at work. Due to the powerful force of socialisation and the widely addicted nature of business systems, the majority of people at work are highly defended most, if not all, of the time. Few people come through socialisation as safe people. Safe people are self-made. That is, they have invested a lot of time, energy and resources into raising their awareness, maturing their emotions and caring for their soul. This is ongoing hard work. Because safe people respect themselves highly and value the effort they have put into their own health, wellbeing and life, they tend to seek out environments where their safety, maturity and wisdom are valued. The consciousness of mainstream society is rising to value the many gifts of a safe person, but you are still more likely to find a safe person in a more nurturing environment than is found in the traditional workplace. Many safe people have capitalised on their self-knowledge, wisdom and understanding of the human psyche and have set up business as therapists, counsellors and consultants, selling for a good fee the insight, wisdom and skills their safety brings.

This is not to say all professionals in these fields are safe—far from it. Many use their knowledge and skills to maintain control in their relationships and encourage their clients to be dependent on them as the 'guru'. Professional training is no guarantee of safety. Safety is about character, not just skills and knowledge. Luckily, however, many people professionals are now recognising this and doing the necessary self-work that leads to them being safe for others.

Although their numbers are increasing, safe people are still rare. They are valuable gems—hard to find, but a prize beyond price. Don't, however, expect safe people to be masters at social etiquette, entertaining conversationalists or obliging. They may from time to time be any of these things, but safe people operate on quite a different agenda.

Robyn, who was for many years my supervisor, was definitely a safe person. She had the disconcerting habit of getting me to laugh at my life's dramas, woes and self-doubts. She had no need to have me feel comfortable and no need to meet my expectations. Her job, as she saw it, was to help people develop. Comfortable, sated people who wallow in self-pity and self-doubt rarely grow. Knowing this, Robyn simply refused to reinforce thought, emotion or behavior patterns that undermined my growth and got in the way of my heroic journey.

Some people, expecting sympathy, expert guidance and 'professional' etiquette, may have found Robyn's frank, no-nonsense humour and insight off-putting. I found it a very growth-inducing approach. Robyn had no need to fix me up, make me better or heal me. She simply used all her years of training and experience to be safe and real with me. I found this so refreshing, so enlivening and so conducive to my advancing on my professional and personal journey. To maintain her professional skills, Robyn did what any 'people expert' worth their salt would do: she just kept working on her growth, her soulfulness and following her heart's desire. In other words, she just kept getting safer.

I spent months looking for a supervisor before I found Robyn. I must have interviewed twenty different psychologists, psychiatrists and psychotherapists before I found someone whom I considered safe. All the others appeared to me to be hiding behind their qualifications, using their degrees and clinical skills to avoid doing their own inner work, escaping their own inner demons. As we have already seen, when people operate from this space they have a tendency to project their limitations, fears and beliefs onto their clients, through whom they then work on their own issues. I didn't want a spiritually and emotionally lazy teacher. I didn't want to be dealing with other people's limitations. I wanted someone who had the courage to keep moving forward, providing me with a role model, companionship and inspiration to follow their lead.

The safe people in our lives don't have to be professionals. If you are truly lucky you will gather around you safe friends, a safe life partner and safe family members. Creating safety in key aspects of our lives is the ideal way to feel supported on our journey through life.

In his inspiring little book *The Power of Purpose*, Richard Leider introduces the concept of a 'nutritious person'. The definition of a nutritious person is that their face lights up when you enter the room, but they have no plans for your improvement. Those on the heroic quest need just as many nutritious people in their lives as they can find. If you don't have more than two nutritious people close at hand, go out and find some—*now*.

Support Groups

Although most workplaces are not conducive to either developing or retaining safe people, support groups can be developed at work and then run in a way that encourages the safety of the members. Support groups can be set up around specific issues—such as women's groups, young people's groups or ex-patriot groups—or they can be set up within existing work and leadership teams. To transform a group of people in an habitually unsafe environment into a safe support group demands three things.

The first is the people involved have to want to work in a different way, learn to be more heroic and be part of a safe environment. The second is that there must be at least one safe person available to teach, guide and facilitate the group. The third is that the group must adopt rules that encourage, support and legitimise safe behaviour. Some people are lucky enough to be part of a work or leadership team that decides to become more supportive. Other people are leaders and decide to encourage their team to follow the heroic path. People like Belinda, who go out and find supportive people and bring them together as a network or team, show us that where there is a will there is a way.

Sometimes, however, even with the best will in the world, people find that in their workplace safety is just impossible under any circumstances. For these people, there are a plethora of support groups available in the community. These groups range from therapeutic groups such as Alcoholics Anonymous, through to awareness-raising groups for just about any minority or interest group you can imagine, through to friendship and religious groups who choose, for their own fulfilment, spiritual development and personal growth to come together under safe conditions.

The rule of thumb with any group is to check out the people, check out the rules and check out your feelings. A lot of people mouth the right words—notice how you feel and trust that. Support groups, if they are safe, are an effective way of edging into the hero's quest. If you cannot create a support group, find one; if you cannot find one, create one, or two or three.

Early on in working with any group, I get them to come up with a set of communication rules. I ask people to remember a real situation they have been in where the communication really flowed well (without the aid of alcohol). We discuss the fact that in every group there are unspoken rules of communication and behaviour called 'group norms'. I ask people to work out the group norms that were operating in the situations of good communication that they have chosen and to frame these norms in terms of discrete behaviours. We then pool our list of norms and come up with a list that looks something like the one below:

> *When someone talks, listen. Don't interrupt.*
> *Anything said within the group is confidential.*
> *Equal time, equal contribution—everybody gets heard, everybody contributes.*
> *Ask for feedback. Avoid judgment. Table your agendas.*
> *Talk for yourself—own your communication.*
> *If you have something to tell someone, speak directly to that person. Clarify objectives and purpose.*
> *Respect each person's opinion and feelings. Respect personal differences.*

After discussing each point to clarify meaning and deal with concerns, I then ask each member of the group to commit to making the listed behaviours the group's communication rules to be followed whenever the group meets. In fact, what we have come up with is a framework for legitimising safety within the group. I have rarely found that I need to enforce these rules. Having devised them for themselves group members usually adopt the rules with pride and self-regulate.

At least half of the groups with which I work are leadership teams. In such groups, some people inevitably have more positional power than others. On top of this, there is usually rivalry over scarce resources and restricted promotional opportunities. I have found, however, that even under these traditionally 'unsafe' conditions people can and do become safe people for each other by agreeing to do so. When this happens, work teams start operating as heroic master mind groups supporting the mutual success, growth and wellbeing of all members. Once this occurs, the competition for resources is replaced by a logical distribution on the basis of strategic need. As success builds, the group and its members attract positive attention and opportunities for promotion are increased all round. Even at work we can create safety, build supportive relationships and network and enhance our heroic learning.

Emotional Support

The emotional support that we receive from safe people is one of life's most priceless intangibles. It doesn't fit neatly on the balance sheet and yet it can make you rich, famous, healthy and soulful. Emotional support vitalises our being, stimulates our growth, enhances our relationships and gives us the insight, backing and reminders we need to follow our hearts' desires in the most heroic and health-giving way. One could almost say that emotional support is the elixir of the gods. Yet it comes not from divine intervention, but from being in a relationship with a safe person.

Let's have a look at how the dynamic works. As we have seen, our socialisation and the operation of society in general and the workplace in particular encourage us to focus our attention on tangible, worldly matters, providing considerable reinforcement for us to deny, repress and ignore our emotions, soul and physical wellbeing. We have also seen that this erodes our human potential, undermines our relationships, generates a whole range of social, physical and psychological problems, and is bad for business. Extending the argument further, we have noted that the way to reverse the deadening of the human heart, mind and soul, the path to building intimate and productive relationships, and the route to organisational and social transformation are through individuals choosing health at every level—raising their awareness, feeling their feelings and consciously deciding to act in constructive ways in relation to their environment. To contemplate living this way, which is exactly the inverse of how most people learnt to survive their socialisation, is decidedly unsettling, psychologically frightening and very hard even to imagine—that is, until we come into intimate contact with a safe person.

When this happens, we gain a window onto another way of being, a healthy, heartfelt, soulful way. We notice that safe people experience real joy, have a deep sense of inner wellbeing and power and have no need to run away from unsettling experiences. They seem as at home with anger, fear, grief and pain as they are with joy, love and compassion. When you are around safe people, you begin to feel your feelings, but there is something more happening. Because of the ability of safe people to relate at a deep, intimate level, when we are around them we begin to re-experience that deep connection that we lost as a child. In the presence of a safe person, we experience ourselves as something more, as part of a whole, no longer alone. This is something for which we have been craving all our lives, and here it is embodied in a human being who looks just like any other human being. Safe people model, and then have us experience, another way to be that feels a whole lot more life giving, nourishing and productive. This gives us incentive to go on, continue and deepen our own heroic quest.

When we leave the sanctuary of a safe person and go out into our daily razzamatazz, we re-experience the reality that has characterised our life experience to date. People play games, deny their emotional reality, punish you for expressing who you really are and expect you to comply to the social norms of business and politics. It is anticipated that you will deny your own needs, meet other people's expectations and speak in half truths. This is so normal, so pervasive and so ever present you forget what you learnt when in safe company. For a while, you remember that there is another way, but there is so much reinforcement of the old patterns that the memory quickly fades. Then it's time for another dip in safe waters.

I find with my clients that if they keep coming back to see me over time, they are able to transfer more and more safety, heroism and health into their own lives. We need constant, ongoing reinforcement to break old patterns, especially when we live in a world that rewards behaviour that is spiritually and emotionally dysfunctional.

Breaking free from the warped patterns of unconscious addiction, emotional and spiritual self-annihilation and dysfunctional relationships that are so prevalent in the wider world, and particularly at work, is a gradual process that requires a lot of support if you are to remember who you really are, gain access to and follow your heart's desire and care for your soul. To do all this in a way that actually increases your success in the world, enables you to master political situations and creates you as a leader is no small undertaking. Finding a safe person who can help you overcome the obstacles, keep your sights set on your goals, learn life giving skills and work through the twists and turns of life and relationships as they happen is essential. It is the most effective way of having your dreams come true. We learnt to operate dysfunctionally in relationships, therefore it is only in relationships that we can reverse this process. It is in a relationship with a safe person that we will find the route to our inner learning, our inner wisdom and our safety. As time goes by, if we stick with the process, we will become safe enough and sufficiently skilled to create safety with anyone, any time, in any situation. When we get to this stage, we really are masters of transformation, who can through magical sleight of hand transform the world around us.

Professional Support—Finding an Heroic Guide

As we have noted, not all safe people make good heroic guides since not all safe people have the depth, intelligence and worldly wisdom to take us through all three stages of the hero's quest.

During the first stage, stage one of our hero's quest, we almost need a good salesperson: someone who knows enough about the benefits of heroism and is far enough down his or her own path to give us a taste of what heroism can do for us. This person also needs to be skilled enough to help us begin to shift our focus to include our inner world, begin to raise our awareness and begin to experience our emotional reality. In my experience, people starting on the hero's quest need a lot of reassurance. They need to be constantly shown how being more heroic will have real, tangible benefits in their life and work. This is easier to do if you can deal with real life and work issues, helping people process them in heroic ways and having them reflect on the personal (inner) and worldly (outer) improvements that accrue from operating heroically. At stage two of our quest, we need a guide who can sit with us as we face our inner fears, doubts and demons—someone who can help us reflect on our early socialisation and remake our decisions in here-and-now situations as they occur. Obviously such a guide will be knowledgeable in and at home with the mysteries of the human psyche. Good stage two guides will be comfortable feeling and expressing their emotions and will help you to uncover your own—not from a place of 'professional distance', but on a human-to-human level. This means that we have to like and trust our stage two guide. We have to believe that he or she understands us and our world. Our stage two guide will need to be very comfortable with silences, unknowing and paradox, since he or she will have to maintain our trust as we face our inner emptiness and come to terms with letting go of outdated world views so we can rest in the fertile bed of anticipation.

'Before the birth of the hero or heroine,' writes Nor Hill in *The Moon and the Virgin*, 'there is often a long period of sterility; and then the child is born supernaturally ... before a time of particular activity in the unconscious there is a tendency towards a long period of complete sterility.' This is often experienced as a period of listlessness, depression and confusion. Life feels stale. It's as if the mind, heart and soul are getting ready for the creative transformation at hand.

Good stage two heroic guides, having been through this process so many times themselves, can give us heart while we endure the nothingness that precedes new life and creation. While we are going through this important second stage of our quest, skilful stage two guides will, drawing on their own knowledge and experience, help us build a bridge between our external reality and our internal world as they unfold before us. This doesn't mean that they will tell us what to do, but rather they will use their wisdom to help us avoid unnecessary pitfalls and deal pragmatically with issues as they arise. This takes stage two outside the normal bounds of therapy, as the stage two guide takes an active and real interest in the emotional, spiritual and physical wellbeing of the heroic quester. Good stage two guides work to the heroic quester's objectives, while always remaining true to themselves.

Skilled stage three guides look much the same as warrior trainers in that they are professional advisers. However, they operate heroically, reminding us of the lessons we have learnt along our heroic path so that we can weave our learning into all our thoughts, actions and responses. Heroic stage three guides help us see and deal with reality differently. They help us bridge the gap between our inner world and our outer day-to-day circumstances and relationships, helping us learn how to bring about magical, sleight-of-hand transformations in our lives, business and world. Actually, stage three is perhaps the most difficult phase in which to find appropriate support. By this time, we will not be satisfied with shallow warrior talk. We want someone who is further down the heroic path than us, someone who can support us to continue on our journey, someone who can help us bring our growing heart and soul into the political and social reality of our world. This is a highly skilled and very exacting task. Finding people who are sufficiently worldly, adequately wise and appropriately heroic is very, very hard.

If our heroic guide does not keep up his or her own growth, we will quickly move past that person. If we are lucky, we will find a guide who can take us through all three stages and keep growing so that he or she is always ahead of us in our journey. If we cannot find such a person, we will need to upgrade our guides as we move through our quest. We may need to have more than one guide at a time, orchestrating the strengths of each to meet our growing, changing needs. We may also choose to work with a variety of specialist guides. I do.

Spiritual Support

For many years, I chose to tread my spiritual path alone. I went on retreat, prayed, meditated and did daily spiritual practice, but I was unable to find a spiritual teacher who met my needs. This wasn't through lack of looking. I asked around and whenever I heard of a spiritual teacher who had helped someone I liked and respected, I would set out to meet this guru. And guru after guru I met. They were Christians, Buddhists and self-appointed masters;

their backgrounds ranged across reincarnation, mysticism and Catholicism. None of their words rang true in my heart. Still I kept searching and praying, searching and praying.

After what seemed like a lifetime (in fact, it was about ten years), a friend introduced me to her spiritual director, who introduced me to his brother. From that very first meeting I knew I had found a soul friend. Here was someone who, after years on his own spiritual quest, knew how to have a soul-to-soul conversation, someone who felt so secure in his soulfulness he had no need to shove dogma, doctrine or rules down my throat, but rather was happy to listen to my soul talk, respecting, validating and illuminating my insights and learning.

Like all good guides, my spiritual director had no need to hide behind his title, position or learning. He shared with me his struggles, his inner journey and the reality of his world. He was a humble, approachable and eminently wise human being. He and I lived in very different worlds and saw things in very different ways, but we related comfortably on the level of our souls. Just being around my spiritual director nurtured my spirit.

Something else happened. The agreement we had was that when we were together we concentrated on soul matters. Just putting the time in my diary and keeping our appointments meant that soul was a high priority in my life. As such, it received attention.

This is what care of the soul is all about—putting our attention, for at least some time in our busy lives, on our spirit. For some people, this happens when they attend church, synagogue, mosque or shrine. For others, it happens reading quietly, listening to music, watching or creating art, singing, dancing or walking in nature. For some folks, soul work includes all of these activities. The really important thing about nurturing your spirit is to pay it attention in whatever way your soul craves. This will be unique and personal. Herein lies its richness.

As we have seen, soulfulness is developed in the day-to-dayness of life. As with emotional support, however, we need constant reminders that the superficiality that is pervasive in the world is not the only way. To learn from the rough and tumble of life, we need times of nurturing, growing, healing and integrating learning into our souls. This process can be heightened and made all the more effective if we find a good guide.

Time taken enriching our souls is time spent in wise-selfishness. If we are to connect spiritually with ourselves and others, if we are to come into relationships soulful and rich of heart, we need to ensure that our souls are well tended. It is very hard to give to others from an empty vessel.

If we don't tend to replenish our soul energy, we will always be running on spiritual empty, not even having enough inner richness to get ourselves through life, let alone being able to share our hearts and souls with others.

Giving and Receiving Emotional and Spiritual Support

Spiritual and emotional support, when expertly given, are remarkably hard to see. Effective support is best judged by the richness of our lives, the ease with which we get things done, our emotional aliveness and flexibility of thought. When we are effectively supported, we are wiser, more intuitive, more compassionate, more in touch with the reality of the world around us and more skilful at relationships. Well-supported people think more laterally and feel calmer, more peaceful and more alive. They act more constructively. In a world that focuses on tangible, measurable outputs, support usually goes unnoticed, unrecognised and unvalued. We don't know what we are missing.

If you want to be a hero, if you want a life that combines the rich fruits of your own humanity with worldly success, you are going to need to treasure, respect and effectively use good support when you find it. To do this, you will need to accept discomfort, learn to listen with the ears of your soul and see with the eyes of your heart. You will need to ask for and stay open to feedback and take the risk of letting down your psychological defences when you are with safe people. This may involve a leap of faith. If you wait until your trust has been earned, your learning may be delayed for years, depending on the nature of your early socialisation.

Some time ago I was working with Eric, a very powerful plant manager. Eric was highly respected in his industry and was probably the most important citizen in the company town built around his factory. He was used to being revered, listened to, heard and obeyed. However, times were changing. His global parent company was going through massive transformation and he had been instructed to find new ways of leading. Eric's superiors felt that this would be very hard for him because he rarely listened to others and was quick to inundate you with his highly defensive opinions. Eric seemed to have made an art form of political posturing.

As I interviewed Eric for a forthcoming workshop, he kept telling me how much he wanted to learn. Each time he said this, I wondered how anyone who didn't listen could learn anything. The more he talked, the more at a loss I felt as to how I could help this man without offending him. Eventually, I asked him if he minded if I gave him some feedback. Eric was surprised, but gave me permission to proceed. I told him how over the past few days a large number of his bosses had spoken to me about him and mentioned that he didn't listen and that this posed a problem. The man was horrified, the blood drained from his face. 'What,' he asked me, 'should I do?' Unable to think of anything more tactful on the spot, I simply answered, 'Keep your mouth shut and your ears open.'

To his great credit, this is exactly what Eric did. By so doing, he learnt more about himself in the following few days than he had learnt in years. He asked for and listened to feedback from his employers and peers, and then let that information into his heart, mind and soul. Through listening, staying open and reflecting, this man gave himself the opportunity to grow and learn at a very deep level. His bosses were amazed—an impossible transformation had taken place.

One of Eric's fears was that if he stopped defending, stopped posturing and started to listen, he would be too vulnerable. He was afraid that the warriors in his factory would see his lack of defensiveness as weaknesses and exploit his vulnerability. He was scared that if he learnt to listen he might no longer be heard.

This fear is so common among apparently powerful leaders it is worth reviewing here. I am constantly amazed just how powerless people feel, even those in positions of great power. I once worked with the divisional top team of a large industrial organisation and had them draw for me the power dynamics in their global company. They drew a stairway to heaven with angels and archangels. Sitting on a throne atop the stairs was GOD, the global managing director. Some years later, I found myself sitting next to GOD, who was battling with introducing a major transformation into his company. When I asked him what was stopping him going ahead, he replied that he wasn't sure he had the power.

If GOD doesn't have the power, I wondered, *who the hell does?* What this man was voicing was his belief that, although in the eyes of the thousands of people he employed he had absolute power, he didn't feel powerful. He therefore went through the motions of power, doing the things he thought powerful people ought to do, but in and of himself he felt vulnerable and disempowered. No wonder leaders spend so much time defending. Those defences aren't to keep other people at bay, but rather to avoid facing their own feelings of inadequacy. When we stop defending and start listening, we realise just how powerless we feel. Ironically, the more we are able to dwell on this realisation, the more comfortable it becomes and the more powerful we feel. We no longer need to defend needlessly, engage in constant chatter and strut our stuff.

As our self-awareness rises, we can combine our growing inner power with our knowledge of who we are, what we want and what we have to offer. By bringing all this into relationship, we start to operate as real leaders—true to ourselves, true to our humanity, aware, powerful and wise. That is what real leadership is all about.

Finding the Time

You may be thinking that finding and using all this support seems like a very time consuming and expensive business. You are right. However, I have found that when people seek, find and use appropriate support, their energy, insight, success and income rise dramatically. For me, the relationship between good-quality support and increased earnings has been exponential. For this to happen, the support does have to be good, by which I mean heroic, wise and intelligent. Poor-quality support can be more trouble, harm and mischief than it is worth. You don't expect to get a good return on a poor investment. It's the same with support. If you invest wisely in high-quality support, you will regain all the time, energy and financial resources you put in many times over. If you invest in poor support, you could lose your shirt.

Unfortunately, most people invest in poor-quality support most of the time. A case in point is the army of warrior trainers that business so happily endows with lucrative training and consulting contracts. However, that is only the tip of the iceberg.

People within organisations spend hours supporting themselves and each other so that they can remain stuck in a rut of social conformity, emotional denial and spiritual flatness. We support each other in burying our hearts' desires, keeping quiet about our challenging ideas and insights, and conforming to mediocrity of thinking and action. Television and other forms of media also support us in staying within the stifling barriers of addictive systems and behaviour. We all invest hundreds if not thousands of hours in gaining and using this kind of support. Why not be selective and take responsibility for the quality of the emotional, spiritual and intellectual support we accept and use? This demands discrimination, judgment and conscious choice. However, living a life full of richness, texture, joy and aliveness makes this well worth the effort.

Practical Support

There is one final kind of support I want to discuss and that is practical support. It used to be that two of the benefits of being an executive were that you received your own office and were entitled to a private secretary. This enabled leaders to create a safe space around themselves at work. Their secretaries became people with whom they could build up a safe relationship, someone they could trust to look after their best interests and provide valuable professional assistance. Secretaries even helped with private matters, such as remembering family birthdays and buying the presents. The support executives received freed them to concentrate on strategic issues and relationships. Not being bothered with short-term arrangements, knowing that there was someone there to help them out, executives were in a position to be optimally effective.

Then along came computers, downsizing, open plan offices and hot desking. Organisations decided that they could do without executives, executives could do without offices and their own desk, and secretaries could work for groups of people. This meant that those executives who kept their jobs had to do more and more for themselves. One of their most valuable support systems was stripped away from them.

In an attempt to save money, companies effectively increased the work load of executives by removing vital support systems. This generally translated into executives spending more time doing day-to-day office and organisational tasks and less time being strategic and long range in their thinking. Instead of having people on relatively inexpensive wages doing the photocopying, organising the travel bookings and ensuring that research for meetings is appropriately organised and to hand, we now have highly paid executives doing these things for themselves. While this may appeal to our desire for egalitarianism, it doesn't make much business sense.

When I was a working mother, I found that the kind of practical support I needed and was prepared to pay for was dinner on the table and someone to clean my house and do the ironing. It used to be that men received these services for free. The women's movement has highlighted this point for years, noting the highly productive unpaid support services provided by women in the home. That most women do upwards of thirty hours unpaid housework and childcare per week on top of any paid work they may do illustrates both how unremitting our need for practical support is and how much we undervalue and fail to reward it.

Today, the invisible support system of the home-based wife has become impossible for most families to afford. With rising inflation, it is a sign of wealth for families to be able to support one home-based parent. So, after a hectic, unsupported day at work, people go home to the cooking, washing, ironing and cleaning, stopping to pick the kids up from childcare on the way. No wonder most people are tired most of the time. Nor is it any wonder that the women who succeed are unlikely to have children and the men who make it to the top of the executive ladder are highly likely to have a home-based wife.

Although we tend to undervalue and overlook support, when we don't have it we certainly feel the lack. Those who are supported stand out from the crowd as successful leaders and achievers. What smart people realise is that support is not a luxury, it is a very expensive secret to making it in the first place. Appropriately supported people succeed in whatever undertaking to which they commit themselves. If we consciously, with discrimination and commitment, invest in a variety of appropriate, high-quality support, we can increase our success in a heartfelt, soulful way. This is surely the secret to sustaining high performance in life and at work.

Chapter 7

Opening the Corporate Heart

It is individuals who change societies, who give birth to ideas,
who by standing out against the tides of opinion, change them.

DORIS LESSING

The Heartless Corporation

When telling people the name of this book, the question I am most often asked is, 'Does the corporation have a heart?'

People generally seem angry with large organisations, which are seen as ruthless, heartless and immoral, spewing out unwanted staff at a frightening rate, breaking the tacit contract of jobs for life in return for worker loyalty. People feel rejected, cheated and resentful. If corporations had a heart, how could they be downsizing, re-engineering and restructuring the way they are? Surely anyone with a heart couldn't cause the level of pain and distress corporations seem to be inflicting on their discarded employees and the environment?

I find this response interesting. There is no doubt that the corporate employment contract is changing. It is also true that many organisations are reducing the size of their workforce and that this is causing many people distress and personal anguish as they reinvent their lives, learn new skills and start out on new careers. What is interesting is the assumption that, once employed by a corporation, people have the right to a job for life. This seems to me to absolve the individual of any responsibility for their own professional development and career management.

For many years, I have talked to executives about managing their own careers, being their own people and creating their own futures. They inevitably look at me and scoff, 'It's all right for you,

you're self-employed.' My response is always, 'So are you, it's just that you don't want to admit it.'

Leadership philosopher Charles Handy (1995) tells us that the number of people in full-time jobs in organisations is now less than half of all adults of working age. He tells us that the emerging configuration in the world of work is a three-ringed circle. The inner ring is the corporate elite, 'entrepreneurs who give their whole life to their business, highly trained executives who step in when the entrepreneurs wear out and the young totally dedicated ladder climbers who want to replace the older executives'. Also in this core are highly skilled technical specialists.

The outer ring consists of itinerant workers, who are brought in as needed and discarded when not. The middle ring consists of what Handy calls the 'portfolio people'. Portfolio people build up a portfolio of skills, achievements, products and services which they sell to a portfolio of clients. When young, portfolio people often take their place in the inner circle to gain experience and then step out on their own, managing their personal assets and careers as one might manage a share portfolio. Unlike the players in the inner circle, portfolio people no longer think in terms of line or upward mobility. Rather they weave a fabric of social, business and community life around themselves. They are, by choice and by necessity, their own masters.

We are, claims Handy, living in an age of discontinuous change. We can no longer predict the future by studying the past. The formula that led to our current success could well be a blueprint of disaster tomorrow. 'The world,' writes Handy, 'at every level has to be reinvented to some extent. Certainty is out, experiment is in.'

As George Bernard Shaw wrote, the future belongs to the unreasonable ones who don't look backwards, but who are certain only of uncertainty and who have the ability and confidence to think completely differently.

A lot of this discontinuous change is being propelled by the new technology. Information technology has changed the game plan beyond recognition. Sophisticated information and global buying opportunities are now available to anyone who owns a computer.

This wide access to computer technology, artificial intelligence and the instant global communication it brings with it is changing the face of corporations and the workforce in general.

I sit in my office in Sydney and communicate with clients all around the world. Through the Internet, I can provide information, answer questions and get to know thousands of people globally. Because of the nature of my work, I spend a lot of time on aeroplanes on my way to visit CEOs around the globe, but those whose work is less people centred can live in any location they please. They can work from home and send their work by computer to their clients, whom they need never see nor meet except by fax, phone or e-mail.

In this rapidly changing world, it seems strange that so many people's relationships to corporations are somehow childlike. We grew up thinking that the contract was that the individual would show up for work and do their best. They would learn those skills that their bosses suggested and, within certain bounds, follow orders. The implicit trade-off was that the corporation would ensure employment for the individual until they decided to leave. Like the dependent child, so many people still rely on the parent for sustenance, trading obedience and loyalty in return.

Often when working with executive groups, I ask them to draw the political dynamic that operates in their organisations and their relationship to that dynamic. Time and again, people draw the 'mother' company with them as a dependent child, striving with all the other dependent children to do the right thing, please mother and earn access to scarce resources. When people say that the corporation doesn't have a heart, what perhaps they are really saying is that the corporation is not fulfilling their expectations of a good mother. It seems to me that this tells us as much about the complainant as it does about the corporation.

Corporation as Parent

A client once suggested that if only he could find and kill the person called 'senior management' in his company, they would get rid of all the problems. It seemed that whenever anything went wrong, it was blamed on some failing by 'senior management'. The old-style employment contract—heavily supported and enforced by trade unions—is very much about insisting that corporations be good parents. That is, that they take responsibility for outcomes, clarify their expectations and intentions, set clear and appropriate boundaries, provide necessary support systems and provide nurturing and acceptance in the form of jobs for life, adequate salaries and comfortable conditions.

If things change, the *corporation* 'should' have known about it beforehand and planned for what was to come. If *they* haven't done this, *they* should quickly regroup, implement proper planning and let the employees know. The employees, of course, will fight to have their needs met, but it is the role of the parent corporation to see this through patiently. Children will be children.

This thought system excuses individuals from taking personal responsibility for their own wellbeing and growth. Choosing to see the corporation as parent frees us from being accountable for making our professional lives work and gives us someone to blame when things don't go our way or turn out as we had hoped. Given the changing nature of work, it is also short-sighted and self-defeating to think this way. Only those who can grow, change and take personal responsibility for their careers, deal effectively with the chaotic nature of change and constantly reinvent themselves will remain marketable in any of the three rings of the global labour marketplace.

Despite this, when the *corporation* finally tells us that we are no longer needed, we feel rejected, like children ousted from the family home, disowned and unloved by the mother. We have not just lost our job; we have lost our sense of belonging, our sense of identity and our guiding hand. We are on our own, responsible for our own lives, our own careers and our own wellbeing. So we rail against the heartless corporation. How *could* they (mummy/daddy) have done this to us? How could they be so heartless?

As I talk with those who have been responsible for terminating the employment of their peers and employees, I hear the anguish in their voices as they describe the horror and pain they felt asking people to leave. They tell me of the reactions of anger, disbelief and shock that people go through on learning that they are no longer needed by their employer. I also hear of the people who, after retrenchment, go on to find new careers, new dignity in self-employment, new energy in finding new paths for growth, employment and lifestyle. It seems that when people use their expulsion from the corporate nest to grow, their banishment from the corporate family actually leads to them growing up and making better, more mature lives for themselves, based not on the assumed parental (corporate) dictum, but on the wants, needs, desires and talents of the individual. The *heartless corporation* is actually giving responsibility, growth and life back to the ousted individual.

It is certainly true that not everybody can cope with this responsibility. Years of deadening their own needs, hearts' desires and soulful yearnings to meet the assumed demands of corporate parents has so robbed people of inner power, direction, maturity and wisdom that many don't know how to cope when the time comes for them to look after themselves. The parent has let them down by not insisting sooner that they take personal responsibility for their lives and grow up spiritually, emotionally and intellectually. Of course, as successful workers must increasingly be the unreasonable ones who can think outside of current parameters and charge forward confidently into the unknown, stunted child folk become increasing liabilities.

I invite you to walk into any major corporation, the more blue chip the better, and look around you. My guess is that you will be hard placed to find anyone, apart from very senior management, who is more than fifty years of age. By the time people make their half century, they have either been moved up or out. Is this further evidence of the heartless corporation or is there some other reason?

As we have seen, the warrior response to corporate life is for the individual to close down his or her emotions and deny his or her spirit. Warriordom demands that we focus outwards, deny our personal difference and march in time to the corporate song. We have also seen that people who close down their emotions and spirit become increasingly inflexible, rigid in thought and action.

They are prone to stress-related illnesses and are generally poor at relationships and dealing with complexity. When ageing is not accompanied by emotional and spiritual growth—that is, by wisdom—the process of rigidity is exacerbated. So what emerges is a picture of ageing children slowly becoming more rigid, staid and inaccessible, demanding that the parent corporation look after them.

We know that in a borderless world, competition has become global. Corporations have to sell their goods and services in crowded international marketplaces where consumers and investors can pick and choose from the best in the world. The death rate of corporations is colossal—few organisations survive more than a few years and even the giants rarely see out their first century. Corporations have to be strong and fit to survive. They can't afford to carry people who have built up fixed attitudes and inner tension rather than growing in wisdom, insight and discernment. Survival of the whole demands that those who haven't improved with age must go. Who are we to blame: the heartless corporation or individuals who have failed to take responsibility for keeping themselves employable?

Of course, the answers aren't easy. Corporations are comprised of people. When we talk about the *corporation*, we are talking about people. People who fill various roles at different times. Sometimes they are employees, sometimes bosses, and often both. So an individual can be in the role of both corporate parent and corporate child, demanding obedience to corporate norms as the parent, and railing against the heartless organisation as the child whenever their needs aren't met or when they find themselves on the corporate scrapheap. This can be clearly evidenced by the fact that corporate dismissals have hit heavily in the once sacred halls of middle and senior management. Charles Handy in *Beyond Certainty* noted that 75 per cent of the new jobless are coming from the ranks of managers, professionals and administrative and technical staff. No longer does status and power render the individual immune from the need to grow, learn and take responsibility for their own career. In the corporate jungle, executives are now less secure than other employees.

An Heroic Answer

We would all like to think that organisations operate rationally and that people function logically within them. We all know deep inside, however, that this is no more than a fairytale, a childish wish list of how things could be in a perfect world. We are all products of our socialisation. Unless we have chosen to do something about it, we operate out of choices we made when we were very young. Each and every person lives a life that is governed by the decisions he or she has made in response to the life experiences he or she has met. The irony is that our earliest decisions, those we made when our brains were maturing, have the greatest bearing on our adult actions, attitudes and beliefs—until, that is, we raise our awareness to the stage where we can consciously choose our actions.

For each of us, the majority of patterns of thought, emotion, action and reaction are unconscious. As a rule of thumb, we have choice over that which is conscious, while what is unconscious rules us. In times of rapid discontinuous change such as the present, the logical and sensible answer would be for organisations to evict those who are slow to adapt, those who are rigid in their thinking and those who cannot keep pace with innovation and change. In other words, organisations would be encouraging people to go on the hero's quest, either within the corporation as ring one people, or outside the organisation as portfolio and ring three people. What makes sense, however, isn't necessarily what actually happens. Let's have a look why.

As we are going through the process of socialisation, driven by childhood imperatives of gaining love and nurture from our care-givers, we hit upon strategies for getting the big people to care for us. These strategies almost always consist of focusing our attention on the big people and what they want of us. If our strategies are sufficiently successful, they become our lifelong patterns of reacting to those in positions of authority.

If our strategies are unsuccessful, we can become rebellious, self-destructive and depressed. These responses, too, become our patterns of dealing with authority figures and life in general. As we grow, we adapt our psychological defences so as to fit into the society around us. We learn to fit in at school (where conformity is a prerequisite for success socially and academically) and at work, but we retain our basic childhood patterning (our inner theatre) until we choose to make it conscious. Only then are we free to choose how we want to think, react and behave.

Organisations, therefore, don't just consist of people. They consist of people and their histories, which have become the unconscious drivers of their adult behaviour. Nowhere is this more potent than in how people respond to any person or institution that they see as having authority. In response to the parent corporation and the surrogate parents (senior management or contract managers), people follow their tried and true responses to the big people. They keep their eyes peeled for the signals they think lead to love, nurture and support. They deny their own needs, talents, realities and soul, to go after the sustenance that the big people bring—the sustenance they have been seeking all their life. In some mad way, we are seeking to regain the unity and comfort we lost at birth and have been seeking ever since. If this sounds a bit bizarre that is because it is bizarre. It is also very human.

Warriors deal with this situation by ignoring or denying it. They continue to focus outwards, increasingly cut off from the pain of their unfulfilled needs and desires. Warriors blame the current parent (authority figure) for life not being all they would want. To insure against ever having to deal with their inner pain and demons, warriors become increasingly defended, pushing their pain and sorrow onto other people, denying others' emotions, desires and soul as forcefully as they deny their own. If warriors feel mistreated, they mistreat. If they feel neglected, they neglect. Warriors explain this away as necessary behaviour given the realities of life, conveniently overlooking that it is the reality of their life, a life which they have co-created through their ongoing choices, actions and beliefs. Denying a situation doesn't make it go away. Emotions, soul and thoughts, if disallowed, don't vanish. They merely go underground, only to spring up in unexpected ways. So, as warriors become more rigid and set in their ways, they also suffer from a range of psychological and physical ailments as their emotions and soul fight to be heard. In short, the warriors are going against the tide. They render themselves increasingly inflexible, constantly escalating their need for security, sameness and conformity—the very opposite of what the current environment has to offer.

Heroes deal with the reality of socialisation and life differently. Realising that they are responsible for their lives through their own choices and actions, they go in search of their inner drivers. They seek to understand not only who they are, but also how they got to be that way, not as some academic or 'feel good' exercise, but so that they can put their learning to use in increasing their effectiveness in the present moment. By noticing how and when they defend, heroes learn about their current moment response and the historical patterns that led to that response. By noticing how they feel in response to every situation, heroes learn the nature and extent of their childhood wounds, they learn about their internal belief systems and they learn to tailor their present moment responses from the conscious perspective of an adult rather than the unconscious driver of a child. By spending time in quiet reflection, exploring the soulful depths of their being, heroes build up their inner resources, becoming their own parent, taking responsibility for meeting their own needs, growing in wisdom, insight and discretion.

Heroes are on the path to mature adulthood—a painful and uncertain path. It is a path that takes our focus away from the razzamatazz of the world around us and puts us in touch with our inner truth, wisdom, pain, heart and soul. From this place, we can see more clearly and respond more truly to the world in which we live. Instead of projecting unconscious childhood images on everyone and everything around them, heroes stand tall as their own people, mature adults in their own right, owning their strengths and their weaknesses in a profound and uncommon way. They take responsibility for their every response to the world they inhabit; they take responsibility for their relationships, their actions, their own growth, wellbeing and emotions. Thus, heroes continue to grow, not just in wisdom and maturity, but also in the flexibility that comes from being in touch with reality as it happens (not as we think it happens when looking through the filter of unconscious childhood patterning).

Heroes, being true to themselves, owning and valuing their individual thinking, emotions and ways of seeing things, are naturally creative. In fact, they find it impossible to be anything but innovative in their way of approaching work, relationships, problems and challenges. They are, without effort, the unreasonable ones. Thus heroes use their hearts and souls to achieve results, enrich their lives, build their relationships and create their future.

People Have Hearts

The truth is the cynics are right. Corporations, still the realm of the warrior and largely devoid of heroes, are heartless. Warriors, in their obsession to deaden their emotions and sell their souls, deny the emotion and soul of everyone around them. If they are in positions of power over in-house staff or outside contractors (i.e. are corporate parents), they do this with added force and potency. Always, however, they are children, blindly striving for love, security and comfort from such an unconscious stance that they inflict pain on others along the way.

The problem isn't that the corporation in its need to remain competitive has to ensure that its staff are constantly learning and growing on every level—emotional, intellectual, spiritual, skill and knowledge—and that those who can't or won't keep up, those who are inflexible and rigid, must go. No, that is just good business—what has to be for the good of the whole. Nor is the problem that new information technology is changing the shape of work and labour markets around the world. No, this is just a fact of life. The real problem is that the majority of business leaders are warriors, who have numbed their humanity, repressed their emotions and spirit, and failed to see past their childhood socialisation. This is the basis of the addictive organisation.

The whole crazy game plan is that by keeping things the same, warriors and their leaders can avoid facing their neurotic patterns of thought, behaviour and emotional response, can avoid facing their pain, and can continue to blame someone or something outside of themselves rather than take personal responsibility for making their lives work. Warriors do this by ensuring that everybody sticks to the nine rules of dysfunctional systems (see chapter 3):

RULE 1   It is not okay to talk about problems.
RULE 2   Feelings should not be expressed openly.
RULE 3   Communication is best if indirect, with one person acting as the messenger between two others.
RULE 4   Be strong, good, right and perfect.
RULE 5   Make us proud.
RULE 6   Don't be selfish.
RULE 7   Do as I say and not as I do.
RULE 8   It is not okay to play or be playful.
RULE 9   Don't rock the boat.

So, the warriors collude to play by the rules and punish anyone who dares to do otherwise. Most of the literature and training of business leaders is about how to be a better warrior, adhere to the rules of addictive systems and avoid noticing the insanity of your behaviour and the needless pain you inflict on others due to your insensitivity. More than that, the training of leaders and the way business is run to the addictive rules take so much time and energy that we are excused for avoiding, repressing and denying responsibility for our own emotions, thoughts and life. We feel we are on the treadmill, that we have no choice but to work at a frantic and exhausting pace, to play the silly office games and sell out who we are. We think being a warrior is the only option which makes sense given that we have to get on with warrior bosses who want us to comply to insane rules of conduct and operation, and threaten (outright or through innuendo) to take away our livelihood if we don't. However, if we don't learn to break the addictive rules, if we don't learn to become unreasonable in our thinking, if we don't take responsibility for our own lives, we are flying in the face of reality and rendering ourselves increasingly unemployable.

We do have hearts and souls. We do have power over our own choices. We are capable of raising our self-awareness and taking responsibility for our present moment emotions, thoughts and actions, and more particularly for the psychological patterns that underlie our adult functioning. However, to access our hearts and souls, to contact and use our inner power, to raise our awareness and take full personal responsibility—in other words, to help ourselves survive in the world of discontinuous change—we will have to break out of the social collusion that keeps business in the realm of the warrior and keeps us rigid and limited in our thinking and conformist in our behaviour. Hence stage one of the hero's journey involves separation and departure. We have to head off on our search for answers outside of the comfort of the known and socially accepted.

This is a terrifying thing to do. As humans, we are social animals; acceptance by the group is so important to us. We fear that by daring to see things differently, think differently, acknowledge that we feel differently from others, we will be scorned, rejected, even annihilated. This, of course, stems from our early childhood experience of learning to fit in to regain our lost state of grace. Yet even knowing this rationally doesn't help all that much as our patterns are so emotionally compelling, all the more so when they are unconscious. When we dare to break the addictive rules (even to ourselves), we stir up all our childhood fears, wounds and pains. For most people, this is enough to have them scurrying back to normality, even though they know that it is killing them emotionally and spiritually.

We constantly read and write about the need for leadership, for social reform, for community, but while ever individuals are too frightened to separate from the known, to head off on the hero's journey, to discover their inner drivers, wounds and world, social organisation and the real quality of people's lives and relationships are unlikely to improve greatly. We will continue to deny ourselves so much of what is possible. We may also be denying ourselves future employment. Moreover, while ever business and business leaders concentrate on the superficial busyness rather than doing the hard work of growing up as people, they will undermine their business success and continue to underperform as corporate citizens. The corporation will go on being seen as heartless. It will also render itself increasingly rigid and therefore ever less competitive.

But what if you are not in a position of power? Perhaps your fears of being punished for being different are real? Well, of course they are. This is why you need an heroic guide. It is also part of the journey; stage two of the hero's quest is, after all, the trials and victories of initiation. The old dictum 'no pain, no gain' holds true.

Most organisations operate in function of the rules of addictive systems. These rules neurotically set out to obliterate free thought and suppress differences in emotional reality at the very time when these are the things most needed to spur creativity, independent thought and experiment. The addictive rules have the effect of eradicating diversity. (This is why women and minorities have had to disguise their difference in order to get to the top.) Irving Janis in studying the historical background to a range of major military disasters, found that in all cases the rules of addictive systems were fiercely obeyed and defended; he called this 'group think'. It appeared that in each military catastrophe that Janis studied there were people in the decision-making team that believed deeply that the decision about to be enacted was wrong. Few, however, were prepared to rock the boat, to express their feelings openly or to raise the problems. It appeared that they chose to go along with a disastrous decision (often sacrificing the lives of others) rather than run the risk of being excluded from the group. Those few hardy souls who dared to voice their concerns were quickly silenced by the 'mindguard', the self-appointed enforcer of the rules, who made it very clear to the dissident that difference was the route to expulsion from the group.

So our fears of going on the hero's journey, of risking thinking, feeling and behaving differently, are well founded if we happen to live and work in addictive systems (and most of us do). However, if individuals don't go on the hero's quest, the system will, like communism, self-destruct. You are damned if you do and damned if you don't. Obeying the political dictum created by the addictive rules will render you increasingly unemployable and your organisation increasingly non-competitive. However, if you disobey the rules, you risk being punished and perhaps thrown out of the inner ring of the corporate elite or losing lucrative corporate contracts if you are already in ring two or three. Our desire for security encourages us to support the political status quo for short-term economic survival. This route, however, guarantees ongoing depreciation of our worth in the labour market.

Heroic guides, those who have been on, survived and know the benefits of the hero's quest, know to the core of their being the inner tension that this situation creates. They know the fears, the delights, the pains and the joys of daring, even in solitude, to think, feel and act differently. They also know that the journey is worth the prize. The prize being not just heart, soul, intimate, fulfilling relationships and community, but also the flexibility, strength and power effectively to apply your personal genius and creativity in your life and work. Heroism is a path for winners who want to sustain their high performance at work, while gaining maximum enjoyment and pleasure from life. Heroes want it all—joy, soulful fulfilment and rich personal relationships, as well as outstanding success in worldly matters. Warriors will settle for the superficial short-term rewards of status, power and wealth. Heroes are greedier. They want a fulfilling, meaningful life as well as the ability to go on making a meaningful contribution to the world at large. The hero's journey, being the search for higher return, is of course a path of higher risk. The lazy, dull and unimaginative have rarely been heroes.

Braiding—The Art of Having It All

One of the things that makes the hero's journey so interesting in the world of work is that work is both a political and a social system. Work by necessity combines the need to achieve goals, push past our limits and perform with our human need for love, companionship and community. Part, therefore, of opening the corporate heart is understanding all these aspects of the workplace so that, as individuals and jointly, we can manage them more effectively. More than that, corporations exhibit the dual aspects of power hierarchies and social systems/communities. These systems work by very different rules—rules that are worth knowing if you are to succeed on your hero's quest.

Biologist Humberto Maturana in *Seized by Agreement, Swamped by Understanding* introduces us to the concept of 'braiding': the need to operate effectively in two apparently competing systems using apparently contradictory ways of thinking, feeling and expressing our experience. Braiding is the art of integrating different parts of ourselves and different aspects of reality. This, of course, is the foundation of creative action, original thought and bold, purposeful action. Heroes are master braiders. Being familiar and comfortable with all parts of themselves, knowledgeable and aware of the intricacies of competing systems, heroes are able to combine politics with intimate relationships, the need to produce at world-class standard with the desire to be loved and accepted unconditionally, the reality of competition for scarce resources with our need to bond and be part of the group. When we start looking at corporations, teams and individual work achievement in this light, we start seeing things very differently.

Warriors tend to be very linear in their thinking—they are masters of the 'either/or' of life. When we see the world as black and white, we miss all the colours of the spectrum that lie in between. Braiding is about learning to live and work in vivid technicolour.

As we saw in chapter 3, we possess emotions as a mere function of being an animal. How effectively we bring our emotions into the human condition depends on how aware we are of our emotions, how effectively we express our emotions (thus converting them to feelings) and how skillfully we bring our feelings into conversation (turning around with the other in the flow of life). We are both rational and emotional animals. Human evolution and growth require that we are as comfortable with our emotions (unexplained and unexpressed) as we are with our feelings (based on self-awareness, reflection and expression of emotion). They require that we can braid the two, bringing all of ourselves into relationships and conversation. Maturana speaks of the braided flow of our emotioning and our reasoning.

Business, the realm of the warrior, knows little of the 'braided flow'. Let's have a look, for instance, at the popular practice of producing value statements. People, usually organisational leaders, get together in a room for a day or two, and discuss what values they think the organisation 'should' have, the values they as strong, caring corporate citizens would be proud to work towards. They discuss these values at some length—argue over words and concepts, and produce a list. This list then becomes the corporate credo, is reproduced for all employees and even sent out to customers. Most of the value statements I have seen say much the same thing. They all claim that what really matters is caring for your staff and customers, being honest, working hard and making a profit. There are individual variations, but the general theme is fairly consistent.

Happy that they have now 'done' their values, the executives set about living by and enforcing the usual rules underlying addictive systems. This is a wonderful example of a feeling/emotion disconnection. The executives have put into words how they would like to feel, which has nothing to do with the emotions they actually experience. This is because executives are usually so totally out of touch with their body-felt senses, with their emotions, that they don't bring them into the equation. They don't braid their rational and emotional selves. They do the logical thing, ignoring their non-rational selves and therefore rendering themselves as hypocrites, who will never be able to live up to their espoused values.

Recently I was sent the executive assessment profile of the CEO of a major corporation. This particular company, like so many others, had created a list of competencies that they believed represented the components of an executive's role. Some of these are listed below:

- Leadership
- Has seasoned philosophy of leadership and business management

- Wears the mantle of leadership conscientiously and confidently
- Reinforces company values and high achievement by drawing attention to exemplars
- Creates heroes and legends

This poor guy had been assessed against more than eighty such competencies. If ever I saw an example of unbraiding, this was it. The words, so precise, so logical and based on such sound theoretical premises seemed to have nothing whatsoever to do with being a human being leading a group of other human beings in the social and political environment we choose to call a corporation. Here, clearly spelt out, were the requisite feelings and behaviours for a CEO—nowhere was there any evidence of the non-rational, emotional reality of a human being in a leadership role. No, leadership by competencies is logical, measured, assessable, sanitised and sanctified. What is amazing is that we spend so much time dealing with this fictional world, rather than daring to braid our logical ideas with our emotional, body-felt sense of what actually happens.

Braiding Social and Political Systems

Unconsciously we operate out of both our non-rational and rational selves all the time in business. As we have seen, we bring our unconscious childhood drivers with us wherever we go and as they pattern our behaviour, particularly in hierarchical systems and situations where power differentials exist, we constantly act out of our non-rational emotions. However, we rarely realise that this is what we are doing, and we go through the pantomime of being logical, rational 'adults' doing what adults are supposed to do—go to work. If we lived and worked in the braided flow, we would be able to identify when we are operating as a function of historical patterning and therefore braid our logic into our non-rational world, reclaiming our right to choose consciously how we behave and react. More than that, if we were in touch with our emotions, we would be able to name them and therefore help others to understand how we are actually responding to what is happening. If we were able to create licence for this—in other words, set up a system where diversity and humanity were valued—we would all feel better and do much better business.

Quite often when working with executive teams, I sit patiently and listen to them having logical discussions about various business issues. The more deeply I listen, the more I realise that absolutely no communication is actually occurring. We are in the unbraided flow. Although logical-sounding words are coming out of people's mouths, they seem to possess no grounding in reality. I have watched executives go through this charade and even agree on an outcome, knowing that the real issues have not been discussed and that no one has any interest or commitment to the agreed conclusion. This is invariably proved to be true when nothing changes and agreements are not enacted.

If, on the other hand, I can interrupt meaningless non-discussions and ask the executives to state how they feel and what action they intend to take based on their feelings, very interesting things happen. In the first instance, they usually fight me. They want to know what feelings have to do with sensible business discourse and why I am wanting them to waste their time when they have real issues to discuss. If, however, I persevere and am persuasive enough, I get them to play my 'silly game', perhaps 'just to please me'. I can then get them to reflect on their emotional response, name it and choose an action based on what they have learnt.

Invariably, the tone of the discussion changes. People feel angry, frustrated, delighted, pleased, questioning, confused, perplexed and anxious. They therefore choose to express a point of view, resolve a conflict, give praise, hunt for answers, ask for feedback, seek clarification and learn to understand what is worrying them. In other words, they choose a positive, self-enhancing action that brings them into real conversation and relationship with their peers. From this, the group is able to have a meaningful discussion of both the rational and non-rational issues, which leads to rapid resolution of the issues in ways that ensure quick and effective implementation of agreed outcomes. This is the 'braided flow' in action.

People in our society aren't very good at braiding at the best of times, but in business we are particularly hopeless. This is because business has the dual aspect of social domain and political system. Maturana in *Seized by Agreement, Swamped by Understanding* tells us that in the social domain the basic emotion is that of love. We seek mutual acceptance of each other and each other's differing realities.

This is not a mawkish sort of system, but in fact underlies the evolution of human kind. We would die without operating at some level where we feel completely accepted for who we are. In such a system, we value others as significant and are willing to disagree and listen. It is this system that constitutes social interaction between people. We have learnt to isolate this system from work. We often decide to work at one place and socialise in another. We may have work friends, but we also have colleagues, whom we keep at a clear distance. In the social system, we are who we are, think what we think and feel how we feel knowing that we will be accepted in our entirety. At work, however, we fear we will be rejected if we don't fulfill our role, complete a task or meet our objectives. This can be quite terrifying because it threatens our way of life and immediate source of income.

While the unknown may open new and more rewarding doors, we inherently distrust it and therefore concentrate on maintaining the status quo through doing what we need to do to read the political writing on the wall and follow its dictums. In fact, this isn't such a bad strategy. In the power hierarchy of the workplace, a very different system of interaction is in operation. Work is the domain of authority. At work, there is a job that needs to be done and there are expectations that need to be fulfilled. Work relations are not social relations. There are tasks to do, objectives to achieve and profits to be made. As work relations are fulfilled, so human relations largely disappear. An important aspect of this way of operating is the need for transparency of the system. What is needed for the authoritative domain to work successfully is for things to be clearly stated and documented. We need accounting systems, controls, ongoing measurement and accountability to ensure workability of the organisation. The needs of the whole system demand a structure and superstructure that is greater than the individual parts.

Both social and authoritative domains have their place. What doesn't work, however, is when we try to keep them in their place. People are people with social needs wherever they go. They are rational and non-rational in whatever environment they happen to be operating. Here again we see the need for braiding. It is not that the authoritative system is cold, hard and inhuman; it is what is necessary for business to operate. The trick is for us to grow sufficiently so that we can braid our social needs with our work needs, recognising from an adult perspective that the corporation is what it is (and not our parent). When this happens, we can function more effectively as human beings and corporations will do better business.

Learning to braid at work is a very heroic adventure. Currently, formal education systems encourage us to keep our emotional self and our rational self separate. Even though this is absolutely impossible to do, we learn that success at school, college and university depends on disowning our emotional self and pretending that we are rational, sane and logical all the time. When I attempted to do a PhD in strategic people leadership, I was unsuccessful. Not because I didn't have the intellect, the commitment or the background, but because I continually wanted to braid. I could always see the emotional and logical side to the argument. I relished the complexity of the human psyche and human interaction. I was forever interweaving disciplines and looking at things from a human as well as a theoretical aspect. It was made very clear to me very early on that good business students didn't think this way. They did logical research on computers building on existing academic theory. The lesson was very clear: disconnect who you are from what you do, or braid and go. I went.

Teams, Networks and Relationships

I am often approached by corporate leaders wanting me to engage in 'team building' exercises with their people. I find this whole notion laughable and quaintly old-fashioned. When I was younger and more silly, I often ran team-building sessions. I took my work very seriously and demanded that all members of the 'team' attend every meeting. I remember the head of one government department bringing me a letter of excuse from his Minister to explain his being late for one of my team-building sessions. Over the years, I found it increasingly difficult to get the whole 'team' in one place at one time. People were on leave, overseas on business or acting in someone else's job. Moreover, the life cycle of teams seemed to be speeding up. I finally gave up completely when working with the top team of one organisation which, by the end of my valiant team-building effort one year later, had none of its original members. They had all been posted elsewhere, retired or otherwise replaced. I decided not to take this personally, but rather to realise that the world had changed. Teams aren't what they used to be. For this fact, I am very grateful.

I recently saw a wonderful cartoon of a 'team': it was a group of ox bodies with human heads. The ox/humans were harnessed into a team being driven and whipped by the team leader. The point being made was that people are different from oxen and from each other. The old concept of teams assumes that individuals abrogate this difference, suppressing their own desires, needs and talents in order to harness their brute force and charge forth in unison in the direction decided by the leader. Unfortunately, most team-building exercises still operate from this paradigm. While the aim is to stir up motivation and excitement in pursuit of a common goal, what is actually promoted is group think and those all-too-familiar rules of addictive systems.

Warriors think they are great team builders. What they actually do, however, is collude to maintain the status quo through uniformity of thought and action. In an environment of discontinuous change, this is nothing short of stupidity. While donning the same colours and forgetting our differences may help us to win a football game, regatta or basketball play-off, it is a pretty silly and unproductive way to operate ongoing relationships in a highly complex, rapidly changing environment where innovation and relationships are of optimal importance. What is needed in today's hyperkinetic world is people who can build enduring and workable relationships which continually change in shape, nature and quality.

Your employee today may well be your boss tomorrow. Today's competitor may well be tomorrow's colleague, boss or employee. That idiot you hate in head office just might be posted tomorrow to be your offsider. We are in an age when relationships have never been more important nor more unstable. Building a fixed entity called a team is a redundant concept; what we need now are hardy, workable relationships that we sculpt and transform according to purpose, need and circumstance. We are in the age of networks that form and re-form, locally, nationally and globally, within, across and between companies.

We can be in many networks simultaneously: a family network, a work team network, a special interest network, a global specialist network and a social network. Heroes know that the really successful networks—those that promote the interests of each individual member, reach the optimal outcome and propel all parties forward—are those networks wherein individual difference is valued and personal and relationship growth is promoted. These are challenging networks of which to be part. To keep pace with your colleagues, to feel the pride of equality of participation and of making a difference, each and every network member has to grow personally through their relationships with their colleagues and the task at hand. This is an enlivening, exciting way to live and work.

Networks are systems of relationships that form and re-form, so let's have a look at relationships and how they work. We have already seen that people are a function of their present situation and their past decisions. When people enter into relationships, they bring all that with them. As we are largely unaware of who we are and how we got to be that way, we relate consciously to a small extent, and unconsciously most of the time. This means that our relationships are fairly hit and miss affairs.

One of the exercises I do with executive groups is called 'neutral mask'. Neutral mask is a technique devised by actor Jacques Le Coq, who used it to help actors develop their stage presence. I use it to help people see how loudly and unknowingly they transmit unconscious material. A neutral mask is made from papier-mâché or leather, and, unlike the human face, is symmetrical. The mask is made without any obvious expression, it is neither smiling, nor frowning, neither tense nor relaxed. When using the mask, we always adopt a ritual that requires people to turn away from the group to don the mask, centre themselves and then, without talking, turn and face the group before carrying out some pre-agreed exercise. What continually stuns people is that without looking at people's faces, without them saying a word, the onlooker can see straight into their psyche. The more personally aware and observant the onlooker, the more accurate and piercing his or her observations, but even unaware oafs can give the mask wearer enough feedback to move that person into extreme discomfort.

What becomes very clear very quickly is that we all transmit huge amounts of unconscious material all of the time. It is as if we are broadcasting to the world more about our psyche than we know ourselves. While this phenomenon becomes more obvious when we don the neutral mask, it is in fact happening all the time. It is just that we fool ourselves that we can use language and our facial expressions to hide the truth. We are wrong. What it does mean is that the less we know about ourselves, the less we are in control of how we relate to others and the less we know what information we actually send them. Bathing in this glorious ignorance, we are continually surprised by the apparently erratic and unpredictable responses we receive from others. Of course, we tell ourselves, they have a problem which they need to fix. What we don't want to admit is that people generally respond to us as a function of how we relate to them on both a conscious and unconscious level. If we want to improve our relationships, we have to increase our awareness so that we know what messages we are sending and ensure that we are sending messages that have at least some chance of getting the response we desire.

Once we start raising our awareness in relationships, we begin to notice just how much we relate in function of historical patterns as against present-moment reality. This is a rather terrifying concept when we first begin to notice it. We like to think that we are in control, that we relate logically and sensibly in a professional adult manner. Forget it. Once we start to notice how we respond, what messages we send and how these relate to our childhood patterns, we realise that unless we do something about it we are prisoners to decisions we made in infancy. Decisions that worked when we were two just may not win us that contract, gain the trust of our peers or get our subordinates to follow us on a risky mission.

To develop and maintain the kind of relationships that we are going to need in the fast-track world of the future, we are going to have to up the ante considerably. To do this, we are going to need a lot more self-awareness and much more skill at braiding our rational and non-rational selves and bringing them, through conversation, into relationships with a sea of people whose roles change continually.

A Word on Politics

While learning to relate as whole, full human beings enlivens individuals, promotes the successful functioning of networks, improves communication, increases innovation, facilitates strategic implementation and boosts performance, do not expect that it will be encouraged by business leaders. On the contrary, if they are living by the rules of addictive systems, you can expect them to wholeheartedly discourage healthy, braided conversation and mature adult relationships. When people and relationships function in a healthy braided way, people are bound to succeed by breaking the rules. This means they will raise and address problems quickly and effectively, they will openly express their feelings, communicate directly and be their own people. They will make themselves proud, listen to and respect their own needs, live in integrity with themselves, be very playful and constantly rock the boat. While this is good for both people and business, it is very bad for those addicted to maintaining the status quo. When healthy people do their thing, it shows up those living by the addictive rules to very bad advantage. Knowing this, those on the hero's journey need to pay very strong heed to the politics. This boils down to three things:

1. Test the waters.
2. Develop a strategy.
3. Get support.

The first thing you will need to do is make an honest assessment of the political lie of the land. Are your superiors sufficiently mature and psychologically healthy enough to deal with heroic relationships? If they are, carefully, very carefully, start braiding more of your emotional self into your relationship with your boss. Test the water. If they can cope with you expressing your truth, asking meaningful questions and operating, at least some of the time, in the social domain, gradually, very gradually, bring more of the heroic you into the relationship.

If you suspect that your boss is a dyed-in-the-wool warrior who will cut heroism off at the knees without thinking twice, you are going to have to be a little more skilful. First, remember that you can grow and develop as a human being and in a whole range of meaningful relationships in your life regardless of your boss's level of maturity, flexibility and insight. Stages one and two of the hero's quest need have nothing to do with anyone but yourself and your closest confidants. It is only when you reach stage three, integrating your learning into society, that your boss needs to be more than simply part of an ongoing lesson in growth, forgiveness and masterful handling of difficult relationships.

By the time you reach stage three, you should be so skilful at relationships, so sure of who you are, what you want and your inner power, that managing the boss will be a piece of cake. Mind you, this is because you will be so aware of your conscious and unconscious communication, so strategic in your approach and so sure of what you want that you could manage Genghis Khan. There is just one thing that you must never, ever forget and that is that your boss is just some man or woman doing a job as best they can given their personal history and all the strengths and weaknesses that that brings with it. The second you forget this and fall back into the childhood pattern of seeing the boss as mom or pop you are sunk. Forget about braiding, forget about strategy, forget about conversation. In fact, forget about everything. Once you have fallen unconsciously back into childhood patterns, once the boss becomes the big person, you don't stand a chance. When this happens, as it inevitably will, remember that it isn't the boss's fault; he or she is simply being themselves. It's you and your childhood patterns that have tripped you up.

All that means is that you need more support. As we saw in chapter 6, support is the key to beginning, staying on and profiting from the hero's journey. You will need emotional support, practical support and political support. This means you will have to go out and find like-minded people in your workplace and form networks with them. You will also need to find support in all the systems in which you interact—family, social, religious and community. You will then be ready to make your 50 per cent of every relationship you are in work for you, taking responsibility for everything you bring into those relationships.

Opening the Corporate Heart

The way to open the corporate heart is for individuals to open their own hearts. To do this without full recognition that corporations are both social and political systems would be naive and rather ill advised. However, with support, self-awareness, skill and commitment, the questing hero can increasingly braid their rational and non-rational selves, thus bringing more of who they are sanely and effectively into work- and home-based relationships. Although this makes good business sense, it can be very threatening to those warriors who are too frightened to grow and change with the times.

With the increased pace of change, there is a very good chance, however, that the warriors, by remaining inflexible, are rendering themselves increasingly redundant. In the chaotic world of today's business and government, all the rules (even the addictive ones) are breaking down. The more heroic you become, the more chance there is that you will overtake your boss on the road to success as well as on the road to mature adult functioning.

What is certain is that if you wait for conditions to be safe, perfect and sure, you will never start. If you hang out for someone (especially your boss) to give you permission to start questing, you may be redundant before you even begin. One of the things we learn from evolution theory is that the dominant species is always the slowest to change. They see less need than others to adapt to changes in the environment as they occur. This is why they often become extinct without realising what has hit them. So just know that your boss (unless he or she is an heroic quester) has a vested interest in keeping things just the way they are, with the systems he or she (the boss) understands and him or her (the boss) in charge. Know also that things are changing at a pace that seems to speed up daily and that if you want to survive, if you want to be a winner in the new system, adapting, changing, growing and remaining flexible are your main chances. The further you move along the hero's journey, the more you shift your centre of power away from the big people and switch into your own knowing, wisdom and growth, the more chance you have of getting (and keeping) it all.

Of course, this means you will have to feel how it feels to be you. You will have to face your inner demons, wound and pains, and take the risk of bringing more of yourself into relationships and increasingly take your own lead. This will make you vulnerable, compassionate and alive. You are the key to opening the corporate heart.

Chapter 8

Heroic Leadership

*The denial of power is as endemic
in our culture as the denial of feelings.*

KEVIN McVEIGH

Researching this chapter was not easy, something which had nothing to do with lack of writing on the subject. Leadership has to be one of the most heavily studied and addressed areas in current literature. The problem is that the leadership literature generally is so dry, so analytical and so devoid of emotion or real understanding of the human psyche that it seems to bear no resemblance to the reality of being a person taking the lead. We are in a period of discontinuous change. A period where the leaders of the future are those who see things differently, forge ahead with independent minds and courageous experimentation to lead the way for the more timid souls.

Moreover, as discussed in chapter 3, leaders will increasingly be assessed not just on their ability to make money for the shareholders, not just on their ability to achieve record profits, but also on their ability to do so in ways that are environmentally sound, humanly enhancing and socially responsible. To be all these things in an environment of chaotic change is no mean feat. We can look back through history and find people who have been better than average leaders on all these counts, but what we don't know—mostly because we haven't looked very hard—is what were the forces operating inside these people's psyches. There are a few notable exceptions to this, such as James Hillman and Manfred Kets De Vries.

What most leadership writers have done, however, is isolate certain behavioural characteristics and attitudes that seem to be shared by great leaders. Corporations have adopted these behaviours and attitudes as 'competencies', which they require their leaders to exhibit. Business schools have set up courses to train aspiring leaders in these leadership competencies. Meanwhile, we all go on complaining that we have never needed leaders more nor had more trouble finding them.

Great leaders, however, weren't trained to follow certain competencies. Great leaders were simply competent. There is a big difference—a difference writers on the subject have overlooked.

Business, having divorced feelings from emotion (i.e. words from body-felt senses), has missed the woods for the trees. Suppose you want to fall in love. You can do all the things someone in love does, such as send flowers and cards, go for moonlit walks together, indulge in romantic picnics and champagne breakfasts. You can see the best shows, dine in the best restaurants, meet each other's families and get to know each other's friends. If, however, there is no physical attraction, no emotional spark, no real liking, and if you share very different interests and values, no amount of acting like you are in love is actually going to make you in love. Being in love is not something that you do. Nor is it something that you achieve. Love is a strong emotion, that comes of its own accord when the conditions, the personalities and the time are right. Love does not come on cue and indeed it often comes when you least expect it or even when you don't want it. None of this has a whole lot to do with you being a loving person. Love comes even to the cold-hearted and ruthless. For these people, however, it rarely lasts.

What we also know about love is that it can build over time. One often hears of couples in arranged marriages who, through sharing their lives, children, troubles and joys over a lifetime, find, almost to their surprise, that they love their spouse even though they originally had no choice over whom they would marry. So, love is mysterious. It has a mind of its own. It is available to all. It can gradually build or be quickly destroyed by those who do not handle it with respect.

As with love, leadership can't be 'done', summoned on cue or even trained into us. Leadership is a gift often unbidden. It can build over time, but cannot be set as a goal and achieved. We can enhance our ability to lead, respect our leadership when it emerges and nurture it at every opportunity, but like love it is mysterious, powerful and has a mind of its own. Unfortunately executives, researchers and business writers have generally chosen to ignore the living reality of leadership. Instead they have worked hard to separate the reality of human heart and soul from the rational analysis of leadership. They have managed to convince us that if we just learn a few skills, practise a few 'competencies' and do a few more courses, we, too, can become leaders.

If we define leadership in terms of the skills, perspective and actions of the warrior, perhaps they are right. If, however, we are looking for more, if we want leaders with heart and soul, leaders with courage based on inner strength, wisdom and grace, if we want leaders with breadth of vision and depth of character, we are going to have to look in new directions, with new eyes and process what we find in new ways.

If we want real leadership, we are going to have to allow leaders to be real people. More than that, we will need to support them in developing themselves to their real depths, not by following some formula devised by studying warriors of old, but by supporting them in finding out who they are and of what they are made. More than this, we are going to have to develop our own heroism so that we can recognise real leadership when we come across it. In these days of the omnipresent media, we are used to judging leadership by 30-second sound bites and attractive appearance, missing entirely the quality of the person behind the public relations image. We want orators, diplomats and 'feel good' specialists, people who can inform, amuse and entertain us, so that we don't have to do the hard work of learning and growing for ourselves. Yet, we want leaders who can get results or, more particularly, who can convince us that they have gotten results. If we later find out that they got their results by exploiting child labour, misinforming the shareholders and bribing the unions, we let out a momentary shriek and then concentrate on admiring the individual's personal net worth, attractive new wife and most recent make-over.

So, good leadership has a lot to do with the leaders, but it also has a lot to do with the followers. Perhaps we have ended up with the leaders we deserve. Perhaps we have been looking for the wrong things in our leaders. Perhaps we have been spending billions of dollars training people the wrong way. Perhaps we are so ignorant about the human heart, mind and soul that we are babes in the woods when it comes to supporting the development of the kinds of leaders we need to guide us into the new age.

Leader as Parent

Unless we have significantly raised our consciousness, we relate to leaders from the perspective of old childhood drivers. Authority figures trigger our childhood patterns of reaction which, unless we are abnormally aware, have us re-enacting the childhood scripts we wrote at the feet of our parents. This habitually makes us see authority figures through the idealised perspective of the child, but also dressed in all the projected angers, pains and distrust that we built up against our parents for the big and small ways they let us down.

As a society, we ask a lot of parents. We ask them to provide children with love, care, emotional, spiritual and intellectual nourishment. We also expect them to provide food, clothing and adequate shelter. As a society, we provide parents with amazingly little support in doing this. Historically humans lived in tribes, then extended family units and then nuclear family groups. Today, however, up to 25 per cent of children are raised by single parents who live alone with their children. We also have a growing number of blended families. In these families, one parent brings his or her children to live with that parent's new partner and, in many cases, the new partner's children. Although children in blended families often end up with more than one mother, more than one father, numerous aunts, uncles and cousins and multiple sets of grandparents, the disharmony that often accompanies divorce can further isolate the children and their custodial parent from ongoing family support. More than that, both single-parent and blended families are often plagued by poverty, having too many mouths to feed and too few bread winners.

These children grow up with parents who are emotionally, physically and spiritually stretched to the limit. This situation is exacerbated by decreasing family support, extended financial demands and the breakdown of traditional realms of spiritual and community support. The quality of parenting that most children receive is less than optimal. Not because parents don't care, but because they have limited resources which are stretched past their ability to cope. As our first model of leadership is in our relationship (or lack thereof) with our parents, this is the source of our earliest and often most potent ideas about leadership. From this perspective, we tend to see leaders as people who look after us and tell us what to do, as well as how and when to do it. We see leaders as knowledgeable, powerful and strong, capable of handling any situation that comes along, never showing us their fears and weaknesses, but simply getting on with the job of making the family, business or world work. In return, we seek to attract and keep the esteem and affection of the leader. We want the leader to notice us, to reward our best efforts with a thank you or word of praise. We want to know that we belong and are appreciated. To achieve this we are prepared to work very hard.

I remember once being told by the leadership team of a large organisation that they were very unhappy about the results of a recent culture survey. It turned out that people throughout their organisation complained that they didn't see the leaders often enough. The leaders, however, were constantly travelling—roaming far and wide to visit their numerous branches. They were constantly meeting staff, noticing their work, asking for their ideas and giving praise. For the staff, however, these visits seemed few and far between. 'How can we,' asked the leaders, 'possibly travel any more? We rarely see our families as it is.'

It seemed to me that the problem wasn't that the leaders didn't travel enough, but that the staff had elevated the leaders to such a position of importance that they were in heavy demand. I could visualise petulant children whining because daddy wasn't home enough. And most daddies aren't home very much, even those who haven't abandoned their families spend so much time at work and travelling that they are ghosts in the night, visiting home far less often than their children would like. So we grow up with the idea of daddies not being available and being stressed, tired and emotionally distant when they are around. Mummies, too, even when they are home all the time, are often tired, overextended and undersupported. So young children learn to 'be good', look after themselves and do whatever seems to work to have their needs met or at least gain some attention. In childhood, we idolise our parents and what they are capable of doing for us. Yet our authority figures receive more than our childhood veneration. They are also the unknowing recipients of projected childhood anger, fears, resentments and frustration.

When it comes to leadership, what we want is very clear—perfection. This means something entirely different to each person. In short, however, we want leaders who care about us (as deeply as the idealised parent), who are omniscient (can foresee the future and plan for it), who are omnipotent (can protect us from harm, injury, pain and loss) and who are tolerant and accepting of our behaviour, attitudes and us being exactly as we are. In return, we seek their approval, yet secretly we don't trust them, don't believe them and doubt their power. When they fall, we see no reason to lend them a hand—after all, they have failed to live up to our expectations.

Under these conditions, it is pretty impossible for any leader to fit the bill. So, as anyone who tries is likely to fail, you may as well go for the image. If you are smooth, attractive and have the right PR machine, at least you can achieve some acclaim.

One of my clients is a short man who told me the following story. He had gotten into a lift on the bottom floor of the high-rise building owned by the company in which he was a general manager. As people entered the elevator, he moved further and further into a rear corner, until he had become invisible to the new entrants. He realised this as the lift ascended and people towards the front started talking about him. What completely amazed him was that the motivations and implications they read into his actions bore no resemblance at all to his own. He realised after much reflection that people were perceiving him not as he was, but as a projection of their childhood images of leadership. He felt there were three solutions to this problem. One was personal, one was relationship and one was marketing. On the personal level, he needed to grow in awareness and inner strength, learning more about himself, what he wanted and where he was going. Secondly, he needed to bring this into deep personal relationship with the people closest to him. Thirdly, he needed to decide the three things he wished to convey to those more distant from him and engage in a marketing campaign to get his message across.

If people respond unconsciously to leaders as a function of their childhoods, rather than who the leader is and how they behave, then leaders are forced to manage impressions skillfully. Unfortunately, we have moved into an era where impression management has become the main game rather than something incidental along the way. As long as we, the followers, remain unconscious of what we project onto our leaders, our leaders will have to manage us as they would children and, in a media age, this means a strong concentration on public image.

Love and Leadership

Impression management in the world of the warrior is obviously very important. However, one cannot help asking whether it is just concern over their leadership skills that keeps leaders so interested in how they appear. Here again we need to look beneath the surface to find out what is actually going on. In chapter 6, we saw that much of the senseless driven behaviour that warriors exhibit in the workplace is propelled not by some logical strategy, nor as a response to the environment around them, but as a neurotic response to feelings of loss of love. Due to our lack of consciousness, we have confused success and power with our desire to be loved and many of us hold the unconscious belief that if only we are sufficiently powerful and successful we will be more lovable. The deep-seated nature of this desire combined with our lack of awareness have us confuse attention and love.

We seek, therefore, to be noticed, even if we have to behave poorly to attract attention. Yet inside we feel hollow, unfulfilled and alone. This, of course, feeds the addiction. As we feel so unfulfilled by what we *are* getting, we seek to get more, rather than realising that no amount of public acclaim, fame, fortune, power or success will compensate for love. Love is its own reward. Only love feeds our need to be loved. Love is not power, status, attention or success. It is an emotion.

Warriors, being totally out of touch with their own emotions and psyche, overlook this fact and become so dazzled by their neurotic games that they become busier and busier in the ceaseless, senseless attempt to fill their inner void with attention, power, status and worldly success. Unfortunately, many leaders are totally in the grip of this crazy line of subliminal reasoning. This is what unconsciously propels many to seek positions of power and authority in the first place. It is also one of the reasons that people fight so fiercely to protect the addictive rules of organisations which inherently support neurotic ambitions and behaviour.

Leaders who seek power and status because of unsurfaced desires for unmet childhood needs cannot be relied upon to make sane, rational decisions that are in the common good. What we would expect from people operating out of such a high level of unconsciousness is exactly what we get: behaviour aimed at winning attention and approval. In other words, warrior leaders are slaves to public opinion and the approval of their bosses and peers. When this is your motivation, impression management becomes exceptionally important. This is why warrior leaders will sacrifice results for the addictive rules. Operating out of the addictive rules, they feel they can sufficiently control the situation and so ensure that they always look good. The addictive system tells us to beware of anyone who raises an issue, uncovers a problem or introduces a new idea that may have the warrior leader look anything less than invincible, omniscient and statesmanlike. It also tells us to beware of anyone who wants to deal with reality rather than massage the warrior leader's public image. The strength of this imperative drives warrior leaders to congregate, read the same journals and conform to the same etiquette, ensuring that they always know the rules by which they will be judged, constantly avoiding those who would open up new avenues for radically different thought and behaviour.

Several years ago I was asked by a professor of strategy to address his MBA class on a concept I had developed called 'Strategy in Motion'. Strategy in Motion is the holistic art of working out what organisations want and then making it happen, bearing in mind that the world is in a constant state of change and that people are more than rational economic units. At the time of addressing this MBA class, I was advising very senior leaders (the students' bosses) and I foolishly thought that I might have carried some weight with the audience. I innocently launched into my lecture on looking at how the business world was changing and how this change would require very different ways of thinking, reacting and behaving for tomorrow's leaders. I spent some time concentrating on the need to develop and braid our emotions with our rational thought if we as leaders were to be optimally effective. It was about this time that the group pounced. They did whatever they could to destroy my arguments and my personal credibility. This was not a gentlemanly intellectual debate; this was a vicious personal attack. I was shocked and surprised and spent some time afterwards working with my professional advisers to uncover what had happened.

The answer gradually emerged. The students I was addressing were part-time students. They were working all day in responsible positions in organisations and were spending their evenings and weekends studying to upgrade their qualifications. The course they had chosen was totally unbraided, there being a total separation of thought and emotion, and a complete denial of the latter. In short, these people were making a huge personal investment and, in many cases, heavy sacrifices to achieve a qualification that I was naively telling them was misguided and obsolete. I had no intention of being insulting, but by telling my truth I had threatened the current cornerstone of their existence. The viciousness of the attack I received could only be explained by understanding the strength of the emotions my address had stirred.

To explain this a little more fully, we need to explore the concept of projective identification. This is a process that happens when individuals, singly or in groups, are unable to deal with strong emotions when they arise. When individuals cannot cope with their emotions, they unconsciously create conditions that enable another person to get a taste of the disturbing emotions that they themselves are unable to handle. In other words, incapable of coping with the emotions themselves, they pass them on to someone else.

What this MBA class passed on to me was a feeling of being attacked at a deep and life-threatening level. They went for the jugular. What they were letting me know, the only way they knew how, was that my innocent description of business trends and suggestions on appropriate responses to such trends felt to them like annihilation. This was a matter of life and death. Obviously, on a rational adult level, this makes no sense at all. On a primal child level, however, it makes perfect sense. If they couldn't get love by doing what they were doing, if all the sacrifice of doing further study wasn't going to lead to more success and power, how could they, as individuals, survive.

It doesn't take a great deal of intelligence to work out that leadership from this place is not very healthy, nor likely to lead the corporation, the society or the world to its fullest possibilities. It is also why warriors will fight so hard to keep things the same and to ensure compliance to the addictive rules.

Upward Management

An improved knowledge of people's psychological drivers gives us greater insight into managing upwards—handling the boss with skill. As we have seen, when most people look up, they see mummy or daddy, and immediately seek to have their childhood needs met. Leaders, however, are likely to have fought hard to succeed because they desperately seek love, attention and affirmation. They want to be stroked and appreciated, as much, if not more, than everybody else. When we approach leaders, as most people do, from an unconscious position of childhood need, we come seeking love, not giving it. When, however, we can see our leaders as human beings doing a job, as much in need of support and care as everybody else, and can approach them from this position, we have a good chance of establishing a productive adult-to-adult working relationship with our leaders. They then come to see us as someone who is dependable, supportive and trustworthy. When we come seeking love, approval and direction our leaders come to see us as dependent children, people who have to be looked after and who are therefore inherently unstable and untrustworthy.

Simon was the managing director of a subsidiary of a large company. He was sent to me by the board because he was seen as needing help with his leadership. It turned out that when Simon had joined his current company, he had come in with a sense of power. He had demanded that he be given his own board of directors and that he report to the managing director of the parent company obliquely through this board. As time went by, the main board decided to abolish the board of the subsidiary. Simon found himself reporting directly to the parent company's managing director through the main board. At about the same time, the main board started to undergo major political turmoil. There was friction between two groups within the board. Somehow in all of this Simon, despite record profits in the company for which he was responsible, became the focus of the board's unfavourable attention. Just before he was sent to see me, he had been asked to find a replacement for himself and plan his staged exit over a period of twelve months. Simon was understandably shocked. He had been nothing but obliging and helpful to the board. His company was performing at the highest level in years. Why was he being evicted from the company's inner sanctum?

As we discussed these issues, we discovered that Simon had grown up as the only child of two powerful and socially well-placed parents. He was used to handling conflict and gaining love by agreeing with his parents and doing what they wanted. He found space to be himself in pursuits outside the home such as sport and at school, where his success was a further stimulus for the attentions and praise of his parents. In other words, he gained love by being obedient and succeeding in socially acceptable ways. He was, of course, using these same tactics with the members of the main board. He was being a good boy, but they weren't responding as his parents had responded.

Faced with internal conflict and infighting, the members of the board felt under threat. They had to make a choice between facing their problems and working them through or remaining unconscious and distracting attention away from their own troubles by using someone else as a scapegoat. Who better to choose than someone who avoided conflict and took the attack lying down, thereby helping the board to offload its emotional garbage and avoid personal responsibility for making their relationships work?

What took place was a perfect example of projective identification. Unable to deal with their own incompetence, the members of the board projected it onto Simon, who began thinking that maybe, despite all evidence to the contrary, the board was right. The combination of the board's behaviour and Simon's eagerness to avoid conflict had the effect of making Simon look even more untrustworthy. Would you trust someone to look after your investment if that person refused to fight for fairness and their own human dignity?

The more Simon stayed in his own patterns of compliance, the more he eroded both his own confidence and his position in the eyes of the board. Once we brought all these things to the surface, it took Simon no time at all to decide that the way out of the situation was to stand up and be counted. He consciously chose to reverse his own childhood patterns, embrace conflict and hand back to the board their problems and discord. In short, he decided that if being a 'good boy' wasn't working, he'd try growing up. When charged unfairly, he would protest, ask searching questions and highlight his company's achievement. Remaining aware of the board members' personal needs for affirmation and esteem, he chose to spend time with each board member in private, helping them to understand that he cared for and supported each of them personally and that his only intention was to gain the maximum result for everybody. Over a period of three months, Simon was told that he no longer had to look for a replacement, his own subsidiary board was re-established and he was given a pay rise. By dealing with each party's need for love, we had solved a major strategic problem.

It's pretty obvious that if people are behaving out of unconscious childhood patterns, they are not likely to perform optimally nor to face the reality of our changing world authentically. Unaware people just don't see straight. If we respond to people and situations as a function of our unmet childhood needs, we are hardly going to make rational decisions based on logical assessment of the situation. That people are unconscious of their deep-seated motivation does not excuse the crazy, irrational behaviour they exhibit. Culling favour, attention and acclaim, projecting uncomfortable emotions onto others and refusing to face up to our own drivers are hardly sound bases for making the world a better place, leading for optimal performance or happy living.

If you doubt that the social dynamics that I have outlined above actually exist, may I invite you to look at what has happened to great leaders who have encouraged people to think past their unconscious childhood patterns. Great leaders who have encouraged people to grow up emotionally and spiritually, if they are skilful in their questioning and persuasive in their storytelling, have always been at risk. Look, for instance, at the fate of John the Baptist, who lost his head to Herod for daring to question Herod's liaison with his sister-in-law. Or Jesus' fate at the hands of the Pharisees, whose power he questioned. Then there are Gandhi, Martin Luther King and Socrates. All people who, through clear thinking, intelligent questioning and powerful storytelling, threatened those in positions of power by having them query their own motivations. When under threat, warriors attack.

Developing Heroic Leadership

This is the climate in which the questing hero must develop. This makes the fear of beginning felt at stage one very real indeed. Deciding to go on the hero's journey can be scary enough when you think all you have to face is your inner demons, but when we see our great heroes brought down by heartless and frightened warriors, it can be all we need to retreat to the comfort of conformity. Most therapeutic techniques demand emotional safety and yet our warriors do their best to show us that the world isn't safe and that we, like them, should become and stay as warriors if we are to succeed. Common sense, however, says that environmental changes will bring rewards to those who are different—the unreasonable ones.

If we overcome our fear of starting on the hero's journey, the threat of attack from warriors who are constantly terrified of searching questions, functional difference and those who stand out from the crowd, can contribute greatly to the trials of stage two. As heroes move forward on their quests, discovering their inner depths, they can be magnificently assisted by warriors whose antics, games and ongoing posturing can provide a plethora of trials through which questing heroes can pit their strength, hone their skills and expand their knowledge so that when these heroes reach stage three, they are well equipped to form the bridge between what they now know is possible and the limited and ill-guided reality of the warrior. All this adds spice and pitch to the hero's journey. That the journey has challenges and hardships only makes it more interesting. The difficulty of the voyage only leads heroes to greater fullness and satisfaction when they succeed.

Warriors will be warriors, but they pay a high price. While they may attain power and success, they never get to really enjoy it, as it is always a substitute, a totally unfulfilling compensation for what they are actually after. Their whole game (and unfortunately their life) is unrewarding and hollow, and no amount of wonderful holidays, beautiful courtesans, glamorous clothes, face lifts, stylish nights out and important friends is going to change that.

What the hero realises, in contrast, is that it doesn't have to be either/or. You can have all the rewards of a warrior and be loved, fulfilled, joyful and at peace. To do this, however, you need to bring to the surface your unmet childhood drivers and deal with them from the grounded perspective of the adult you now are. Know yourself is wise advice for the would-be hero.

This is easier to say than to do. For one thing, it is very difficult to see ourselves exactly as we are. This is where the heroic guide comes in. An heroic guide can hold up a mirror for us in which we can more clearly see ourselves and our motivations. We can also seek and listen carefully to feedback—remembering always that feedback tells us as much about the giver as it does about the receiver. Again, this is why the heroic guide is a good source of feedback. Knowing themselves and their motivations, heroic guides (being well down the track on the hero's quest) are much less likely to project their unconscious fears, doubts and concerns onto you.

Receiving clear, accurate feedback isn't necessarily comfortable. Who likes to see their own warts, scars and inadequacies? Who wants to feel their own pains and wounds, or deal with their inner demons? The difference between heroic questers and warriors is that heroes choose to deal with their unconscious matter, to take personal responsibility for their hurts, whereas warriors choose to remain unconscious and project their fears, doubts, scars and injuries onto others. Through their own growth, no matter how uncomfortable that may be, heroes learn to see the world as it actually is, whereas warriors see reality through a veil of unconscious projections that have much more to do with yesterday than today. When the world was more static and less complex, when change was continuous rather than discontinuous, the warrior's ways worked perfectly well. Today, remaining in the unconscious world of an infant is a recipe for disaster, both on a personal level for the warrior and an interpersonal level for everyone they affect. Nobody can force warriors to go on the hero's quest. They must choose to do that for themselves. However, everybody suffers if they don't.

My big complaint about most leadership and organisational change programs is that they introduce skills, techniques and competencies. These simply help the warrior to be a better warrior for a short period of time, i.e. they assist the continuation of the unconscious game when what is needed is for warriors to feel the need to go questing so that they can change their game altogether. We need support, however, to change our game. We need strong people around us providing truthful and helpful feedback. We need other heroes who can share the trials and tribulations of their journey with us. We need heroic guides to hold up the mirror, support our courage and lend us their wisdom. We need political support so that we can withstand the neurotic games of the warriors. We need emotional support so that our need for love is sufficiently met so that we don't have to displace this outwards, thus fostering our neurotic compensations. We need spiritual support so that we can remember that the quest is worth the prize, that we are not alone and that we are part of the human community. We need opportunities to tell our stories, speak our emotional truths, thus learning more and more about who we are. If we have all these things we might be able to deal with the truth of our inner world, the shocking reality of our unconscious realm. If we have all these things, we may come to accept the fullness of our own humanity.

'When we recognise our shortcomings, acknowledge and accept them openly, true wisdom is ours,' write Chungliang Al Huang and Jerry Lynch in *Mentoring*, then 'we open up to the greatness within us'. However, they warn us not to expect perfection. It is perfectly human to have weaknesses, faults, doubts and fears which we may never understand or overcome. The aim of the exercise isn't to live up to some ideal standard of excellence (the eighty competencies for human perfection don't exist). The heroes' goal is to make conscious who they are so that they have choice over their actions and responses, not so they can control themselves and the world around them. In fact, our perceived 'imperfections' may actually be our greatest strengths. Al Huang and Lynch remind us that many twisted, knotted trees reach old age precisely because they are useless to the builder. Perfect trees make great furniture.

I find this time and again with my clients. The leader that thinks he is too soft has great strengths in building compassionate, intimate relationships that lead to deals based on outstanding trust. The woman who feels she is rejected by those around her realises that it is her strength and competence that is causing others to find her powerful and unapproachable because of their own fears of inadequacy. The quiet, 'shy' person turns out to be a great observer of human behaviour and becomes a great writer, the sensitive person turns out to be a budding hero; the warrior, through self-awareness, turns his strength to great personal and strategic advantage. Women, having spent years in child rearing, develop patience, understanding and interpersonal skills that take them later in life to leadership positions of great heights. The rape survivor discovers an inner strength and ability to help others of which they were previously unaware.

In truth, humanity is wonderful, if we choose to see it that way, raise our consciousness, accept the truth of who we are and learn at the level of heart and soul from everything that happens to us. This, of course, is the road to wisdom and inner peace. It is also the way to see reality as it is, which in turn allows us to think and act strategically.

Strategic Leadership

Leadership in conditions of discontinuous change is 'like being a catcher in a trapeze act hanging from a high wire shouting to your people, "Yo. Jump. Trust me. No I haven't done it before either."' Leading people courageously into an unknown future is a terrifying responsibility, especially when we can no longer rely on trends from the past to guide the way. Apart from a radical self-confidence on the level of heart and soul, heroic success in leadership under conditions of chaotic change demands that we learn to see patterns and opportunities as they emerge. In times of discontinuous change, we can no longer rely on specific cause-and-effect links. Now we have to rearrange paradoxes using intuition and newly developed perception. This is best done through dynamic, challenging debate amd conversations with others. Strategic leadership in times of rapid change, therefore, involves building strong, robust relationships, raising our awareness of ourselves, others and our environment, and growing personally in terms of heroic self-confidence, emotional maturity, ability to relate on a dynamic and meaningful level, and learning to create meaning from paradox and rapidly changing patterns.

This, says Ralph Stacey in *Managing Chaos*, is the foundation of strategic thinking. When strategy is a static form of analysis resulting in a blueprint for action, it is just too slow and out of date for today's world. Leaders need to be thinking, acting and relating strategically all the time, continuously perceiving, processing, conversing, debating, acting and reviewing. They don't have time to wait for the documentation to be written.

Strategy is simply jargon for being sufficiently clear about what you want and sufficiently in touch with yourself, those around you and your environment to be in a position to create, notice and capitalise on opportunities, thus ensuring you achieve your long- and medium-term objectives. In a changing world, this means you have to think constantly on your feet, be continually reading and re-reading the environment and have relationships with all-important parties that are strong enough to withstand the constant twists and turns that successfully traversing changing terrain demands.

This is a reality-based model of leadership and strategy which rests on two basic premises:

1. People will be people (which means you constantly have to relate on both an emotional and rational level, dealing with your own and other people's conscious and unconscious drivers).

2. Reality is ambiguous, paradoxical, chaotic and always changing—the recipes of the past may be worse than inadequate in helping you to achieve your strategic goals. They may actually undermine your chances of doing so.

Thus strategic leadership is about being sufficiently emotionally robust that you can dwell in a place of conscious uncertainty and active relationship for long enough to allow change in your ways of perceiving and acting in the world. This is an extremely challenging path psychologically.

The hero has no difficulties dealing with these facts. The warrior pretends that they don't exist or can be overcome by tricks, new techniques, better means of control or impression management. Warriors fool themselves into believing that by staying physically fit (so they can manage the stress), learning to acquire better skills in oratory and 'media management', employing the best consultants in strategic analysis and bringing in the specialist in culture change, all will be well. Deep in their hearts, however, they know that it is all too slow, too cumbersome and too inefficient.

There is a radically different and effective alternative. This is to clarify your thinking (through seeing things differently), raise your self-awareness (thus freeing up your private blocks to strategic vision and personal effectiveness), develop your relationships on an intimate level (which is the place of radical trust) and get in touch with your emotions, heart and soul, thus unleashing your intuition and putting yourself in immediate contact with the world as it changes. In short, the route to strategic leadership is the hero's quest.

Heroic Heart—Tough Love

As we have seen, the fears that warriors face when contemplating the hero's quest are that they will become too vulnerable, too open and too tender. They think that their defensive warrior ways protect them from the dangers of competition and attack, and allow them to survive and succeed in the rough and tumble of business. Yet, heroes are actually much tougher than warriors. Let's have a look why.

Warriors, as we have seen, are driven by the unconscious craving to compensate for unmet childhood needs. This makes them very susceptible to the approval, acclaim, affirmation and attention of others. Due to differences in personal socialisation, the defences that individuals build around their inner drivers are unique to them. One person may be a pleaser, another creates attention by being a bully, another makes embarrassing mistakes or plays the fool. All these defences are aimed at protecting the individual from feeling their own pain and gaining enough compensation to fill the void left by childhood deficit. These defences and the childhood patterns they mask become the warrior's Achilles heel, their Shakespearean tragic flaw. Furthermore, being unconscious, these personal weaknesses lie in the individual's blind spot, meaning that they often surface only when it is too late to take appropriate corrective action.

Some years ago, I worked with a man who had been employed by a large public company to bring about massive cultural change. My client, let's call him Peter, was a highly intelligent, creative person with a very charismatic personality. He saw his task as a guerilla war, empowering the legions of foot solders within the organisation to take up the instruments of personal liberation by working stealthily and strategically together to ease power away from the organisation's leaders, who Peter saw as the dishonest 'forces of darkness'.

Originally, because of his creativity, intelligence and personal charisma, the change program was a great success. As people felt more powerful and as they worked more cooperatively with their peers, their work performance improved markedly. The organisation's leaders, despite the obvious increase in effectiveness in those areas where Peter and his team worked, were not happy. They exhibited their unhappiness by making Peter and his team redundant just as their programs were really taking off and gaining momentum. The corporation's leaders claimed that the organisation no longer needed in-house change agents and a decision had been made to terminate the expense of carrying such a unit.

Peter's warrior ways had worked to some degree, but something obviously had gone wrong. In my personal sessions with Peter, I discovered that he had been the eldest male in a family of ten children. His father was the 'typical absent-minded professor', who apparently had no time or interest in children. He was constantly engrossed in a book or his own thoughts, making him totally unavailable to his offspring. Peter's mother was so fully occupied bearing and caring for her brood that she, too, was emotionally out of reach. Peter learnt early that contacting the big people on any emotional level was impossible. He therefore decided to get his love needs met by his siblings and became 'king of the kids'. He organised his brothers and sisters into a rebellious crew who ran the home to their own objectives, meeting their own needs, supporting each other and creating their own subculture.

Secretly Peter resented his father ferociously—a fact that he acknowledged, but refused to deal with in any depth. 'Why cause problems and bring up old issues,' he protested. The old issues, however, kept coming up by themselves. By playing out his old patterns, by getting his love needs met at forty-six years of age in the same way he had at six years of age, Peter tripped himself up. The organisation's leaders had become the father whom he so deeply resented. He unconsciously transmitted this to them at every meeting. He refused to listen to their fears and doubts, and continually refused to acknowledge their needs. Still 'king of the kids', he had stirred up the little people, which only served to increase the unconscious insecurities of the bosses. Peter was devastated when he and his team were evicted from the corporate nest. From where I sat, Peter, through his refusal to deal with unconscious childhood patterns, hurts and fears, had brought the situation on himself.

Warriors do this to themselves time and again. They insanely believe that by repressing, ignoring and denying their psychological make-up, they can remain strong, in control and invincible. In fact, they simply undermine their ability to choose strategically sound and personally enhancing actions, responses and relationships.

I spend a lot of time talking with clients about 'tough love'. Originally a concept developed to help parents deal with wayward teenagers, tough love is about realising how your patterns of relationship, response and behaviour are affecting your way of being in the world around you. Most of us have a tendency to save those we care about or those we want to impress from the consequences of their actions. While this reinforces in others their dependence on us, it also reinforces their inappropriate, negative and self-destructive behaviour. It is as if we collude with those we protect to keep our relationship with them, their behaviour and thus our lives the same, even if the same is not what we claim we want. Of course, you've guessed that the reason we do this is we want love and we are frightened that if we stand up to people, give honest feedback or simply let them feel the consequences of their actions they will withdraw their love. In some weird, neurotic way, we also think that by colluding with them to keep things the same we can remain in control. By letting the people around us hear, see and feel the truth, we fear that they will grow and change and we will lose control or, more terrifyingly, be left alone. So we actually save others, not as we so often claim, because we love them but because we fear the emotional consequences for ourselves if we don't.

Warriors are masters of collusion. In order to maintain control and in their habitual compensation for unmet childhood needs, they continually save anyone who is significant to them. This, of course, keeps people dependent, stunts their growth, promotes the status quo and helps the warrior to feel more in control. It also gives them something to complain about and allows them to feel superior.

Tough love is simply getting out of your own way for long enough to allow people to feel the consequences of their actions. So, if your children take drugs, you allow them to go to gaol. You don't cover up, lie and cheat for them (to protect the family name or their chances of making you proud through undertaking a career in law). If your boss wants you to cover him while he slips out with his mistress every second lunch hour, you find some polite way of refusing and, if confronted, tell your truth. If your employees are not performing to expectations, you tell them so clearly and honestly, providing guidelines for sought-after improvements and openly spelling out your expectations. If you are given the boss's son as an offsider and he isn't up to scratch, you get out of the way and let him fall on his face, thus allowing him to learn how he needs to grow and improve.

Tough love requires incredible inner strength, tenacity, integrity, courage and skill in communication. It also requires considerable support from like-minded others. We are quick in our society to brand as heartless someone who doesn't mop up, fish out and save others from the consequences of their actions— particularly in corporations where the addictive rules insist that there are no problems, that everyone must be strong, good, right and perfect, and where we must never be 'selfish', the social pressure to avoid tough love is colossal. Telling the truth, letting people learn from their mistakes and dealing with conflict that arises when we don't save people are guaranteed ways to rock the boat, something most warriors go out of their way to avoid.

If, however, we don't practise tough love, people don't mature emotionally. By protecting others, we rob them of the opportunity to learn at a deep, personal level; we hinder their progress on the hero's quest and train them to be and remain as warriors. This not only limits their chances for deep personal fulfilment and strategic success in a rapidly changing world, but it also undermines the organisation's possibilities for outstanding success. Saving, colluding with and protecting others is a sure-fire way to avoid becoming a 'learning organisation'. Learning organisations practise tough love, support people to go on the hero's quest and insist that all the addictive rules of organisations are broken all the time.

Graham is one of my big success stories. He was the managing director of a successful family company and as such was responsible for the employment of several of his relatives, one of whom (Linden) had for several years been receiving a huge salary (around $500, 000) for, it appeared, doing very little. Everybody resented Linden—his siblings, his staff and Graham all complained to each other that Linden was a wastrel who took a lot and contributed very little. To his face, they treated Linden politely; behind his back, they all whinged about his lack of competence and greed. This situation had been going on for decades, with the offender being continually 'saved' by everybody, including, in fact especially, Graham. Nobody had ever expressed to poor Linden how angry and resentful he or she was that he received such a large salary and contributed apparently so little.

Graham, a true heroic quester, came to understand the reasons behind his 'saviour behaviour' and the resentment that it incurred. More than that, he came to see how totally unfair it was to Linden to not provide honest feedback, thus giving him the dignity of making real choices about his behaviour. Furthermore, because no one had ever told Linden how he or she felt, he had never seen any reason for, nor been given the opportunities to, engage in serious ongoing training. Linden was being kept by the entire family as a man-child, living in a web of lies and deceit all woven to 'protect' his feelings.

When the showdown actually happened and Graham told Linden of his disappointment and resentment about Linden's salary viz-a-viz his added value to the firm, Linden was given an opportunity to behave like a man, which to his great credit he did. Linden took the criticism on the chin, agreed to lower his salary, engage in serious training and commit to meeting clearly spelt out objectives. For the first time in his working life, Linden had been given and had taken the opportunity of being his own man. He had been given the opportunity to grow, which he wisely took. The amount of courage that it took for Graham to break the family silence and speak the truth was colossal. He and I spent weeks working through his childhood issues about family, relationships and rescuing others. We also practised the skills of giving clear, honest feedback in a non-threatening and relationship enhancing way. This was done largely through the use of 'I' statements described in full in *Peaceful Chaos*.

Through the heroic practice of tough love, Graham was not only able to help Linden grow and regain his dignity, but also to improve his relationships and become a valuable asset to the company. Through this process, Graham and Linden's relationship improved markedly as their mutual respect grew. While Graham had risked giving up control in order to tell Linden the truth (thus triggering his fears of vulnerability and loss of love), the toughness of his actions set an heroic example of leadership that Linden was then able to follow.

While warriors toe the line, stick to the status quo and avoid rocking the boat, heroes do what needs to be done, say what needs to be said and ask what needs to be asked. In short, they lead the way forward rather than fighting to hold on to their current position. This tends to make heroic leaders look rather eccentric. Contrary to popular rhetoric, leaders are not good 'team players'. Heroic leaders are too strongly themselves. Being true to their own opinion, beliefs, intuitions and vision, heroic leaders continually disagree, stir up conflict and refuse to go along with the pack. They are mavericks and nonconformists. What makes the difference between a ratbag and a hero is that heroic leaders have superb skills in relationship and communication. They might ruffle your feathers, but somehow they can make you feel good about it and motivate you to follow their lead, even while you fume that your sensibilities have been affronted.

Heroic leaders are very real, very alive and outrageously themselves. This is so novel, so unusual in organisations and a society where conformity is so dearly sought and heavily rewarded, that heroic leaders can take your breath away. In doing this, they well up both our love and admiration (particularly our childhood needs for heroic parenting) and our anger and resentment (particularly our childhood projections of anger, fear, doubt and pain.) They both attract and repel us. If we want good leadership, if we want to play our part in making the world a better place, we are going to have to grow to the extent that we can bring to the surface and make conscious our response to heroic leaders—real people who are taking the lead. Otherwise, out of our own lack of awareness, we may serve to thwart, undermine and disempower the very people who are likely to lead us forward to a better world.

Of course, the more we do this, the more we discover that we, too, are heroic leaders. In supporting our leaders, we learn and grow; we, too, go on the heroic quest. As we do this, we may find, quite to our surprise, that we, too, have created a following—people who turn to us for guidance and support, people who seek our wisdom, insight and vision. In working to support those who are on the heroic quest, we may well find that we, without asking to do so, have become leaders in our own right. If we then cherish this gift of leadership, cherish our own heart and soul, constantly raise our awareness, build and use our support systems and nurture our relationships, we may discover in the depths of our being the courage, clarity, integrity, strength and purpose that make us stand out from the crowd. When you stride forward from this position, you are likely to notice that there is a whole mass of people following you. Not because you crave and have sought their affirmation or acclaim, not because you have exploited their need for parental love and guidance, not because you have successfully managed your public image, but because you are a real person with strong relationships who knows what he or she wants and where he or she is going. As you let go of the trapeze bar and lurch forward, you are likely to find hundreds of loving hands stretched out before you, offering real commitment, real energy, real relationship and real love. By being true to yourself, you are likely to find all the things that those who drive themselves forward in delusion so desperately crave and never achieve.

By gaining yourself, knowing yourself, trusting yourself and accepting yourself (warts and all), you will become the kind of leader that the world so desperately needs. With so much inside you, however, you will remain your own person and thus lead from a place so strong, so secure and so powerful you will never lose your way, no matter how turbulent the weather, or rough the terrain. You will have discovered the secret to heroic leadership.

Chapter 9

The Heroic Mysteries

Infinite nature, which is boundless Spirit, unutterable,
not intelligible, outside of all imagination, beyond all essence,
unnamable, known only to the heart.

ROBERT FLUDD, HISTORY OF MACROCOSM

Many of the things that happen to us as we travel along the heroic path surpass rational understanding. Although it includes the realm of emotion, heroic endeavour is much more than that. So much of what I see in my own life and in the lives of my heroic clients transcends the boundaries of logic. There is something quite mystical about the heroic journey, something that I would rather gratefully and unquestionably receive than analyse. As the nuclear physicists have discovered, often in our endeavours to understand and explain, we can actually change, even destroy, the phenomena we are trying to diagnose. There is a fragility in the great powers of the mysterious, a fragility that we must respect and cherish if we are to work skilfully with those powers and put them to good use.

The Sacred Doll

Mary has been one of my clients for some years. When she first came to see me, she had just been asked to act in an organisation development role, having previously been a specialist in equal employment opportunities. In our early sessions, Mary created a vision of how she would like her life to be. This included marrying her current partner, feeling more powerful and confident in herself and being permanently appointed to her new role (which would constitute a promotion and thus bring with it a raise in her income and allocation of a car). She also had some ambitious work-based goals.

Within a period of nine months, Mary had achieved her vision in all but one key area. She had indeed met her work-based targets, had had a romantic wedding and, she claimed, was for the first time in her life, worry free. It was almost as if her confidence and inner feelings of power had grown to such an extent that there was no room for the normal self-doubts and small worries that had previously preoccupied her mind. Mary's income had risen, as she had hoped, but through the unexpected source of an inheritance. Despite some impressive achievements at work, however, Mary still found that she had not been confirmed in her new role. She also felt that the salary she was receiving was way below what she believed she deserved. The car, too, was yet to materialise.

At this stage, Mary participated in a group session on neutral masks (see chapter 7). It is a mysterious thing, but when different people put on one of those papier-mâché masks and turn silently to face the group, unexplainable things happen. Some people look older, some younger, some smaller, some bigger, some smarter, some more stupid. This all happens with their face concealed and in total silence. A fifty-year-old woman, masked, may present as a twenty-year-old girl, a thirty-year-old woman as a teenage boy, a sweet-natured man as a jolly, green giant and another as Darth Vader. When the group provides these individuals with feedback, we discover that the fifty-year-old woman feels like a twenty-year-old trapped in an ageing body. The middle-aged woman lives her life full of energy and constant activity, only putting down the paint brush to pick up the tennis racket. The sweet-natured man is frightened of his personal power and Darth Vader is a man who is desperately trying to be cleaner than clean. With his words and face, he can belie his darker side; masked, his shadow shines brightly for all to see.

When Mary put on the neutral mask and turned to face the group, I saw a sacred doll. Other people in the group politely acknowledged my impression, but quickly slipped on to more explainable images. Still, Mary was for me a sacred doll and only a sacred doll. Later in the session, Mary raised with the group that she had her annual performance review the next day and that she wanted our support to help her achieve the promotion and the raise she felt she deserved. We asked questions, listened and some offered advice. I was still struck by this image of the sacred doll and raised the issue again.

It was at this point that Mary told us that in the previous year she had indeed been given sacred dolls by two different people. One doll was a model from the British Museum of an Egyptian original, the other was a Balinese ritual doll. They were, she said, somehow very special to her. Knowing this I persisted. How would a sacred doll approach the forthcoming performance appraisal? As Mary and I pursued this, I suggested that a sacred doll would surely tell a mysterious and wonderful story about how she had achieved the wonders of the previous year and how those who were near her would be able to use her magic to achieve their own miracles. So together we wove the magic story that Mary would tell the following day. As a prompt, and for emotional support, I suggested that she put one of the dolls in her briefcase and take it with her to the meeting.

At home that evening, standing before the dolls on her mantelpiece, Mary tried to decide which doll would be the more appropriate to take. 'Which doll am I?' she asked herself. Just then the words 'Smell me' floated into her consciousness. She realised that they came from the television program her children were watching nearby. Bending to smell the two dolls, she realised that the Egyptian doll was stone and had no scent; the other, the Balinese doll, was made of sandalwood and had a strong aroma. This, she knew, was the doll she must take to her meeting. So, armed with her sacred doll and her magic story, she walked confidently into her boss's office at the appointed time, clear in her objectives and sure of her right to achieve them.

The next day I received a message: 'I have achieved my goals, beyond my wildest dreams.'

Apparently Mary's boss was so impressed with her and so in agreement with her proposal for promotion that he had taken her request straight to the organisation's chief executive. He, too, was impressed and had called Mary into his office. Mary repeated her story and to her utter amazement was promoted not the one level she had hoped for, but received a rise of several levels and was told that she was to be the first woman in the organisation's top team. She received a $30, 000 per annum pay rise and was immediately issued a car. Within ten minutes, she was attending her first executive committee meeting.

I'm sure that there are all sorts of logical explanations that one can find for this series of events, but I no longer ask rational questions. Too many times I have seen unexpected coincidences link with unexpectedly wonderful results, which seem to stem from nothing but a dream and an openness to experience and believe. Jungians may tell you that this is synchronicity; for me, even giving the mysterious flow of life a name somehow gets in the way of the wonders that are possible when we raise our awareness and let life happen.

Turning up the Volume

When I was in my early thirties I started hearing the voices, words ringing in my head telling me to do things that I didn't really understand. I thought I was going mad and consulted a psychiatrist who told me I was one of the sanest people he had ever met. Still the voices continued. I found that the only way I could have peace was to do what the voices told me. If I didn't follow their instructions, disastrous things happened to me. So I learnt (probably for the first time in my life) to be obedient. I started to listen to the voices and follow their lead. At the time, I was attempting to rebuild my business after my daughter's long illness and the voices told me to do things in a very non-conventional way. So, I was very selective as to which clients I would see (being deeply in debt, I was in no position to be choosy). I insisted on clients coming to me for personal interviews before any workshops. Further, I demanded that I establish a strong personal relationship with the boss before working with any teams and used techniques that at the time people found very unusual. I did very little direct marketing; instead, I wrote a lot of articles and gave a lot of speeches, highlighting the difference in my approach and being very clear that if people wanted the traditional I was not their person.

Back then, most people thought I was crazy. Whenever I attended professional meetings of consultants, psychologists or psychotherapists, they found my approach bizarre. Therapy and business they told me didn't match, and anyway my approach didn't fit comfortably in either camp and was therefore obviously wrong. The voices, however, didn't think so and I had to live with them every day. Looking back now, I see that my intuition, which chose to make itself audible, had more sense than my rational mind. There was no way that I was going to get out of the hole I was in by following the traditional routes. On my own, I didn't have the confidence to strike out as distinctly different, but my intuitive voices did.

Recently, in an interview for a research project based on a major organisational change process that I am overseeing, the story of my voices came to light.

'Do you have a sense for the people you're working with,' asked the interviewer 'that they have this other presence that speaks, too, that there is a voice … that if they listen to it or are open to listen to it a bit more it might help them?'

'Oh, sure,' I replied. 'Where I was lucky was that mine shouted at me. I didn't have a choice to listen to it, it was just in my head shouting so I had to.' Then I recapped, 'Most of the business people I meet could well have voices in there shouting and they manage to turn the volume down so far that they can only hear a tiny whisper.' Surely, when our intuitive knowing insistently makes itself heard, in ways we can no longer ignore, we are receiving the gift of leadership. This can happen at any time along the road on the hero's quest. It can be what sends us off on the journey in the first place. It can be what sustains us as we go through the trials of initiation or it can be what gives us the strength and the wisdom to build the bridges back into society as we ourselves become heroic guides. What is certain is that while we can do a lot of things to turn up the volume so that we can hear the voices when they come, we cannot force them to materialise. No, their creation, transmission and content are their own. We only have control over the reception and what we do with the messages when they are received.

Increased responsiveness to the mysterious flow of life is, however, one of the key rewards of the hero's journey. When we can tune in to intuitive knowing, life becomes simpler, our goals become clearer and reaching them becomes faster—in some cases, almost instantaneous.

The Promotion

Geoff was a chief executive of a manufacturing organisation whose spiralling success evidenced his skills as a leader. He was a very personable man and totally dedicated to his organisation, its people and their success. He was also a loving family man, the head of a large clan which included five grandchildren. Geoff had come to see me because his human resource people felt that he needed to upgrade his perspective on leadership and had convinced him that I could help. I found him a very private man, much more comfortable talking about business or family than about himself. It seemed that while he had no shortage of visions for his company, he was very out of touch with his own desires, inner drivers and personal dreams. Geoff had been coming to see me regularly for more than a year when his secretary asked for an urgent, extended appointment. I curiously awaited this meeting to find out what had occurred. Geoff's company was the division of an upbeat multinational that was very serious about succession planning. They kept an eye on all their executives around the globe to ensure that they were always training the next generation of leaders. It appeared that Geoff's company had been chosen as an excellent training ground for the next round of global chiefs.

As Geoff was sixty-ish, a decision had been made in global head office to start winding down his career, thus making his position available to a younger man. So Geoff had received a phone call telling him that he was to return to the head office, where he would be given an adviser's position, initially full-time. This would give him opportunities to rebuild his contacts (he had been an expatriate for many years by that time). Geoff was told that he could then work part-time until he could support himself with director's and consulting fees.

Geoff didn't like this at all. He wasn't ready to go into a staff position and wind down. More than that, his company was in an interesting and exciting growth phase that he didn't want to miss. He was filled with anger, disappointment, grief and the will to fight. This incident gave Geoff and me an opportunity to start looking at some of the more personal areas that he had chosen to avoid. It turned out that he hadn't, in fact, thought much about retirement—he had been too busy running a company. His wife didn't want to move back to their country of origin and he didn't want to let go of the reins of power just yet. I discovered that Geoff and his wife had never talked in any depth about what they would do when Geoff left his current posting. They hadn't faced their fears and doubts about the future. It seemed that this was the time to do so. In fact, the company's suggestion that he move home in time to build up his contacts so that he could move out into useful full- or part-time employment made sense, but Geoff wasn't ready to accept what the company was offering.

On my prompting, Geoff and his wife went away together for a weekend to discuss what they wanted for themselves as a couple. How did they want to live the rest of their lives in a work and a personal sense? How were they going to finance their latter years and what were their immediate desires for Geoff professionally?

Geoff fought me on this last one. What a waste of time working out what he wanted when the company had told him what was going to happen. I, however, was insistent. Working out what you want can be a more powerful process than we imagine. I had convinced him that, even if it came to nothing, the process was worth exploring.

On their return from their planning weekend, Geoff rang. He had decided that he wanted one more active posting as a chief executive, then he and his wife were happy to return home to rebuild their contacts while working in a staff position, initially full-time and then part-time. He had decided what financial compensation he wanted from the company and he had developed a clear timeline. 'What,' he wanted to know, 'do I do now?' So

I discussed with him the well-used technique of 'visualise and advertise'. Tell people what you want and visualise them giving it to you. Geoff was a practical, sensible man, but he was prepared to try anything.

Three days later, he rang. The company had offered him a promotion. He was to head up a strategically important and politically sensitive joint venture in Asia. It was felt that he was the best man for the job given his skills and experience. It was agreed that this would be his last active posting and his terms and conditions for being repatriated were accepted exactly as he had put them forward.

'Congratulations on pulling that one off,' I told him. 'Oh,' he replied, 'but I didn't do anything.'

That's what he thought. When we are clear about what we want and are upfront about it, when we work on ourselves, our perspective and our relationships, when we acknowledge and are true to our desires and souls' yearnings, all sorts of unexpectedly wonderful things happen.

We can choose to ignore this and put things down to good or bad luck, or we can improve our luck by taking responsibility for being responsive to our heart's desire and soul's calls. When we listen to the Angel of Destiny, she very often returns the favour and listens to us.

Control Versus the Flow of Life

This is a very different process from the power of positive thinking or mind control. These techniques are implicitly premised on the superiority of man above nature, even above the forces of the Divine. I find this level of arrogance unappealing. I also find it foolish. Believing that through force of will we can think the world into being what we want it to be simply ignores the complexity of the human psyche, nature and life. Nature is never entirely positive, nor entirely negative—night always follows day. When we live by force of will, desperately seeking to create positive outcomes, we invite the Angel of the Night to sneak up, unbidden, unseen and uninvited. In my experience, this is never the optimal way of greeting the misfortunes, hardships, disasters and ailments of life that the Dark Angel brings.

However, when we are clear about what we want, when we come to know who we are, when we dare to dream, to listen to our heart's desires and soul's yearnings, then we invite the Angel of Destiny to bring forth her gifts. More than that, we are ready to receive her and what she has to offer because we have respectfully and lovingly prepared ourselves. We have opened our hearts and minds to the possibilities that lie ahead. By developing our relationships, we have prepared the ground for whatever comes— success, struggle, joy or failure. Wisdom tells us that when we invite in the Angel of Destiny, she will bring with her what she wills. If, however, we have listened closely to our inner knowing and transmit out through the ether what it is we desire, it is quite uncanny how often our dreams are fulfilled.

Fate is kind, but you do have to let her know what you want. But Fate doesn't respond kindly to being manipulated, conned, forced or coerced. Fate doesn't fall for the PR image. She dishes out the good and the bad. Those who respect the flow of life, the powers of creation and the forces of nature are ready for whatever comes and make the most of every situation, learning, growing and strengthening through every twist and turn along the road. These heroic questers, through respectful observance of the laws of nature, win at every turn. They also seem to have a disproportionate number of their wishes come true.

Hearing the Oracle

When we choose to live the way of the hero, to pay respectful attention to the Angel of Destiny, we are well advised to increase our ability to hear the Oracle when he calls. The great philosopher Socrates lived his life in the company of his daemon. This was the voice in his head that told him what to do. It asked him questions and generally operated as his guiding force, his own private oracle. Socrates' daemon told him not to escape his execution. It is as if it were concerned with the integrity of his soul.

Indigenous cultures such as the Native Americans or the Australian Aboriginal peoples receive much communication through personal visions and the ebb and flow of nature. When Cyclone Tracy demolished the Australian city of Darwin, it was members of the white population who were killed. The Aboriginal peoples had left town some days before—the land, the animals, birds and trees had told them they were not safe and it was time to move on.

Some may scoff and many will ridicule, but too many of us have had strong premonitions that when followed have saved our lives, prevented a disastrous outcome or helped us be ready to deal with an unexpected situation to dismiss their importance. The further we move along the hero's journey, the more messages we receive. As we raise our awareness, we simply begin to see and hear things that were probably always there, but we had failed to see or hear before. As we get more in touch with our true selves, we somehow connect with the universal force of nature. The more we own who we are, the more we clarify what we want, the truer we are to our heart's desires and soul's yearnings, the clearer, more relevant and more timely are the signs, messages and premonitions.

In a rapidly changing environment, at a time of discontinuous change, this is a great gift—a gift one learns to cherish and treat with great respect. When we are in touch with the mysteries of our own nature and we thus connect with the mysteries of universal nature, we can think, react, prepare and act at astonishing speed. This then frees us up to spend time doing what we need to be doing in order to maintain our intuitive knowing and instinctive hearing at a premium level. In *Peaceful Chaos*, I called this 'strategic thinking time'.

Strategic Thinking Time

Strategic thinking time is the time we take out of our busy schedules to support our ability to think strategically, that is, to think in an holistic, dynamic, clear way about what we want and how we are going to achieve it. Strategic thinking time is that time when we allow a change to happen in our perspective. This happens when we relax, build nurturing relationships, play and become so involved with what we are doing that we can suspend thought. Strategic thinking time therefore includes times when we clear our minds, making room for new, more creative ways forward. Strategic thinking time may be seen by warriors as time wasted, but that is only because they don't know or respect the mysteries.

Strategic thinking time is that time we spend in daily meditation, prayer or personal reflection. It is the time we spend walking quietly in nature, contemplating a flower or a bird, listening to music, singing with friends, reading poetry and great prose. I like to spend strategic thinking time in the great art galleries of the world, where I engage for hours with the works of Michelangelo, Titian, Turner, Renoir, Van Gogh and Rubens.

Children are wonderful companions for strategic thinking time; they help us forget our worries, fear and inhibitions and can remind us of our great capacity for play. I watch my neighbour on summer evenings, strategic thinking with his baby son in their pool where they laugh, play and enjoy the luxury of being free and close and alive. For me, an hour's yoga, a massage or a Feldenkreis lesson promotes the highest quality of strategic capacity. A morning at church, an evening with friends, an afternoon of lovemaking, all seem to make the Oracle easier to hear and interpret.

In our ongoing busyness, strategic thinking time is the first to go. Warriors throw it out without thinking or drown it out with drugs and alcohol. Heroes plan for it, capture it at every opportunity and build it into their personal and professional development. For a hero, ten to fifteen hours a week strategic thinking time is nothing. (This equates to approximately two hours a day or one hour each weekday and one full day on the weekend.) You may think this is self-indulgent. Well, it doesn't have to be.

One can strategic think while doing the dishes, mopping the floors or mowing the grass. The strategic thinking comes with the change of pace, the inner reflection and the knack of learning to flow with the activity at hand. Heroes know the great return they will get from an investment in strategic thinking time, not just in the short term, through being less stressed, more relaxed, fuller and more joyous, but in the long term, through making the right decisions and seeing things as they really are, rather than responding with a knee-jerk reaction. More than that, heroes know that in a dynamic world, relationships are everything and strategic thinking time promotes our ability to relate and the quality of the relationships we have. Soul-filled joy, laughter and intimate sharing make the hard times easier to weather.

Spotting the Daemon

'I know nothing,' wrote Keats, 'but the holiness of the Heart's affections and the Truth of the Imagination.'

Why don't business courses teach us more poetry? The muses have always known the truth—that the soul languishes in the sterile world of thoughts. 'O,' prayed Keats, 'for a life of sensations rather than thoughts.' Our warrior ways have led us to discard the sensations of emotion that fuel our soul and feed our heart. In so doing, we have forgotten how to feel alive and how to see what is best in ourselves, others and the world around us. In overlooking the finest things in life, we have reduced ourselves, our relationships and our society to so much less than is possible. We have overlooked the power of dreams and belief. We have sought mere survival, forgoing the passionate richness and fullness of a life well lived. James Hillman (1996) tells us that when we are not looking with the eye of the heart, we are indeed blind, for we do not see ourselves or others as the bearers of imaginative truth. When we see others for less than they are, they rarely give us their best. More sorrowfully, we rob them of the incentive and even the opportunity to see the best in themselves.

When I sit in my studio and a new client walks in the door, I am excited. I know that the person is already perfectly themselves and that together we are going on a journey that will help them move that perfection to greater depths, as their heart and soul begins to soar. In each client, I look for and see what is possible on the levels of heart, soul, mind and imaginative creation in the world. In a way, I expect more of my clients than they expect of themselves. After all, they come looking for ways of being a better leader and initially, for most of them, that means a more skilful warrior. I look past their defences to their heroic possibilities shining through so brightly in the inner realm of their beings.

This is the gift that others have given me—a family friend who encouraged me to leave home and go to university; the professor who tutored me in physics; the head of department who challenged me to go for and get the highest honours that the university had to offer; clients like David Judd who believed in my ability to take them and their people to new levels of heart, soul and professional success; Robyn, my supervisor; and Gerald, my spiritual director. All these people have seen the greatness lying deep within me and supported me to see the depths of goodness and potential in all that I meet. This is the wonder of the hero's journey. You not only get to take it, you get to share it, to pass it on. In approaching our own heart and soul, we get to approach the heart and soul of others. If we take this with us to the workplace, we get to approach the corporate heart.

Conclusion

Every Sunday I attend mass. Apart from the inspiring homily from the priest, a Jesuit more than seventy years wise, I am continually uplifted by the other members of the congregation. Those in wheelchairs are escorted by loving family members, as are those who are blind. Those who are old and infirm are supported by each other, or by a caring Sister. Each week I witness the strength of the human spirit. I come face to face with the fact that, while today I am fit, strong and mobile, at the end of the day I am only human. My time, too, will come for suffering, hardship and old age. I am reminded that it is in our suffering that we discover the strength of our being. It is through our wounds that we test the boundaries of who we are. It is in coming to terms with our weaknesses that we grow stronger.

As someone who spends much of their time in the warrior world of business where vulnerability and weakness are scorned, my weekly excursions into the real world remind me just how much business misses by encouraging warriors to avoid learning from failure, vulnerability and the normal ebb and flow of life. Not being a signed-up member of the congregation, I don't get to take communion with my fellow worshippers—the church still holds fast to its rules—but no restrictions stop me from drinking in the strength of faith, hope and spirit that I meet in our small chapel. The priest, Father Paul, who runs the services also works as a hospital chaplain. He told me that one of the great joys of that work is that when people are really sick, when they are ailing and especially when they are facing death, they often let down their walls of psychological defence. When this happens, the depth and glory of who they are shines forth. Paul reported of the great sense of awe and feeling of privilege that he experiences when encountering the human spirit at this level.

'However,' he said, 'when people recover their walls go back up and they walk away—back to normality.' There must always be a few, however, who having been through such a strong experience, having seen themselves in a new light, having heard the call to the hero's quest, decide to go on the journey. What is incredible is that so many choose not to heed the call when it comes, decide to push away the wonder of who they are and return to the normality of being less than they now have seen is possible.

If I have one wish, it is that you, having read this book, will heed the call to the hero's quest next time it comes your way—whether it be through disaster, illness, a chance meeting, inspiration, intuition or in response to a book, film, story, poem or song. May you rise to the call next time you hear, see or smell it, laying aside your timid, self-effacing, dry self-limitations and daring to see who you are in your truest and brightest light.

If my prayer is granted you, too, will go on the hero's quest. For it is only when a significant number of individuals take up the challenge to be all that they can be that the business world will change. It is only when individuals in their thousands decide to go on the hero's quest that society will evolve into the kind of place we want for ourselves and our children. It is only when we, each and every one of us, in all our human imperfection, decide to take full personal responsibility for making the world a better place, through being all that we can be, that real enduring change will occur.

The wonder, the great wonder, of this way of thinking, living and working, is that it feels so alive, so rich and so full that every living second becomes a reason to give thanks just for the privilege of being alive. Every living second becomes a psalm of praise not just for the good times, not just for the wins, but for every aspect of our life—the whole emotional, spiritual and interpersonal range of experience. Life on the hero's quest then becomes an ongoing chorus of thanksgiving just for the wonder of life itself.

Bibliography

Al Huang, Chungliang & Lynch, Jerry, *Mentoring: The Tao of Giving and Receiving Wisdom*, HarperSanFrancisco, San Francisco, 1995, p. 37.

Barker, Joel, *The Business of Paradigms* (video), ChartHouse Learning, Minnesota, 1990.

Beatty, Jack, 'The Body Snatchers', *Australian Financial Review* (online version), September 2001.

Bennis, Warren, *Why Leaders Can't Lead: The Unconscious Conspiracy Continues*, Jossey-Bass Publishers, San Francisco, 1989, p. 59.

Bennis, Warren, *Coaching the Team*, BBC Training Videos, UK, 1991.

Bennis, Warren, *Behavior On Line Conversations*, http://www. behavior.net/column/bennis/index.html.

Bernstein, Aaron, 'Too Much Corporate Power', *Business Week* (online version), 11 September 2000.

Bowman, Karlyn & Ladd, Everett, 'Opinion pulse', *American Enterprise*, Jan/Feb 1993, p. 86, from Hood, John, *The Heroic Enterprise: Business and the Common Good*, Simon & Schuster, 1996, p. xiv.

Boyers, Karla, 'Business soul', *Association Management*, Feb. 1996, p. 44.

Cairnes, Margot, *Peaceful Chaos: The Art of Leadership in Times of Rapid Change*, The Change Dynamic, Sydney, 1992.

Cairnes, Margot, *Reaching for the Stars: The Politics and Process of Bringing Vision to Reality*, The Change Dynamic, Sydney, 1994.

Cairnes, Margot, 'Achieving personal success: Standing tall against the odds', *The Whole Person*, Mar./Apr. 1995, p. 27.

Campbell, Joseph, *The Hero of a Thousand Faces*, Fontana Press, London, 1993.

Chappell, Tom, 'Business soul', *Association Management*, Feb. 1996, p. 46.

Collins, Jim, *Good to Great: Why Some Companies Make the Leap and Others Don't*, HarperBusiness, New York, 2002.

De Bono, Edward, *Six Thinking Hats*, Penguin, London, 1990.

De Castella, Nicholas (unpub.), *Passionately Alive, Passionately Alive*, 44

Rutland St, Clifton Hill, Victoria 3068, Australia.

Fell, L., Russell, D. & Stewart, A., *Seized by Agreement, Swamped by Understanding*, Hawkesbury University Press, Richmond, Australia, 1994.

Gleick, James, *Chaos*, Penguin, London, 1988, p.

Goleman, Daniel, *Emotional Intelligence: Why It Can Matter More than IQ*, Bloomsbury, London, 1996.

Hammerschlag, Carl A., *The Dancing Healers: A Doctor's Journey of Healing with Native Americans*, HarperCollins, New York, 1988.

Hammerschlag, Carl A., *The Theft of the Spirit: A Journey to Spiritual Healing with Native Americans*, Simon & Schuster, New York, 1993.

Hancock, LynNell, 'Breaking point', *Newsweek*, 6 Mar 1995, p. 58. Handy, Charles, *Beyond Certainty: The Changing Worlds of Organisations*, Hutchinson, London, 1995.

Heisenberg, Werner, *Physics and Philosophy*, Harper Torchbooks, New York, 1958, p. 107.

Hill, Napoleon, *Think and Grow Rich*, Ballantine Books, New York, 1959.

Hill, Nor, *The Moon and the Virgin: Reflections on the Archetypal Feminine*, The Women's Press, London., 1990.

Hillman, James, 'The great mother, her son, her hero and the puer', from Berry, Patricia (ed.) *Fathers and Mothers* (audio and journal), 1990, 2nd ed., Spring Publications, Texas.

Hillman, James, *The Soul's Code: In Search of Character and Calling*, Random House, New York, 1996.

Hillman, James & Ventura, Michael, *We've Had a Hundred Years of Psychotherapy and the World's Getting Worse*, HarperCollins, New York, 1992.

Holder, Robert & McKinney, Richard, 'Corporate change and the hero's quest', *World Business Academy Perspectives*, 1992, vol. 6 no. 4, p. 40.

Houston, Jean, *The Search for the Beloved: Journeys in Sacred Psychology*, J. P. Tarcher, California, 1987, p. 12.

Irving, Janis, 'Group think', *Psychology Today*, Nov. 1971, pp. 43–6.

James, Jennifer, *Thinking in the Future Tense: Leadership Skills for a New Age*, Simon & Schuster, New York, 1996.

Kets De Vries, Manfred, *Fools and Imposters: Essays on the Psychology of Leadership*, Jossey-Bass Publishers, San Francisco, 1993.

Kirschenbaum, Howard & Land Henderson, Valerie (eds.), *Carl Rogers Dialogues*, Constable & Co., London, 1990.

Leider, Richard, *The Power of Purpose*, Ballantine Books, New York, 1985. Lowen, Alexander, *Fear of Life*, Macmillan, New York, 1980.

Lowen, Alexander, *The Spirituality of the Body*, Macmillan, New York, 1990.

Maturana, Umberto, 'Reality: The search for objectivity or the quest for a compelling argument', *The Irish Journal of Psychology*, 1988, vol. 9 no. 1, pp. 25–82.

Maturana, U. & Varela, F., *The Tree of Knowledge: The Biological Roots of Human Understanding*, Shambala, Boston, 1987.

May, Rollo, *The Cry for Myth*, Dell, New York, 1991.

Maynard, Herman & Mehrtens, Susan, *The Fourth Wave: Business in the 21st Century*, Berret-Koehler Publishers, San Francisco, 1996.

Moore, Thomas, *Care of the Soul: A Guide for Culminating Depth and Sacredness in Everyday Life*, HarperPerennial, New York, 1992.

Nevis, E., Lancourt, J. & Vassallo, H., *Intentional Revolutions: A Seven Point Strategy for Transforming Organisations*, Jossey-Bass Publishers, San Francisco, 1996, pp. 14–15.

Nouwen, Henri, *Reaching out: The Three Movements of the Spiritual Life*, HarperCollins, London, 1975, pp. 71–2.

Peck, Dr M. Scott, *The Road Less Traveled*, Arrow Books, London, 1978.

Peck, Dr M. Scott, *Further along the Road Less Traveled: The Unending Journey Toward Spiritual Growth*, Simon & Schuster, New York, 1993.

Popcorn, Faith, *The Popcorn Report: Targeting Your Life*, Doubleday, USA, 1991.

Priognes, Ilya, *Brain/Mind Bulletin*, 21 May 1979.

Quinn, Robert, *Beyond Rational Management*, Jossey-Bass, San Francisco, 1988.

Reynolds, David, *Constructive Living*, University Press of Hawaii, Hawaii, 1984.

Rogers, Carl, *Freedom to Learn: A View of What Education Might Become*, Charles E Merrill Publishing Company, Ohio, 1979.

Rothenberg, Albert, *Creativity and Madness: New Findings and Old Stereotypes*, John Hopkins University Press, Baltimore, 1990.

Rothman, Stanley & Lerner, Robert, 1990 study from Novak, Michael,

Business as a Calling: Work and the Examined Life, Simon & Schuster, New York, 1996, pp. 43–4.

Sardallo, Robert, *Love and the Soul*, New York Publishers, New York, 1995. Scettler J., 'Leadership in corporate America', *Training*, Minneapolis,

Sept. 2002, Vol. 39 No. 9.

Seligman, Martin, *Learned Optimism*, Random House Australia, Sydney, 1992, p. 10.

Stacey, Ralph, *Managing Chaos: Dynamic Business Strategies in an Unpredictable World*, Kogan Page, London, 1992.

Stubby, Robert, 'Inside the chemically dependent marriage: Denial and manipulation', *Co-Dependence: An Emerging Issue*, Health Communications, Hollywood Beach, Florida, 1984.

Thomas, Peters & Waterman, Robert, *In Search of Excellence*, Warner Books, New York, 1982.

Wheatley, Margaret, *Leadership and the New Science: Learning about Organization from an Orderly Universe*, Berrett-Koehler Publishers, San Francisco, 1992, p. 20.

Wilson Schaef, Anne, *Beyond Therapy Beyond Science: A New Model for Healing the Whole Person*, HarperCollins, New York, 1992.

Wilson Schaef, Anne & Fassel, Diane, *The Addictive Organisation*, HarperCollins, New York, 1988.

Yalom, Irvin D., *Love's Executioner and Other Tales of Psychotherapy*, Penguin, UK, 1989, pp. 167–86.

Zohar, Danah & Marshall, Ian, *SQ: Spiritual Intelligence, The Ultimate Intelligence*, Bloomsbury Publishing, London, 2000.

Index

All those who wish to explore the author's services or support her mission are welcome to visit:

Zaffyre International
www.zaffyre.com

If you wish to contact the author, you may do so by e-mail to:
mcairnes@zaffyre.com

Other books by Margot Cairnes

Boardrooms That Work

Peaceful Chaos: The Art of Leadership in Times of Rapid Change

Reaching for the Stars: The Politics and Process of Bringing Vision into Reality

Staying Sane in a Changing World

PROOFREADING CORRECTIONS
By Leigh Robshaw & Josie Gagliano